Microformats
Made Simple

Emily P. Lewis

Technical Review by Tantek Çelik

Microformats Made Simple
Emily P. Lewis

New Riders
1249 Eighth Street
Berkeley, CA 94710
510/524-2178
510/524-2221 (fax)

Find us on the web at: www.newriders.com
To report errors, please send a note to errata@peachpit.com

New Riders is an imprint of Peachpit, a division of Pearson Education.
Copyright @ 2010 by Emily Lewis

Acquisition and Development Editor: Wendy Sharp
Copy Editor: Jacqueline Aaron
Production Editor: Myrna Vladic
Compositor: David Van Ness
Indexer: Emily Glossbrenner, FireCrystal Communications
Cover Design: Mimi Heft
Interior Design: Kathleen Cunningham

ISBN 13:   978-0-321-66077-0
ISBN 10:   0-321-66077-3

9 8 7 6 5 4 3 2 1

Printed and bound in the United States of America

Acknowledgments

To Tantek Çelik, not only for lending his technical expertise, but also for all his work making microformats a reality and for his ongoing advocacy.

To everyone at Peachpit New Riders who had a hand in the creation of this book, especially Jacqueline Aaron and Wendy Sharp. And a special thanks to Wendy for taking a chance on a new author and being patient with and supportive of me as I learned *how* to write this book.

To Jason Nakai, for coming up with designs for my CSS chapter on very short notice and for being my safe place to fall when I thought I was going to completely lose my mind.

To Ian Pitts, for being the best boss I've ever had and for encouraging me to continually push my skills and knowledge.

To my colleagues, friends, and family who have provided unwavering support, not only for this book but also for me as I expand my horizons: Erin Lewis, Erin Shutes, Jen Schwedler, Tracy Teague, Theresa Ball, Chris Harrison, Virginia DeBolt, Chris Kenworthy, Trevor Gryffyn, Mark Casias, Suellen Maneely, Laurie Varela, Sarah Mitchell, Chris Heilmann, Jeff Croft, Jeremy Keith, Jason Beaird, Jeremy Abbott, Joe Lewis, Ben Ward, Stephanie Sullivan, and Andy Clarke.

To the designers, developers, and fellow web geeks who inspire me and keep the bar high: Greg Storey, D. Keith Robinson, Dan Rubin, Nick Finck, Leslie Camacho, Nevin Lyne, J. Cornellus, Derek Featherstone, Lea Alcantara, Ryan Irelan, Jonathan Snook, Ryan Masuga, Whitney Hess, Rob Jones, Chris Pederick, Jason Santa Maria, James Craig, Eric Meyer, Jeffrey Zeldman, Michael Boyink, Cameron Moll, Ethan Marcotte, Roger Johansson, Shaun Inman, Molly Holzschlag, Andy Budd, Simon Collison, Doug Bowman, Dave Shea, Chris Messina, John Allsopp, Dan Cederholm, Aaron Walter, Nicole Sullivan, and dozens of others.

To the readers of A Blog Not Limited and all my social-network friends, for being interested in what I have to say and spreading the word.

To my local community of geeks, especially Webuquerque and ABQ Web Geeks, for keeping me sane, engaged, and full of beer twice a month.

To anyone I overlooked, you know I love you.

And finally, to you. Thank you for reading! I hope you enjoy the book and learn a little something in the process.

Contents

Chapter 1

Introduction

What Are Microformats?

Microformats are simple, open design patterns based on existing standards that you use to describe common web content, including people, places, events, links, and much more.

Existing standards? Yes. HTML (Hypertext Markup Language) and CSS (Cascading Style Sheets). That's it. Seriously. No fancy software. No new languages. Just markup and `class` patterns using two of the most basic building blocks of the web today.

Which is why microformats are so simple and easy-to-use.

Humans first, machines second

The markup and `class` patterns you use to define microformats are designed for humans first, machines second.

What does that mean? Basically, the content "contained" by microformats is consumed by humans, such as a person's name as viewed on the web in a browser. From the user's perspective, web content using microformats is indistinguishable from content without. People just get the content. The microformats are invisible.

But the true power of microformats is the second part. The data patterns of microformats allow machines—computers, user agents, applications, and the like, not *The Terminator*—to extract that human-readable content for a wide range of uses.

For example, if you use the hCard microformat for a person's contact information, the Operator plug-in for Mozilla Firefox extracts that contact information and allows the user to save it to his computer's address book, rather than having to manually copy or type the information.

With microformats, you write your content and markup once, but make it available to a potentially infinite number of uses.

Meaning through semantics

One of the reasons microformats are so simple is they rely on structure. This is something every website already has: structure through markup. Microformats just take it to another level with specifically defined structures for particular web content.

But structure by itself isn't everything. *Semantics* are essential to microformats. They give structure meaning through the use of semantic markup and CSS. And we can all use a bit more meaning in our lives, can't we?

POSH

What is semantic markup? It is markup that describes the content itself, not its presentation. And because geeks *love* acronyms, semantic markup is also known as **POSH** (Plain Old Semantic HTML).

This concept is part of today's web standards that encourage the separation of content from presentation. No more `<font>` tags. No more `<b>` tags. No more `<tables>` for layout.

Instead, semantic markup means using `<ul>` for a list, `<p>` for a paragraph, and `<h1>` for a headline. Meanwhile the presentation, such as bold type or layout, is controlled via CSS.

In addition to being semantic, POSH markup must be valid. All that means is your markup must validate against the assigned DOCTYPE. And there are plenty of tools to help you validate, including the W3C's (World Wide Web Consortium) Markup Validation Service (http://validator.w3.org/). Couldn't be easier.

With this book, you won't just become a microformats master, you'll also learn about POSH. All of the examples in this book use POSH, and I explain my logic behind the semantic markup used.

And I should mention that all of the examples of and references to markup are XHTML. This is simply my personal preference, not a requirement. If your language of choice is HTML 4, go for it. If you are exploring the forthcoming (I'm using that term loosely) HTML5, no problem. Remember, microformats rely on markup attributes that are inherently supported in all versions of HTML 3 and later.

With all that microformatty and POSHy goodness (and my charming tongue-in-cheek wit) you are really going to get your money's worth with this book. Lucky you!

Semantic CSS

I've mentioned that in POSH, CSS controls presentation. But it's not just CSS, it's *semantic* and *valid* CSS. Semantic CSS simply extends the notion of describing what the content is (rather than what it will look like), to `class` and `id` naming.

For example, rather than assigning `class="rightColumn"` to a section of related content, you assign `class="relatedContent"`. This helps you account for a future possibility that the presentation of the content changes to be positioned on the left.

It is important to note, though, that the `class` attribute is part of HTML, not CSS. Further, the use of `class` in microformats isn't primarily for presentation purposes. Granted, CSS styling is the most common use of `class`, but the HTML specification indicates that `class` has several roles, including for general purpose user-agent processing. It is this general pur-pose role that drives the use of `class` in microformats: to add semantic context to web content.

Still, I personally like to think that microformats support the notion of semantic CSS. Each microformat has unique and semantic `class` names (along with other metadata) that are assigned to markup to describe the content. For example, hCard uses `class="url"` for a person's website address. And if you choose to style your content with CSS, these `class` names give you a semantic hook to do just that.

As for the CSS validation that POSH requires, you simply validate your CSS against the version/profile you are using (just as with your markup). It doesn't matter whether it is CSS 1 or CSS 3. Whatever you choose to use is fine, as long as it validates. Once again, the W3C offers a CSS validation tool (http://jigsaw.w3.org/) that will validate your CSS against a selected profile. Easy peasy.

Some Background

I've talked a bit about semantics, but I feel it is important to distinguish this concept from that of the Semantic Web.

The Semantic Web

The Semantic Web was proposed as a replacement for the current Document or Presentation Web, where content publishers produce two versions of their content: one for human consumption and one, using RDF (Resource Description Framework), for machines.

Sir Tim Berners-Lee, who envisioned the concept, explains:

"... most information on the web is designed for human consumption, and ... the structure of the data is not evident to a robot browsing the web. ... the Semantic Web approach instead develops languages for expressing information in a machine-processable form." (www.w3.org/DesignIssues/Semantic.html)

Microformats are *not* a formal specification of the Semantic Web. But because they embrace the idea of information for *both* humans and machines, they support the Semantic Web's goal of human and machine consumption. Yet unlike the Semantic Web, which advocates separate machine versions of content, microformats encourage making human-readable content more machine-readable.

Why is machine readability important? Because computers don't necessarily understand human-readable content. And computers could care less about what your content looks like. Computers care about the data and information on the page, and being able to meaningfully identify that data. Microformats and POSH help with that identification.

For example, a search-engine spider likes to know which content is a headline, and using <h1> gives that content the extra "headline" meaning so the spider can easily identify it. Not to mention, this can offer the bonus of organically boosting your search engine optimization (SEO).

A brief history of microformats

At present, the Semantic Web isn't fully realized. But that doesn't mean folks don't want semantics to enrich web content *now*. In fact, during the early 2000s, web designers began using semantic HTML (now referred to as POSH), as well as semantic CSS. Then, in 2003, the microformats initiative kicked off with the rel="friend" XFN (XHTML Friends Network) proposal.

The microformats community decided early on that one way toward the Semantic Web was to utilize *existing technologies* to add semantic value to content. As part of the GMPG (Global Multimedia Protocols Group) work, three HTML attributes were identified that could be utilized for that purpose: class, rel, and rev.

They then defined the core microformats principles, each aimed at ensuring the desired semantics would be created via a controlled, standardized process:

- Solve a specific problem.

- Be as simple as possible.

- Design for humans first, machine second.

- Use widely adopted standards.

- Be modular and embeddable.

- Encourage the "spirit of the web" through decentralization.

And that brings us to today, where we have eight stable, standard microformat specifications:

- hCalendar for events

- hCard for people, places, and organizations

- rel-license for licensed content

- rel-nofollow for limiting user-agent link analysis on hyperlinks

- rel-tag for indicating a link destination is to a page about a keyword (tag) for the current page

- VoteLinks for indicating endorsement, disagreement, or neutrality of the destination of a hyperlink

- XFN for representing human relationships in links

- XOXO (Extensible Open XHTML Outlines) for indicating outlines and blogrolls

We also have 15 draft microformats, (with more being considered all the time):

- adr for specifying address information

- geo for indicating geographic coordinates

- hAtom for content that can be syndicated

- hAudio for audio recordings

- hMedia for publishing images, audio and other media

- hProduct for consumer products

- hRecipe for food and beverage recipes

- hResume for résumés and CVs (curricula vitae)

- hReview for reviews of things like products, services, and businesses

- rel-directory for indicating the destination of a link is a directory listing that contains an entry for the current page

- rel-enclosure for indicating attachments that can be downloaded and cached

- rel-home for specifying the link to a site's home page

- rel-payment for payment mechanisms

- robots exclusion to indicate page-specific direction for web crawlers on any content

- xFolk for collections of bookmarks

Everyone's doing it

It's been six years since the microformats initiative began, and *millions* of sites are using them:

XFN

- According to Yahoo! SearchMonkey results, there are 445,000,000 web pages using XFN.

- Online identity consolidation services like Plaxo and claimID use XFN to identify online social relationships.

- Google's Social Graph API (Application Programming Interface) uses XFN for data visualization of social relationships

- Social networks like Twitter, Flickr, and LinkedIn use XFN for friends and followers.

hCard

- Yahoo! SearchMonkey shows 1,370,000,000 results for hCard.

- Google Maps uses hCard, while Google's Rich Snippets feature leverages hCard to display more contextually-relevant search result information.

- Both Twitter and Last.fm apply hCard to their users' profile pages.

- Yahoo! Local and MapQuest Local apply hCard to their search results.

- Technorati's microformats search indexes hCard.

rel-license

- Creative Commons uses rel-license in its generated license markup.

- Both Google and Yahoo! offer search engines that can filter results based on rel-license content.

hReview

- There are 37,200,000 pages using hReview, according to SearchMonkey

- Google's Rich Snippets use hReview for search result information.

- Cork'd Tasting Notes uses hReview.

- Both Yahoo! Local's user feedback and ratings apply hReview, as does its broader search results. Yahoo! Tech's reviews also use hReview.

- Technorati searches for hReview from submitted URLs (Uniform Resource Locators)

hCalendar

- SearchMonkey reports 36,900,000 results for hCard.

- Yahoo! Upcoming uses hCalendar for all events, as do Facebook and Last.fm.

- Event-based search results in Yahoo! Local are marked up with hCalendar. Same with MapQuest Local.

- Technorati also indexes hCalendar information for its microformats search.

And, of course, I use microformats all over my blog, my design portfolio, and my work sites.

The list goes on an on, but I won't bore you any further. Want to see more microformats in the wild? Go to http://microformats.org/wiki/examples-in-the-wild.

All these microformat implementations are getting you excited, right? You don't want to be left out in the cold, do you? You want to be one of the cool kids. So get on board and start using microformats today! Do it. Do it. Seriously. *Do it.*

Core Concepts

Since I know you are now an eager beaver (peer pressure *can* be quite effective) and want to dive straight into microformats, please be patient as I first cover some of the common elements and core concepts of microformats.

I know, I know, you just want the examples. But trust me. Understanding the foundations of microformats will make it easier for you to conceptualize them once we get into the examples. Really, trust me.

Basic syntax

Let's start with syntax, and it is going to *blow your mind* how simple it is.

While I've stressed the importance of POSH in microformats, the truth is that markup tags have virtually nothing to do with the syntax of microformats. Do not misunderstand, though. Good, valid, and semantic markup is essential for an *effective* microformat implementation.

If you are going to bother adding semantic richness to your content with microformats, why dilute that with crap markup? POSH helps ensure that your content has the greatest semantic value possible.

That said, the keys to microformats are classes and other metadata. Technically, you can use any markup as long as the `class` and attribute values follow the microformats specifications. But really, "any markup" simply isn't good enough. Be committed to quality and professionalism and use POSH with your microformats. Hell, you should use POSH, period.

So, how about a look at the most basic of microformats, rel-me, which uses the `rel` attribute in links for identity consolidation (associating one page about a person to other pages about that same person):

```
<a href="http://www.ablognotlimited.com" rel="me">A Blog Not
Limited</a>
```

In this example, the addition of `rel="me"` indicates that the link destination references a page about me or for which I am responsible.

Taking this same content a bit further, let's look at the basic syntax for hCard:

```
<p class="vcard"><a href="http://www.ablognotlimited.com"
rel="me" class="fn url">Emily Lewis</a></p>
```

In this example, I changed the displayed content of the link to be my name. As this is contact information, I added the `class` value `vcard` to the `<p>` to designate the content as contact information.

Next, I added `class="fn url"` to my link, which indicates that the link destination is my website and the link content is my name. And, you will note, I retained the `rel="me"` value because you can (and should) combine microformats where it makes sense.

That's it. A few `class` values, a `rel` attribute value, and I've got two micro-formats in action. Is your mind effectively blown? *Sweet.*

Terminology

Now that I've covered the basic syntax, let's talk terminology.

Elementals and compounds

There are elemental microformats and compound microformats.

Elemental microformats contain a single attribute and value, such as the rel-me microformat I demonstrated earlier. Typically, elementals are used as building blocks for compound microformats.

Compound microformats, such as hCard, are slightly more involved and are comprised of properties and subproperties.

Properties and subproperties

Each compound microformat has a root property, which is assigned to the root markup element containing the content. An example of a root prop-erty is the `class="vcard"` assigned to markup containing contact infor-mation (as in my previous example).

Root properties cannot be combined with any other properties. For example, `class="vcard fn"` would be invalid. Further, root properties are required for each microformat.

In addition to the root property, compound microformats have properties, some of which are required, some of which are optional. The only required property for hCard, for example, is `class="fn"` to indicate the person's formatted name. All other properties, such as `class="url"`, are optional.

Compound microformats also have subproperties. In a sense, these are like children of properties. For example, the `adr` property, which indicates a person's address, has several subproperties to give even more semantic detail:

```
<div class="vcard">
    <p class="fn">Emily Lewis</p>
    <p class="adr">
        <span class="street-address">1234 Microformats
Avenue</span>,
        <span class="locality">Albuquerque</span>,
        <span class="region">New Mexico</span>
        <span class="postal-code">87106</span>
    </p>
</div>
```

And there are other `adr` subproperties I didn't include in this example. But subproperties are entirely optional. If you have the content to support them all, then use them all. No limits. But if you don't, no worries.

However, you do have to use *at least one* of the subproperties.

A few final points about properties and subproperties. First, they cannot be combined. So, for example, in hCard, `class="adr street-address"` is incorrect.

And, second, all properties and subproperties are case sensitive, as are all `class` names in HTML.

XMDP

All microformats have an associated **XMDP** (XHTML Metadata Profile), which defines the metadata and `classes` that are specified in the given microformat. And each profile has a unique **URI** (Uniform Resource Identifier) that is used for referencing it on web pages containing the microformat it defines.

For example, the profile URI for XFN is http://gmpg.org/xfn/11, while the profile URI for hCalendar is http://microformats.org/profile/hcalendar/.

Referencing profiles   To reference a profile on your web page, you simply add the `profile` attribute to your page's `<head>` element:

```
<head profile="http://gmpg.org/xfn/11">
```

And if you are using more than one microformat on your page, the W3C allows multiple `profile` values, separated by a white space. For example, if you have both XFN and hCalendar on your page, you would use this:

```
<head profile="http://gmpg.org/xfn/11 http://microformats.
org/profile/hcalendar/">
```

There is also work on a combined profile URI for all microformat specifications. So if you are using more than one stable, formal microformat on your web page, you can use this combined profile, rather than listing all of the individual profiles for each microformat.

For *draft* microformats, you need to specify the profile for that particular microformat. If you are referencing *both* draft microformats and stable specifications, you can use the combined profile URI along with the profiles for drafts.

Referencing these profiles in pages that contain microformats is recommended, but not required. This could change in the future, though, so I personally recommend including them by default.

Also, the profile URIs, themselves, are subject to change. In fact, I have it on good authority that some of them will be changing soon. The profiles referenced here and in other chapters reflect the profiles that are valid as of this writing. By the time you are reading this, they could change. So please be diligent and check http://microformats.org/profile/ to see what the most current profile URIs are. Sorry, I can't see into the future.

Drafts and specifications

I've mentioned drafts and specifications a few times already. I suppose it might be helpful to explain these to you.

Formal specifications   What I've referred to as microformat specifications are those that are formal and stable. These aren't going to change. Use them without concern of having to revisit your markup.

An added bonus of using formal microformat specifications is there tends to be much more development of tools to leverage these microformats. This is because they are stable. Developers can write to them without concern of change.

Drafts   *Draft* microformats, meanwhile, are those that are relatively far along in the specification process but haven't been formally completed. And that means these can (and probably will) change to some degree before becoming a formal specification.

As such, there can be challenges in implementing drafts:

- Less information about the properties and subproperties of drafts may be available, making comprehension and implementation comparatively more difficult.

- Open, unresolved issues can affect how a draft is implemented, making revisiting markup more likely.

- Fewer tools, such as generators and parsers, are available for drafts. This makes sense, though: why develop a tool when the specification isn't finalized? Just means more work for the developers.

- What tools are available may not be as up-to-date as the draft itself, making those tools less useful.

What to use   There's no doubt that you should embrace the formal specifications. But should you use drafts? Personally, I say absolutely! I subscribe to the notion that web technologies are, inherently, moving targets. Maybe slow-moving targets, but subject to change nonetheless. Just consider HTML 4, XHTML, and HTML5.

Specifications evolve to meet changing needs and technologies. Yet that doesn't mean I won't implement something in which I strongly believe, like microformats. But that's me. You decide for yourself.

But at least consider that, to stay ahead in today's web field, being able to understand and adapt to new and changing technologies separates the wheat from the chaff. You don't want to be chaff, do you?

Combining microformats

One of the best things about microformats is that they can be easily combined. As long as it makes contextual sense, you should combine microformats whenever possible. This adds more semantic value to your content and gives machines even more data that can be extracted and made available to your users.

In one of my earlier examples, I combined rel-me and hCard. A more involved example combines hCard with hCalendar:

```
<dl class="vevent">
    <dt class="summary"><a href="http://groups.adobe.
com/posts/d95482d8f6" class="url">Web Standards &amp;
Accessibility With Dreamweaver</a></dt>
        <dd class="dtstart"><span class="value-title" title=
"2009-05-06T18:30:00"> </span>May 6, 2009 at 6:30pm</dd>
```

(continues on next page)

```
        <dd class="location vcard">
            <span class="fn org">Uptown Sports Bar &amp; Grill,
            <span class="adr">
                <span class="locality">Albuquerque</span>,
                <abbr class="region" title="New Mexico">NM
</abbr>
</dl>
```

This example describes an event with a time and a date, but I also include content about its location: a restaurant name and address. As such, it makes contextual sense to add hCard information to describe the venue.

Design patterns

The building blocks of microformats are design patterns you use across different specifications. Before diving into specific microformats, you should first understand these patterns. And I'm happy to take you on this exciting, educational journey.

Class design pattern

The **class design pattern** is the core of microformats. It is the pattern of assigning the requisite `class` value (property or subproperty) to a *semantic* element.

That's it. And you've already seen it:

```
<p class="vcard"><a href="http://www.ablognotlimited.com"
rel="me" class="fn url">Emily Lewis</a></p>
```

Just in case it is necessary to point out, you can use multiple `class` values as I've done in the above example.

Rel design pattern

Another common pattern is the **rel design pattern**, which you use to indicate the meaning of hyperlinks. (I'm calling this a pattern, but it's actually simply using the `rel` attribute as it was defined in the HTML 4 specification.)

And, just like the class design pattern, you've already seen this one in my previous examples:

```
<a href="http://www.ablognotlimited.com" rel="me">A Blog Not
Limited</a>
```

That's all there is to it. Nuff said.

Abbr design pattern

The **abbr design pattern** takes advantage of the `<abbr>` element, which, as part of the HTML 4 specification, is used to expand abbreviated content. As part of microformats, `<abbr>` is frequently applied to short human-readable content for which you want an expanded abbreviation that not only provides more precise human-readable information, but is also useful for machines. To do this, you contain the content with the `<abbr>` element and define the machine data as the `title` attribute value, such as for country abbreviations:

```
<abbr title="United States of America">USA</abbr>
```

However, microformats discourage the use of the abbr design pattern simply to add more human-friendly content. The logic is that if someone doesn't want to make his content visible, adding the content "invisibly" shouldn't be encouraged. Here's an example:

```
<abbr title="Emily Lewis">Emily</abbr>
```

The microformats initiative believes that invisible metadata is unreliable metadata (a lesson learned from the historical failure of `<meta>` keywords).

Include design pattern

The **include design pattern** allows you to include a portion of data from one area of a page into another area of the same page. This means you can reuse the content without having to repeat the information.

This pattern is primarily used in the hResume format, which often references multiple hCards for the same person. By utilizing the include design pattern, you don't have to repeat a person's name information for every hCard reference, which would go against the accepted and expected content format for résumés.

Here's how it works in hResume. For the first hCard instance, you assign an id (which, I hope I don't have to tell you, must be a *unique* value):

```
<div class="vcard" id="emily">
```

Then, in later hCard instances, you add a link assigned `class="include"` with an `href` value equal to the `id` value:

```
<a class="include" href="#emily">Emily Lewis</a>
```

The only caveat to this include design pattern is that the link displays in the browser. This isn't what one would expect to see in a résumé: multiple links of a person's name. I usually address this problem with CSS to hide the content (via `display:none`) so that the link doesn't appear multiple times.

Hiding content via CSS is, generally speaking, a no-no in my book because I feel if the content is there, it should be visible. But there are exceptions to every rule, and I'm nothing if not flexible.

Regardless, this is the recommended include design pattern for microformats. There is an alternative approach that utilizes `<object>`. However, since the `<object>` include pattern isn't recommended (due to browser display inconsistencies), I won't go into detail about it. Go look it up if you must.

DATETIME DESIGN PATTERN

The **datetime design pattern** is currently deprecated in favor of the value class pattern. You shouldn't use it anymore: instead, use the value class pattern. But you still might need to understand it, especially because historically its structure was an argument against using microformats (more about that later in the chapter.)

The datetime design pattern utilizes the abbr design pattern for date and time information:

```
<abbr class="dtstart" title="2009-05-06T18:30:00">May 6, 2009 at 6:30pm</abbr>
```

In the above example, the `<abbr>` element has a `title` attribute of "2009-05-06T18:30:00," while the contained content is "May 6, 2009 at 6:30pm."

Note that the machine-readable values for date-time is in the International Standards Organization (ISO) 8601 format, which specifies numeric representations of dates and times.

For dates, the format is YYYY-MM-DD, where *YYYY* represents the four-digit year, *MM* represents the two-digit month, and *DD* represents the two-digit day.

For times of day, the format is hh:mm:ss, where *hh* represents the number of hours that have passed since midnight, *mm* represents the number of minutes that have passed since the start of the hour, and *ss* represents the number of seconds passed since the start of the minute.

When combining dates with times of day, you simply join the two above formats with a *T*: YYYY-MM-DDThh:mm:ss.

Value class pattern

The **value class pattern** is one of the new patterns in microformats. It is used when only a part of an element's content is intended as the value of a microformat property. For example, the telephone property in hCard:

```
<p class="tel"><span class="type">Work</span>: <span
class="value">555-123-4567</span></p>
```

In this example, `class="value"` is applied to the segment of content that is the intended machine value for `tel`.

The value class pattern can also be used when an element's human-readable content needs to be split up to provide valid machine data, such as localized telephone numbers:

```
<p class="tel"><span class="type">Work</span>: <span
class="value">+44</span> (0) <span class="value">1223 123
123</span></p>
```

In this example, the content displayed to users includes a *0* to indicate local dialing. However, including the *0* in the machine data makes the number invalid. The solution? Contain the necessary machine data in `<span class="value">` elements, and machines know to concatenate the inner text of those elements into a single data string.

Value-title subset   In discussing the datetime design pattern (which uses `<abbr>` for dates and times), I mentioned some accessibility issues. The primary accessibility concern with the use of `<abbr>` for dates and times is how screen readers expand `title` values: sometimes (depending on the screen reader, how it is configured, and so on) they read the full ISO 8601 value, which can be confusing to screen reader users. So, the value class pattern offers the **value-title subset** for authors who want an alternative to using `<abbr>` for date and time information.

With the value-title subset, you contain your date and time information with `<span class="value-title">` (instead of an `<abbr>`) which is then assigned an ISO 8601 `title` value. Parsers can then extract the machine data from the `title`, not the inner text:

```
<p class="dtstart"><span class="value-title" title="2009-05-
18T13:00:00">May 18, 2009 at 1pm</span></p>
```

However, ISO 8601 data in the `title` attribute of any element displays as a tooltip on browsers. This is a usability challenge for folks who have no idea what ISO 8601 is or why the tooltip is there. Remember, microformats should be invisible to the user.

So another option for the value-title subset relies on an empty `<span class="value-title">` assigned the ISO 8601 `title` value:

```
<p class="dtstart">
    <span class="title-value" title="2009-05-18T13:00:00">
</span>May 18, 2009 at 1pm
</p>
```

Note that the `<span>` isn't actually empty. It contains a single space character, but no other content. This eliminates the display of any tooltip on the browser, but machines still get the ISO 8601 data.

Also note that in this empty value-title implementation, the empty `<span>` immediately follows the parent element, appearing before the human-readable content and without any additional nesting.

And this value-title subset isn't limited to date-time information. It is also useful for localization purposes, such as telephone types in hCard.

```
<p class="tel">
    <span class="type">
        <span class="value-title" title="cell">mobile</span>
    </span>
    <span class="value">+44 1234 123 123</span>
</p>
```

In this example, *mobile* is displayed to the user, while machines will recognize the requisite hCard property value of `cell` for the telephone `type`.

The value class pattern is the most flexible of all microformats patterns because it allows authors to *choose which method is ideal for their content and sites*.

Furthermore, all of my examples have used `<span>`s, but that markup element isn't tied to the value class pattern (or the value-title subset). You can use any element that makes semantic sense, whether it is `<strong>`, `<em>`, `<p>`, etc.

A word of (slight) caution

It is important to realize that this brand-spanking-new pattern is only *somewhat* supported by machines, though it is gaining traction every day in existing transformers like Optimus (http://microformatique.com/optimus/) and X2V (http://suda.co.uk/projects/X2V/).

The rules for parsing this pattern are not completely finalized, nor is the current documentation. However, they are fairly solid.

Still, you should use this pattern with the awareness that future changes to documentation and parsing rules may affect the pages on which you implement it.

Also note that the value class pattern is, perhaps, the most complicated in microformats. The above was just a cursory review. I will go into further detail as it applies to various microformat implementations. Don't worry, you'll get this if you haven't already. Plus, how else am I to ensure that you'll keep reading?

Global Benefits

I've covered a lot about microformats thus far, but I've yet to go into much detail about the benefits. Let's do that now.

While each microformat has its own specific benefits, there are global benefits to microformats in general.

SEO

During my earlier discussion of semantics, I briefly mentioned SEO (search engine optimization). Since this is one area of the web in which many companies are deeply invested, it is worth mentioning again.

Organic SEO can be challenging. It depends on a wide range of factors, not the least of which is quality content. But if you have quality content, you can add even more value with the semantics inherent in microformats.

Let's consider rel-me and Google. Google likes the extra semantic hook of `rel="me"` on links because it indicates that the link destination references a page about a person. I use rel-me on my blog, as well as on my design portfolio. And most, if not all, of the social networks I use also assign rel-me to my profile links.

What this tells Google is that all of these pages are about me. So when I search for my name on Google, the sites using rel-me on links to pages about me have a potentially higher page rank than others. And I stress *potentially*. Page rank is determined by more than just a single semantic addition. But it certainly helps, especially when used with POSH.

And there is no doubt that the two biggest search engines out there, Google and Yahoo!, are embracing microformats to enhance their search results. Google's Rich Snippets supports microformats and RDFa for content about people (hCard) and reviews (hReview) to provide more information in their search results.

Similarly, Yahoo! SearchMonkey encourages site developers and owners to add microformats to certain content in order to provide enhanced search results in Yahoo! Search Gallery.

Frankly, I think you would be remiss if you didn't implement (at least) the specific microformats Yahoo! and Google are using to improve their search results.

Extensible data publishing

With microformats, you are essentially publishing your content for multiple uses.

Content by itself supports user access. Adding POSH to the equation gives search engines the semantic value it needs to evaluate that content. Throw microformats into the mix and search engines get even more semantic value. And your users get a potentially unlimited number of ways to utilize that content.

How so? Through the myriad parsers and extractors available that can take microformatted content and convert it to XML (Extensible Markup Language), JSON (JavaScript Object Notation), RSS (Really Simple Syndication), and so on—whatever format in which you want to publish your data. Yet you only have to write the content once.

For example, by using hCard with contact information, you automatically make it possible for that information to be converted into a downloadable vCard, which can then be used by programs such as Microsoft's Outlook and Apple's Address Book.

Standards

Microformats encourage standards. And not just today's web standards regarding semantics and separation of content from presentation, but standards in terms of design and development processes.

Consider a large, and possibly distributed, web team working on an expansive corporate site. If that team uses microformats, they don't need to discuss *how* to mark up content. Further, with consistent markup, CSS development is easier and faster. Even better, that team can then extract microformatted content for custom web applications on the site, such as an employee directory that can be downloaded directly from web content.

All of this combined leads to more efficient use of time and resources, which leads to more cost-effective development.

And I'll say it again: following standards is, at least in my opinion, the benchmark of a true professional who cares about the quality of his work.

Simplicity

I hope I've made it apparent already how simple microformats are. If I haven't, I promise to prove it in the following chapters. For now, take my word for it. *They are simple.*

But what is the value of this simplicity? Basically, anyone can implement microformats as long as they have a fundamental understanding of XHTML. In fact, you don't even need to know CSS; you just have to understand the application of class values in markup.

Simplicity also means that microformats have a minimal learning curve, so it doesn't take a lot of time to grok them and start implementing right away.

Styling hooks

While this may not be a typical "business case" benefit, it is one I think any web designer or front-end developer would appreciate (if it isn't apparent to them already). Because microformats rely on classes and attributes, they are perfectly suited for easier styling.

How? Microformats already have their own classes (properties and sub-properties). You don't need to create new classes for styling your content; you just use the ones defined in your microformat. Less time is required to think about (semantic) class names, leaving you more time to focus on the styles themselves.

But that doesn't mean you are restricted to only the classes from microformats. The W3C allows combining class selectors, so you can add as many classes as you like to your microformatted content.

And if you like to define your CSS rules based on elements, rather than declaring rules for specific `classes`, microformats don't prohibit you from doing so.

Even better, because several microformats take advantage of XHTML attributes, you can also use CSS attribute selectors to define specific styles based on attributes.

For example, via CSS, you can add an icon to the beginning of links with `rel="license"`, rather than applying a `class` or, worst case (and perhaps bad practice), adding that icon inline with your markup.

Here's what that might look like in your CSS:

```
a[rel~="license"]:before {content: url(copyright.png);}
```

All of today's standards-compliant browsers support CSS attribute selectors. Which, obviously, means Microsoft Internet Explorer (IE) 6—the crap browser of the web world—doesn't. But it is 2009, people. Embrace progressive enhancement and screw IE 6.

Challenges

With the good comes the not-so-good. Despite their simplicity and benefits, microformats have faced some challenges.

Usability and accessibility concerns

When I detailed the datetime design pattern, I mentioned that, historically, it posed one of the arguments against microformats. In fact, the British Broadcasting Company (BBC), which had adopted microformats early on, decided to drop microformats that used this datetime design pattern.

The pattern had two problems. Used in conjunction with the abbr design pattern, the machine-readable ISO 8601 date-time information defined in the `title` attribute displays as a browser tooltip when users hover over the content. Not everyone understands this ISO 8601 information, so this can pose a usability issue.

And because screen readers read/speak `title` attribute values, in a screen reader set to expand abbreviations, `<abbr title="2008-09-30">` would be read aloud as "two thousand eight dash zero nine dash thirty." In 2007, the Web Standards Project dubbed this problem "hAccessibility."

Another common usability concern was related to a lack of localization in the property values used by some microformats. For example, the hCard subproperty values for indicating telephone type (for example, home, cell, work, and so on) are localized for American-English.

If I were to list my cell phone number in my hCard, I would use `<span class="type">cell</span>`. That is appropriate, since I'm American and that value has meaning to me.

However, British-English refers to cell phones as *mobile* phones. Yet mobile isn't a valid value for hCard telephone types, and thus can cause confusion to users.

The good news

With the recent release of the value class pattern, these issues are largely addressed. As developers update their tools and markup to recognize this new pattern, these problems will likely go the way of the dodo bird.

Unnecessary markup?

During my foray into the wonderful world of microformats, I discovered many people blogging and commenting that microformats require unnecessary and excessive markup. This is a misperception, although it's one I think was unintentionally propagated by less-than-ideal examples of microformats.

Case in point is the Microformats Wiki (http://microformats.org/wiki), which is a fount of useful information—but sometimes also a fount of microformat examples that don't use POSH, instead relying on nonsemantic `<div>`s and `<span>`s—markup diseases known as "divitis" and "spanitis."

The reality is, and I will demonstrate it throughout this book, that microformats can and should rely on clean, semantic markup that is appropriate to the content. `<div>` and `<span>` elements are not required for microformats. They work, just like any markup would work, but they are not part of the specifications and are not required.

As for the argument of excessive `classes`, I think some people (wrongly) believe that the defined `class` values for microformats can't be used as CSS hooks, necessitating the use of additional `class` values. I've already explained that they can and should be. No new `classes` are needed for styling microformats.

All that said, though, there are situations when an extra `<span>` or `<div>` may be needed. But that happens in markup development, regardless of the presence of microformats. Can you say `<div class="wrap">`? It is just a reality of our current markup specifications. Sometimes you need non-semantic elements to achieve presentational goals.

So, if you're OK with adding a few `<div>`s or `<span>`s for presentation, how can you argue intelligently against adding them for semantic richness?

Adoption

The last challenge that I see facing microformats is slow adoption. Personally, I think part of the problem is lack of awareness, but also there aren't enough tools available that take advantage of microformats. As of this writing, most browsers require plugins or extensions to provide a nice microformats user experience (although both Firefox and Opera have *some* native support).

These browser plug-ins, scripts, extractors, and parsers, are great tools. But they are mainly known about by geeks—and a comparatively small number of geeks at that. Unfortunately, most everyday users don't know about or take advantage of browser plug-ins, much less seek custom applications.

What's the solution? I like to think that if more folks implemented micro-formats on their sites, then browser developers would see the advantage of offering native tools for discovering and working with microformats.

Also, as more people publish microformats, developers have even more structured data to work with and create tools to help publishing and consumption. In fact, this is already happening, with Microsoft's Oomph Microformats Toolkit (http://visitmix.com/Lab/oomph/).

And as search engines take more and more advantage of the extra seman-tics microformats offer, they deliver better and more relevant results. This benefits search engine users (which is pretty much everyone), so publishers would be remiss to pass up on an opportunity to make their content more searchable and usable.

This future-gazing isn't unrealistic. It isn't even a distant reality. Which is one of the many reasons I choose to implement microformats wherever possible. Maybe by the time you finish this book, you'll agree with me. And then we can form a club. And get T-shirts.

Why a Book on Microformats?

Yeah, I know, you want to get to the meat of microformats. I get it, I'm impatient too. Go ahead and skip to the next chapter if you just can't wait any longer. Or, you can indulge me in my explanation of why I wanted to write a book on microformats. Your call, but you *will* hurt my feelings if you ignore this part.

Microformats are inherently simple. I've said it a dozen times already and, by the end of this book, I'll probably have said it a hundred times. But despite the fact of this simplicity, microformats continue to stump some folks.

Too techy

Why? I think the biggest suspect is that most available information about microformats makes them seem intimidating.

I've already touched on the abundance of less-than-ideal examples of microformats on the wiki (I'd normally call them crap examples, but I'm trying to be diplomatic here). But another problem that plagues the wiki is technical jargon.

Every page on the wiki is filled with tons of great information. But the information is described in language that I know I find challenging to comprehend even when my brain is fully functioning (which, sadly, is not often enough).

Lest I sound too negative about the wiki, the community is actively working on interative improvements to the content and examples. So, maybe by the time you read this, many of these criticisms will be addressed (fingers crossed!)

More conversational

Since microformats are so simple, the language used to explain them should be as well. And I'm aiming to do that with this book.

As I hope I've already demonstrated, microformats can be explained using conversational, easy-to-understand language and practical examples. And I throw in a bit of humor—ahem, my pathetic attempt at humor—because even I can admit that microformats aren't necessarily sexy, so discussions about them might need a little extra something to keep your attention.

Practical examples

I also believe that a key to encouraging broader use of microformats is to show the different ways they can be implemented. This book will not only explain each microformat, but also show multiple examples for each using different context and content.

And, of course, all examples will use POSH.

Diplomacy and new developments

Another reason for this book is to talk about microformats diplomatically. Yes, I do love them, but that doesn't mean that I don't recognize their issues and limitations. And I believe that talking about these issues and limitations is essential for moving forward and encouraging broader acceptance of microformats.

I also wanted to write about the new developments in microformats that address historical accessibility and usability concerns, namely the value class pattern that I've already shared with you.

Finally, I wanted to cover several draft microformats. Even though they aren't formal specifications, they are invaluable in demonstrating all the different types of content that can benefit from microformats.

I heart microformats

And if you haven't guessed it by now, I love microformats. They use what I already know. They are easy to implement. They add semantics to my content. They have potential for future technologies. What's not to love?

So since I love microformats, why not write a book about them? Share my love with the world. Wait, that sounds wrong . . . well, you catch my drift, right?

And that brings us to the end of this chapter. Thanks for sticking around. Now let's dive into the heart of microformats with some great POSHy examples.

Chapter 2

Defining Outlines: XOXO

What Is XOXO?

Since we are just getting started, I thought it would make sense to begin with one of the simplest microformats. You know, ease into things. So, here we go with XOXO.

Nope, it's not about kisses and hugs (although my grandmother would've disagreed). **XOXO** stands for Extensible Open XHTML Outlines, and it is the microformat applied to outline content on the web.

What is considered outline content? Basically, it's content that would be contained by XHTML list elements, such as actual outlines, blogrolls, site maps, even presentations.

What's the point?

Other than adding semantic value, using XOXO with outline content allows machines (remember, those are computers, user agents, applications, and so on, not *The Terminator*) to extract outline content from the page and transform it into XML, JSON, RSS, or whatever data structure you desire.

Let's say, for example, you have a site map marked up using nested lists. If you use the XOXO microformat on this site map, you allow a simple program (which doesn't have to be customized for your page) to extract that content and convert it into a Google Sitemap. Google Sitemaps, as you probably know, can help the search engine crawl your site more intelligently, which may help with SEO.

Profile

Like most of the microformat specifications, XOXO has its own profile. You reference its profile in your `<head>` element:

```
<head profile="http://microformats.org/profile/xoxo">
```

And for clarity's sake, profiles are not required, only recommended.

Basic syntax

The syntax for XOXO is ridiculously simple. You just add the required root property `xoxo` to a list, such as in this example of a linkroll (**Figure 2.1**):

```
<ul class="xoxo">
    <li><a href="http://www.ablognotlimited.com/">A Blog Not
Limited</a></li>
    <li><a href="http://www.alistapart.com/">A List Apart
</a></li>
    <li><a href="http://microformats.org/wiki/Main_Page">
Microformats Wiki</a></li>
</ul>
```

Figure 2.1
Unstyled browser view
of a simple linkroll
using XOXO.

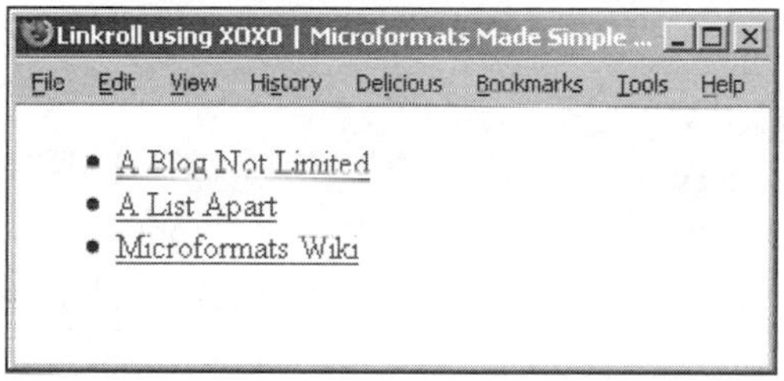

That's it.

XOXO is one of the few microformats that *does* require specific markup. As I mentioned, the `class="xoxo"` is applied to either a `<ul>` or `<ol>` list element. Pick the one that is most semantically appropriate for your content

Once you've decided on the appropriate list element, you'll need to keep a few things in mind in terms of the structure of your list content:

- The `<ul>` or `<ol>` is the container for your outline items. It is the root element of your outline and must be assigned `class="xoxo"`.

- The `<li>`s within your list contain the outline content, which can be a single bit of text, a paragraph, or even nested lists. In the case of nested lists, you can use `<ol>`, `<ul>`, or `<dl>`.

- The only element of a `<ul>` or an `<ol>` that can be a child is an `<li>`. So if you are nesting markup, nest inside the `<li>`s, *not* the `<ul>` or `<ol>`.

And them's the basics.

ORDERED OR UNORDERED: CHOOSING THE RIGHT LIST ELEMENT

Remember all that talk about POSH in Chapter 1? Well, now we're going to talk POSH specifics about list elements. This should help you decide which list element makes the most sense for your content.

There are three types of lists in XHTML: ordered lists (`<ol>`), unordered lists (`<ul>`), and definition lists (`<dl>`). For the purposes of the XOXO discussion, I'm focusing on ordered lists and unordered lists. (I will cover details about definition lists later, so don't get your panties in a bunch.)

First, when should you use a list element? Use it whenever you have a series of related content items that would make sense organized in a group or a list (duh)—for example, navigation links, a group of tags or keywords, a shopping list, a set of instructions, and so on.

Once you have this sort of content, you need to determine which list element, ordered or unordered, is the most semantically suitable for your content.

Unordered lists group or organize content regardless of any sequence or suggested ordering. The lists are sometimes referred to as *bulleted* because the default browser rendering of `<ul>` has a bullet preceding each `<li>`.

Ordered lists, meanwhile, should be used with content that has a specific order or sequence.

Different from unordered lists, `<ol>`s render with a sequential number preceding each `<li>`, which indicates the order in the list.

Not only do `<ol>`s and `<ul>`s render differently on the browser, but also their semantic meaning is different. User agents—such as screen readers, nongraphical browsers, and search engines—interpret the content contained by an `<ol>` as having a sequence, and the content contained by a `<ul>` as not having a sequence.

But other than the rendering and semantics, `<ul>`s and `<ol>`s have the same characteristics:

- Child elements are list items (`<li>`).

- `<li>`s can contain most block-level and inline elements, including `<h1>`, `<p>`, `<img />`, and other lists, known as **nested lists.**

- Nested lists—in fact, all content—must be contained by the child `<li>`, *not* the parent `<ol>` or `<ul>`.

And both `<ul>`s and `<ol>`s can be styled in any fashion. The presentation is only limited to your own CSS skills and imagination.

Now you know about ordered and unordered lists. *And knowing is half the battle.* Go forth and mark up your lists' content confidently.

Detailed content? Detailed markup.

Of course, if you want to get into further detail with your content structure and metadata, you can. It just isn't required for XOXO.

If your outline content contains in-depth information (opposed to brief text descriptions), be sure to mark up that content semantically. Remember,

`<li>`s can contain most elements, so if you have headline content, use the appropriate element (`<h1>`–`<h6>`). If you have paragraph content, use `<p>`. If you have more list content, use `<ul>`, `<ol>`, or `<dl>`.

Or when URLs are included for an item in your outline, the `<a>` *can* be assigned attributes to provide further detail:

- `title` attribute, to give further descriptive detail about the link

- `type` attribute, to indicate the MIME (Multipurpose Internet Mail Extensions) type of the `href` destination

- `rel` attribute, to indicate (via XFN) the relationship of the `href` destination to your outline

- `rev` attribute, to indicate the relationship of your outline to the `href` destination

These are just extras, though, not required attributes for the links in your outline. But if you have the information, why not add it? The more detail, the more power your content has.

For even more content power (I'm starting to sound like a dish detergent ad), if it makes sense to apply another microformat to any of that content, do it.

If you have contact information, use hCard. For event information, hCalendar. And so on. Of course, we have yet to cover those microformats in detail, but keep in mind that combining microformats where appropriate is, as Martha Stewart would say, "a good thing."

Practical markup

So now you know the basic syntax for XOXO, and you know all about XHTML list elements. Let's put all of this into action with some practical examples.

S5 presentation using `<ol>`

I mentioned earlier that outline content can be a presentation. In fact, renowned CSS guru Eric Meyer developed a web-based presentation system that uses XOXO: S5 (Simple Standards-Based Slide Show System).

S5 was developed so that, with a single XHTML page, you can have a web-based slide show along with a printer-friendly version. Not to mention, all of the content in S5 is accessible to search engines for lots of SEO goodness.

I've used S5 for many of my own presentations. Here's an excerpt:

A fair amount of markup, JavaScript, and CSS is required to get S5 to work completely. But since this book is about microformats, I won't be talking about any of that. Plus, it's all already well documented at http://meyerweb.com/eric/tools/s5/. See for yourself.

```
<ol class="presentation">
    <li class="slide">
        <h1>What Are Web Standards?</h1>
        <div class="slidecontent">
            <ul>
                <li>Technologies, specifications and guide
lines for creating and interpreting web-based content</li>
                <li>Designed to future-proof web content and
make that content accessible to as many users as possible</li>
                <li>Encompasses Structural Languages (XHTML,
<acronym title="eXtensible Markup Language">XML</acronym>),
Presentation Languages (CSS, <acronym title="Mathematical
Markup Language">MathML</acronym>, <acronym title="Scalable
Vector Graphics">SVG</acronym>), Object Models (<acronym
title="Document Object Model">DOM</acronym>) and Scripting
Languages (JavaScript/ECMAScript)</li>
            </ul>
        </div>
    </li>
    <li class="slide">
        <h1>The Holy Grail</h1>
        <div class="slidecontent">
            <ul>
                <li>Valid markup and styles</li>
                <li>Semantic markup and styles</li>
                <li>Separation of content (XHTML),
presentation (CSS) and behavior (JavaScript)</li>
                <li><em>Works</em> in <em>any</em> web
browser</li>
            </ul>
        </div>
    </li>
    <li class="slide">
        <h1>It All Starts With Valid Markup</h1>
        <div class="slidecontent">
```

```
        <ul>
            <li>Valid means that the syntax of your
markup is correct</li>
            <li>Correct according to the definitions of
your DOCTYPE</li>
            <li>DOCTYPE also ensures browsers render
your pages in Standards mode = more consistent display</li>
        </ul>
    </div>
  </li>
</ol>
```

As you can see, it is just a list containing detailed content that I've marked up to reflect the proper semantic structure.

Required root property: xoxo

To implement XOXO on this slideshow is really quite simple. I just apply `class="xoxo"` to the `<ol>`, and all of my displayed slide content is contained within each `<li>`.

```
<ol class="presentation xoxo">
```

All the other classes you see applied to the various elements just support the CSS and JavaScript that enable the slideshow to display and function as intended (**Figure 2.2**). So while these aren't necessary for XOXO, they do illustrate that you can style microformats any way your heart desires.

Figure 2.2
Styled browser view, using the core S5 CSS, of three presentation "slides."

And to illustrate the power of CSS and POSH, here is the unstyled view of the presentation in a single web page that contains all of the content, completely accessible to all devices, search engines, and users (**Figure 2.3**).

Figure 2.3
Unstyled browser view
of the S5 presentation
using an ordered list
with XOXO.

The logic behind the markup

Now, as I promised in Chapter 1, we'll discuss the logic behind the markup in each example. Here goes.

You will note that the S5 markup utilizes an `<ol>` as its root element. That is because the slides have a sequential order to them: slide one, slide two, slide three, . . . you get the picture.

Because there is a sequence to the slides that is important to the content, an `<ol>` is the correct list element to use. Even better, because `<li>`s can contain most block-level elements, using an `<ol>` doesn't restrict what type of content the `<li>`s can contain.

Of course, this presentation could've also used a series of `<div>`s rather than an `<ol>`. In fact, there *is* a non-XOXO S5 version. But personally, I feel the `<ol>` is more semantic because of its inherent sequential nature. Not to mention, XOXO only works with the `<ol>`-based version.

Site map using nested `<ul>`s

I also referenced a site map as an example of outline content. So let's see how that would look with XOXO, using a simple site map for a fictional company that sells widgets and sprockets.

```
<ul>
    <li><a href="/" rel="home">Home</a></li>
    <li><a href="/Products/">Products</a>
        <ul>
            <li><a href="/Products/Widgets/">Widgets</a>
                <ul>
                    <li><a href="/Products/Widgets/Blue/">
Blue Widgets</a></li>
                    <li><a href="/Products/Widgets/Red/">
Red Widgets</a></li>
                    <li><a href="/Products/Widgets/Green/">
Green Widgets</a></li>
                </ul>
            </li>
            <li><a href="/Products/Sprockets/">Sprockets</a>
                <ul>
                    <li><a href="/Products/Sprockets/
Orange/">Orange Sprockets</a></li>
                    <li><a href="/Products/Sprockets/
Purple/">Purple Sprockets</a></li>
                    <li><a href="/Products/Sprockets/
Yellow/">Yellow Sprockets</a></li>
                </ul>
            </li>
        </ul>
    </li>
    <li><a href="/Services/">Services</a>
        <ul>
            <li><a href="/Services/Installation/">
Installation</a></li>
            <li><a href="/Services/Removal/">Removal</a></li>
        </ul>
    </li>
    <li><a href="/About/">About</a>
        <ul>
```

(continues on next page)

```
              <li><a href="/About/Press/">Press Room</a></li>
              <li><a href="/About/Events">Calendar of Events
</a></li>
        </ul>
    </li>
    <li><a href="/Contact/">Contact Us</a></li>
</ul>
```

Required root property: `xoxo`

Once again, to apply XOXO to this site map, I add `class="xoxo"` to my
root `<ul>`:

```
<ul class="xoxo">
```

As with the S5 markup example, the only things essential for XOXO are a
list element assigned `class="xoxo"`, and nested lists properly contained
by `<li>`s.

Are you starting to see how simple XOXO is? Good. That's what I want
to hear.

The logic behind the markup

For a site map, at least how I see it, there isn't an inherent sequential order
to the content. It is just a list of links to pages on a site. As such, a `<ul>`
makes the most semantic sense to me. There is a hierarchy, though, which
is why this example uses nested lists to give the content a structure suggesting sections and subsections (**Figure 2.4**).

Figure 2.4
Unstyled browser view
of a simple site map
using nested ordered
lists with XOXO.

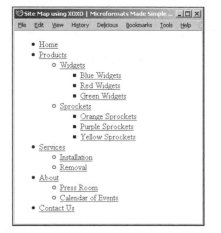

Table of contents using nested `<ol>`s

Another possible type of outline content may be a table of contents for a lengthy online article to help users navigate to specific content. I've been guilty of verbosity with some of my microformats blog posts, and in retrospect, a table of contents might have been useful. Here's how I'd do it now:

```
<ol>
    <li>Getting Semantic With Microformats, Part 3: hCard
        <ol>
            <li><a href="#origins">Origins: vCard</a></li>
            <li><a href="#peopleOrgCoPlaces">People,
Organizations, Companies &amp; Places</a></li>
            <li><a href="#me">A Person, Namely Me</a>
                <ol>
                    <li><a href="#personalIdentity">Personal
Identity Information</a>
                        <ol>
                            <li><a href="#sidebarDates">
Sidebar: Dates</a></li>
                        </ol>
                    </li>
                    <li><a href="#subProperties">
Sub-Properties</a></li>
                    <li><a href="#emailPhone">Email &amp;
Phone Information</a></li>
                    <li><a href="#address">Address
Information</a>
                        <ol>
                            <li><a href="#sidebarAddress">
Sidebar: address</a></li>
                        </ol>
                    </li>
                    <li><a href="#webSite">Web Site
Information</a></li>
                    <li><a href="#final">Final Product</a>
</li>
                    <li><a href="#add">Add to Address Book
</a></li>
                </ol>
            </li>
```

(continues on next page)

```
                <li><a href="#rules">Some Rules &amp; A Reminder
</a></li>
                <li><a href="#profile">Let's Not Forget the
Profile</a></li>
                <li><a href="#naturalLanguage">Natural Language
hCard</a>
                    <ol>
                        <li><a href="#differences">The
Differences</a></li>
                    </ol>
                </li>
                <li><a href="#combining">Combining hCard &amp;
XFN</a></li>
                <li><a href="#orgCo">Organizations &amp;
Companies</a></li>
                <li><a href="#places">Places</a></li>
                <li><a href="#benefits">Let's Talk Benefits</a>
                    <ol>
                        <li><a href="#semantics">Semantics</a>
</li>
                        <li><a href="#sharing">Share Contact
Information</a>
                            <ol>
                                <li><a href="#firefox">Firefox
</a></li>
                                <li><a href="#safari">Safari
</a></li>
                                <li><a href="#bookmarklets">
Bookmarklets</a></li>
                            </ol>
                        </li>
                        <li><a href="#search">Search</a></li>
                        <li><a href="#social">Social Networks
</a></li>
                    </ol>
                </li>
                <li><a href="#tools">Tools to Make It Easier</
a></li>
                <li><a href="#more">There Is So Much More</a>
</li>
                <li><a href="#part4">Coming In Part 4</a></li>
```

```
        </ol>
    </li>
</ol>
```

Required root property: `xoxo`

Let me say it one more time: all you need to do to your POSHified content
to utilize XOXO is add `class="xoxo"`:

```
<ol class="xoxo">
```

The logic behind the markup

For this table of contents, I used the same concept as that of the site map,
but with nested <ol>s. Why ordered lists? Because tables of content are, by
nature, sequential, so the <ol> gives me that sequential meaning through
the structure of the element (**Figure 2.5**).

Figure 2.5
Unstyled browser
view of a simple table
of contents using
nested ordered lists
with XOXO.

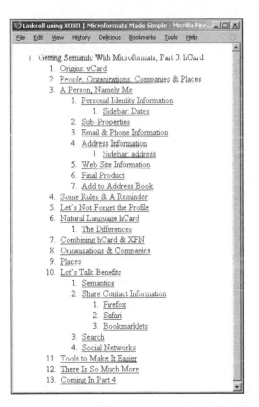

You did it!

And that concludes our first look at a microformat. I *told* you it was easy.

Next up, we're going to take a look at the `rel`- and `rev`-based microformats, which give semantic meaning about the relationship of links to their destination `hrefs`.

Chapter 3

Defining Links:
rel and rev

Link Relationships

Another set of microformats that are extremely easy to understand and implement are those used to define **link relationships**.

What are link relationships? First, let's consider links. There are two types: hyperlinks and links to external resources. Hyperlinks point to any resource on the web such as another HTML page, an image, an audio file, and so on, and they are clickable in the browser, allowing the user to navigate to the referenced resource.

The second type of links are those to external resources that a web page references, frequently appearing in the `<head>`. Both utilize the `href` attribute to indicate the destination resource, but each has its own syntax:

A basic hyperlink uses the `<a>` element:

```
<a href="http://www.ablognotlimited.com/">A Blog Not
Limited</a>
```

And a basic external resource link uses `<link />`:

```
<link href="/styles/global.css" rel="stylesheet" />
```

You will note that in the `<link />` example, there is a `rel="stylesheet"` attribute-value pair. This indicates the relationship—a style sheet—of the destination resource (global.css) to the page on which it is referenced. And I'm sure this example is one with which you're familiar.

So, in essence, link relationships are a way for you to indicate the *type* of resource an `href` references.

Microformats take link relationships a step further. They let you assign semantic values to hyperlinks in order to indicate the relationship of the destination `href` to the current web page (via `rel`), as well as indicate whether or not you endorse the destination `href` (via `rev`).

rel

The `rel` attribute is used as part of several elemental microformats. When applied to a hyperlink (`<a>`), `rel` specifies the relationship of the linked resource (`href` value) to the page on which the link appears.

Another thing to keep in mind about `rel`: you can assign multiple values.

So, let's dive in.

Formal specifications

As I mentioned in Chapter 1, there are formal specifications and drafts. I'm going to cover *all* of the `rel` microformats in this chapter. Fasten your seatbelts!

rel-license

You use the rel-license microformat to indicate the link to a web page's license, such as a Creative Commons license.

On my blog, I copyright my content with Creative Commons. As such, I provide a link to that license:

```
<a href="http://creativecommons.org/licenses/by-nc-nd/3.0/"
rel="license">copyright</a>
```

And to give that link more semantic value, I indicate the link relationship with `rel="license"`.

Profile   Of course, because I'm using a microformat, I want to be sure to include the necessary profile in my document `<head>`:

```
<head profile="http://microformats.org/profile/rel-license">
```

And that's all there is to it

Benefits   For you folks who need a greater reason than semantic value, there are a handful of benefits rel-license offers, thanks to some nifty web tools.

The Tails Export plug-in for Mozilla Firefox automatically recognizes links assigned rel-license and lets users go directly to the link destination and view the HTML source of the link (**Figure 3.1**).

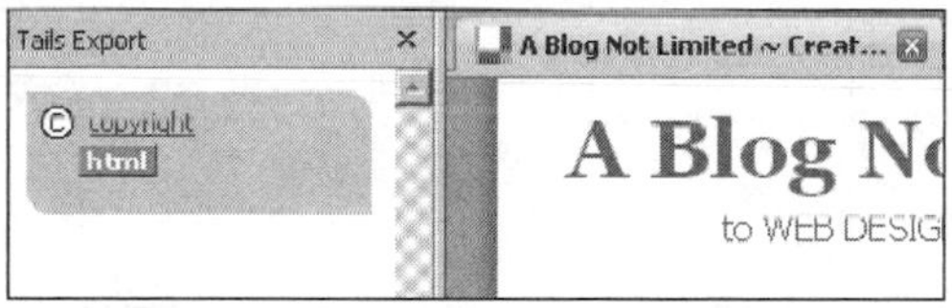

Figure 3.1
View of the Tails
Export identification
of rel-license

There are also major search engines that have created specialized searches that filter content based on the availability of a license: Yahoo's

Creative Commons Search (**Figure 3.2**) and Google's Usage Rights option in Advanced Search (**Figure 3.3**).

Figure 3.2
Yahoo's Creative
Commons Search

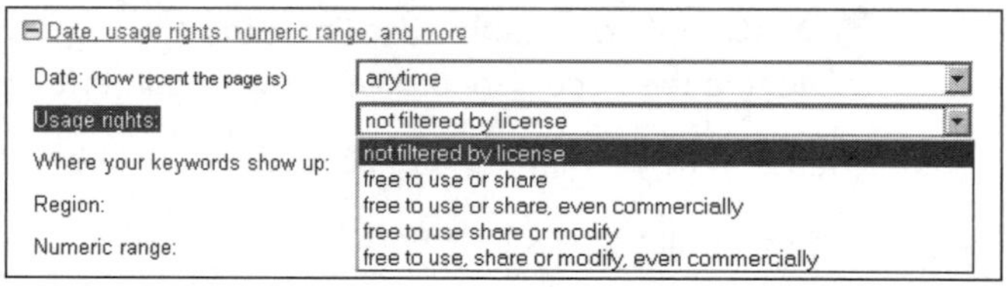

Figure 3.3
Google's Usage Rights
options in its Advanced
Search

And by using rel-license, you are keeping good company: Creative Commons uses rel-license in its generated markup (**Figure 3.4**):

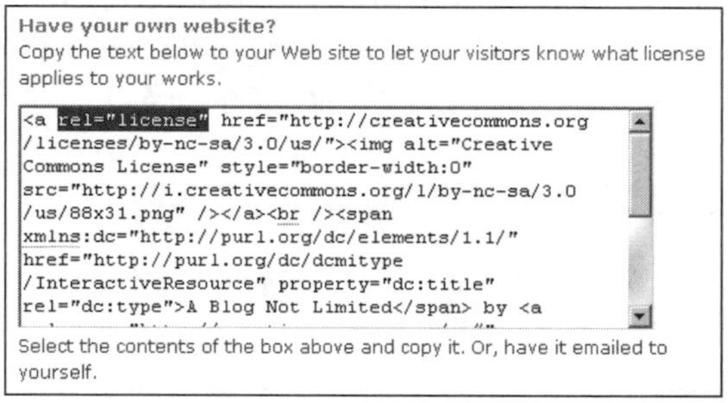

Figure 3.4
Generated markup from
Creative Commons for
license links

rel-tag

Another `rel`-based microformat is rel-tag, which is used on hyperlinks that indicate what a given web page—or part of that page—is about. This is commonly known as **tagging** and is widely used on blogs, where authors assign **tags** to their blog posts. I use it myself:

```
<a href="http://www.ablognotlimited.com/articles/tag/
microformats/" rel="tag">microformats</a>
```

And where I include tag links, I always specify `rel="tag"` in the `<a>`. I even assign `rel="tag"` to my blog's category links, since they, too, describe what my pages are about.

Other than specifying the `rel` value, the only other requirement of rel-tag is that the destination `href` must have the actual tag content as the final segment of the logical URL.

```
http://www.ablognotlimited.com/articles/tag/microformats/
```

This is known as the **tag space.** And any web page that utilizes a logical URL can be used as a tag space.

URLS: LOGICAL VS. PHYSICAL

In describing the tag space, I mentioned logical URLs. Figured I might as well explain this, so as to continue with keeping things simple.

A logical URL indicates a resource, whereas a physical URL indicates a content type. The example URL I used in the rel-tag illustration above is logical. A physical URL would look like this:

```
http://www.ablognotlimited.com/articles/tag/microformats.html
```

Notice how the physical URL contains an extension of .html? That says the URL points to an HTML page—a MIME type. This *cannot* be used as a tag space.

Profile   But let's not forget the profile:

```
<head profile="http://microformats.org/profile/rel-tag">
```

Benefits   *Of course* there are benefits to using rel-tag (other than semantics).

Do you use Firefox? Then get the Operator plug-in. It recognizes rel-tag links on web pages and provides searches across other websites (such as Flickr, Amazon, Technorati, YouTube) based on the tag (**Figure 3.5**):

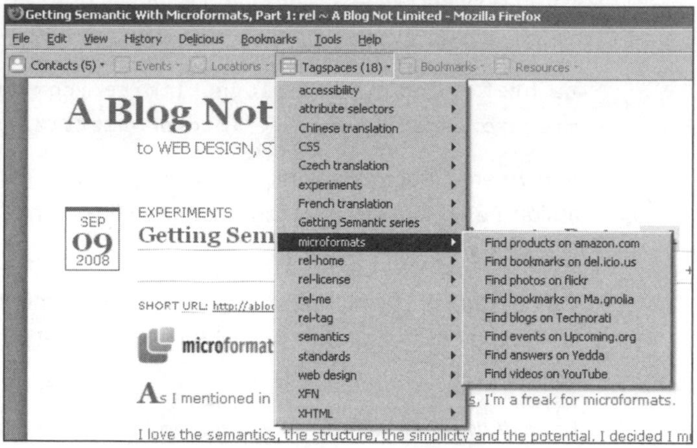

Figure 3.5
The Operator plug-in for Mozilla Firefox recognizes rel-tag and offers tag-specific searches of popular websites.

And Technorati Tags (http://technorati.com/tag) indexes rel-tags to provide tag-specific searches of content across the web.

There are dozens of rel-tag implementations in the wild. Here are just a few:

- Huffduffer, the audio podcasting service, uses rel-tag on all of its tag links, making it easier for users to find other similarly tagged content on the site.

- Opera, the browser developer, uses rel-tag for tag links on all My Opera blog entries, as well as on its own Dev Opera articles.

- Google, too, assigns rel-tag to its blog-post tag links.

So, join the cool kids. Add rel-tag to your tag links.

rel-nofollow

The last of the `rel`-based formal specifications is rel-nofollow, which is used to instruct spiders (like search engines) *not* to follow a link. Not follow a link? Yep.

Before I explain further, you should understand that search engines typically give higher page ranks to pages that have lots of links to them. The search assumption is that if you link to a page, you are indicating it has value.

But what if you have a link on your site that is intended to give your users a destination for more information, yet you don't care to offer that link any additional weight or a higher rank in search engines? An example of this might be links in comments posted to your blog, particularly those from spammers.

If you don't want to promote those links in the eyes of search engines, you just add `rel="nofollow"` to the `<a>`s:

```
<a href="http://www.commenter.com/" rel="nofollow">Commenter
</a>
```

Profile   Just like the other `rel` microformats I've covered so far, rel-nofollow has a profile:

```
<head profile="http://microformats.org/profile/rel-nofollow">
```

Benefits countered by issues   I've already explained the primary benefit of rel-nofollow: you prevent raising the search engine rank of a given link. And that's about it.

While this is a powerful benefit (at least in my opinion), there are a number of folks who do not support this approach—for a variety of reasons:

- Some argue that `rel` values should strictly indicate the *relationship* of a link destination to its source. From that perspective, rel-nofollow indicates a behavior, which is contrary to the link relationship concept inherent in link-based microformats.

- Others suggest the value name is inaccurate. Specifically, rel-nofollow doesn't restrict search engines from *following* a link (as a robots.txt would), but instead tells spiders not to raise the rank of the link.

- Still others are concerned about rampant, indiscriminate use of rel-nofollow on links to legitimate sites, which could adversely affect their search-engine ranking.

Nonetheless, rel-nofollow is widely used.

- Many social networks apply `rel="nofollow"` to links on users' profiles, including Twitter, Flickr, and Facebook.

- Wikipedia uses rel-nofollow on all of its external links.

- And even Google has advised rel-nofollow be applied to links in paid advertisements, links to content that the site owner doesn't trust, and links to password-protected sections of sites.

As for what you should do, I would encourage you to consider your links carefully and then decide if rel-nofollow is appropriate.

If you choose *not* to use this particular microformat, I promise I won't kick you out of the club—you know, the one we're going to get T-shirts for.

Drafts

Now it's time to head into the draft link-based microformats. Remember, drafts are those microformats that have yet to be formally approved, so they are in a state of some (likely minimal) flux.

rel-home

Wanna guess what rel-home does? You got it—rel-home indicates that the destination of the specified link is the site's home page.

For the most part, rel-home is used for site navigation, but it also provides some indication of the broader site structure to individual pages. Can I get a "Hell, yeah!" for meaning and semantics?

Unlike the `rel` microformats I've already covered, which are only used with `<a>`s, rel-home can be used two ways: on hyperlinks and on links to external resources.

On my blog, I use it both ways. In the `<head>` of my site documents I include this:

```
<link href="http://www.ablognotlimited.com/" title="Home
page" rel="home" />
```

Figure 3.6
Opera's Navigation toolbar recognizes rel-home in `<link />`s.

This particular implementation was developed so that browsers could easily detect a site's home page and provide users a hotkey or shortcut to navigate to the site's home page. Unfortunately, browser support pretty much sucks. At present, only Opera supports this (**Figure 3.6**).

The other implementation for rel-home is just like that of the other `rel`-based microformats. For links to a site's home page, you specify `rel="home"` on the `<a>`:

```
<a href="http://www.ablognotlimited.com" rel="home">A Blog
Not Limited</a>
```

Profile   Note that rel-home does *not* have a profile URI. So you can skip referencing a profile in your `<head>` when using rel-home.

But in case you are interested, you'll find the XMDP for rel-home on the Microformats Wiki: http://microformats.org/wiki/rel-home.

Benefits While I mentioned that the use of `rel="home"` in a `<link />` element aids in navigation (at least in Opera), it also provides broader accessibility. Several text-only browsers, like Links and Lynx, display rel-home metadata as a navigation link at the top of pages.

Unfortunately, that's about it in terms of the benefits. However, if more browsers begin supporting rel-home, you can imagine how useful it would be for navigation and accessibility.

And I, myself, have no problem adding a few semantic tidbits to my pages—especially if they can be utilized in the future.

rel-directory

Next up, rel-directory. This draft microformat indicates that the `href` destination of a link is to a directory that contains (or should contain) a reference to the page containing the link.

Now you may ask, what is considered a directory? Well, the Open Directory Project is a great example. It is "the largest, most comprehensive human-edited directory of the web." And it has spawned several more focused directories:

* ChefMoz for restaurants

* MusicMoz for music

* Open Site, an online encyclopedia

So let's say you've written an article about adoption, which would be a good fit for Open Directory Project in the Home section, under Family and then Adoption.

All you need to do is add a link in your adoption article page that directs to the appropriate Open Directory Project path, and then assign `rel="directory"`:

```
<a href="http://www.dmoz.org/Home/Family/Adoption/"
rel="directory">Adoption</a>
```

Profile Like rel-home, rel-directory does *not* have a profile URI. The rel-directory XMDP is, however, included on the Microformats Wiki: http://microformats.org/wiki/rel-directory.

Still, no need to reference any profile when using rel-directory.

Benefits   The rel-directory draft is designed to build distributed, open directories. So by using rel-directory on links that you wish to be included in a directory, you are, theoretically, "populating" the directory remotely. You don't have to submit your page to the directory itself. And meanwhile you, as the content owner, can control the place(s) your site is found.

Technorati's Blog Directory at http://technorati.com/blogs/directory/ automatically adds blogs it discovers that use rel-directory.

Imagine you maintain your company's intranet, which has a directory list-ing with links to employee profiles. If this employee directory is anything like the one I work with, it is manually entered data from Human Resources that has to be imported on a (hopefully) regular basis. Which means it is constantly out-of-date and a major pain in the ass to maintain.

But what if those employee-profile pages featured links to the direc-tory's alphabetical listing? And what if those links were assigned `rel="directory"`?

You could easily create a web application (remember the machines) that parses the information and extracts the links, dynamically creating a direc-tory. And not just any directory. A directory that links to profiles that each employee updates themselves. Less work for Human Resources. More timely information. Easier maintenance.

I'm sold.

rel-enclosure

You use the rel-enclosure draft microformat to indicate links to files (video, audio, and so on) that can be downloaded and cached. An example might be if you provided a link to a video recording on your site that was intended to be downloaded, rather than streamed online.

For such links, you simply add `rel="enclosure"` to the `<a>`:

```
<a href="http://yoursite.com/files/video.mov"
rel="enclosure">download the video</a>
```

Profile   Just like the other `rel`-based drafts, rel-enclosure doesn't have a profile URI, but the rel-directory XMDP *is* included on the Microformats Wiki: http://microformats.org/wiki/rel-enclosure.

Benefits   Other than a bit of semantic meaning for your file links, rel-enclosure has some benefit for feeds. If you have a blog that generates a feed and you want to include a link to a file, you should use rel-enclosure on that link.

Why? Because best practices for feed syndication suggest that adding `rel="enclosure"` to your file links can help services like FeedBurner identify the links and convert them to **enclosures** in your feed.

What are enclosures? Basically, they are the files in your feed that readers, such as Google Reader, convert into playable files. Enclosures are essential for things like podcasting.

rel-payment

The last `rel`-based draft microformat is rel-payment, and you use it to indicate link destinations that show or give support (not necessarily financial, despite the name) to the source page.

This might be a link to your organization's fund-raising page that directs users on how to make donations. It could be a link on an online retail site that points to a page where a given product can be purchased. It could even be an affiliate link, such as Amazon's affiliate program.

However, rel-payment is not used on links that actually facilitate a purchase or payment. It is only appropriate for destinations that provide information about or a means to offer support.

So, for those types of links, you add `rel="payment"`:

```
<a href="http://nonprofit.org/fundraising/" rel="payment">
learn about our fundraising program</a>
```

Profile   Again, no profile for rel-payment. The rel-payment XMDP is on the Microformats Wiki: http://microformats.org/wiki/rel-payment.

Benefits   One of the intended benefits of this draft microformat is to allow content aggregators, like feed readers, to easily identify these links so they can be, perhaps, presented differently—such as with a special "donate" or "purchase" indicator.

But that is an intended benefit. As of yet, this is not a reality.

rev

The last link-based microformat utilizes a hyperlink attribute I've not yet covered: `rev`.

You use the `rev` attribute to indicate a reverse relationship with a link destination. So, unlike `rel` (which indicates the relationship of the link destination to the source page), `rev` indicates the relationship of the source page to the link destination.

REV: THE MISUNDERSTOOD ATTRIBUTE

My brief introduction to `rev` may not have been quite enough to explain this infrequently used attribute. So let me go into a bit more detail.

First, let's revisit `rel`. Using rel-license, for example, I'm stating the link on my source page points to a destination that contains my copyright license information. In a way, you can think of it as a "forward" relationship.

```
<a href="http://creativecommons.org/
licenses/by-nc-nd/3.0/" rel="license">
copyright</a>
```

Let's make this clearer by translating it into English:

http://creativecommons.org/licenses/by-nc-nd/3.0/ is the license of this current page.

Conversely, `rev` indicates a reverse relationship. So let's say I have an index page, which contains links to certain sections of my site. For those links, I could include `rev="index"`.

```
<a href="http://www.mysite.com/
purplewidgets/" rev="index">purple
widgets</a>
```

Now the English translation would be this:

The current page is the index for http://www.mysite.com/purplewidgets/.

Despite this (meager) explanation of `rev`, you may still be confused about it. And you wouldn't be alone.

A lot of web designers and developers (myself included) have a hard time grokking `rev` and, as such, it has been ignored entirely or used improperly.

In fact, as of this writing, `rev` has even been removed from the HTML5 specification. Even the microformats community advises against the use of `rev` (the exception being as part of VoteLinks, which was grandfathered).

It is entirely possible, though, that this could change. Recently there has been an astounding amount of discussion regarding the `rev` attribute for links to short URLs, using `rel="canonical"`.

I won't even begin to address this particular point, as it is a rapidly moving target and debatable implementation. However, it is worth mentioning, since `rev` has traditionally gotten such a bad rap. It may make a comeback.

VoteLinks

VoteLinks is a formal link-based microformat, and it uses the `rev` attribute on links to `href` destinations for which you wish to indicate support, lack of support, or neutrality.

For these sorts of links, you add the `rev` attribute to your `<a>` with one of the following values:

- `vote-for`, to indicate that you support the link destination

- `vote-against`, to indicate that you do not support the link destination

- `vote-abstain`, to indicate you don't have an opinion about the link destination

Profile   VoteLinks has its own profile:

```
<head profile="http://microformats.org/profile/vote-links">
```

Benefits   As a link-relationship microformat, VoteLinks lets you specify via hyperlinks whether or not you approve of a link destination. By themselves, without any semantics, search engines automatically treat hyperlinks to other sites as endorsements of those sites. VoteLinks was developed so that content authors could indicate if they did or didn't endorse a site via those hyperlinks.

So, if you include a hyperlink to a product you don't care for (and maybe you aren't a fan of rel-nofollow), you could simply add `rev="vote-against"`.

By default, links that lack the VoteLinks microformat are assumed to have a `rev="vote-for"` or `rev="vote-abstain"` value, depending on the machine that is interpreting them.

Another benefit of VoteLinks is in the creation of distributed voting and reputation systems, such as Folksr. However, I *should* mention that you have to submit your site to Folksr for it to index your VoteLinks; it doesn't seek out websites.

The beauty of distributed voting systems, as opposed to polling and traditional voting, is that content authors retain control of their votes because they control the data.

VOTELINKS OR HREVIEW?

I haven't yet covered hReview (that will be in Chapter 10), but I do want to mention it since I'm talking about endorsements with VoteLinks.

VoteLinks, as an elemental microformat, is extremely simple. And it only indicates endorsement (or lack thereof) via a link relationship. If that is all you want to do, then VoteLinks is the solution.

But what if you want to indicate more than just for, against, or neutral? What if you want to explain *why* you do or do not endorse something?

That's where hReview comes in. It is a compound microformat that gives you even more semantic options for endorsing or pooh-poohing something.

From that perspective, I prefer hReview. The more information, the better, as far as I'm concerned. That is not to say, though, that VoteLinks doesn't have a purpose.

For things like my Delicious linkroll, `rev="vote-for"` is perfect. I don't want to explain why I bookmark everything, I just want to show my endorsement of those link destinations.

Combining Your Elementals

I talked about combining microformats in Chapter 1, and I'm going to talk about it again in relation to the link-based microformats.

Where it makes contextual sense, you should definitely combine these elemental microformats.

rel-nofollow and VoteLinks

If you are using rel-nofollow, for example, you may also want to indicate a lack of support for that link, not just deter spiders from giving it additional weight. Sounds like the perfect use of rel-nofollow *and* VoteLinks, no?

Let's take an example from my blog. I posted an article raving about a new vacuum cleaner I had purchased. But in the discussion I mention the vacuum I had previously owned (and hated). Yet, in the spirit of giving my users a wealth of information, I provided a link to the hated brand:

This VoteLinks markup is styled with CSS in Chapter 12 (page 274).

```
<a href="http://www.vacuumthatsucksbutnotinagoodway.com"
rel="nofollow" rev="vote-against">Vacuum</a>
```

By applying both microformats, I'm telling the spiders to ignore my link when determining page rank for the site, *and* I'm telling vote counters that I vote against that particular vacuum.

rel-tag and rel-directory

Another good combination of `rel`-based microformats is rel-tag and rel-directory. As I mentioned in my explanation of rel-directory, you have a link with an `href` value of a directory URL.

In the case of the Open Directory Project, these URLs are logical and, as such, make perfect tag spaces. Which means you can use both `rel` values together:

```
<a href="http://www.dmoz.org/Home/Family/Adoption/"
rel="directory tag">Adoption</a>
```

By combining these two, you indicate that the link is both a tag *and* a directory listing for the page.

Not Enough Benefit?

Now that we are nearing the end of this chapter, you may be asking yourself how implementing these link-based microformats benefits you—particularly the drafts, which have comparatively fewer tools to leverage them and implementations to reference.

I already talked extensively about the benefits of semantics and structured data in Chapter 1, so I won't repeat myself (for now). What I will mention again, though, is that just because all of the technology isn't yet in place to leverage microformats to their fullest doesn't mean the technology won't ever be there.

I believe it will. I believe that broader use of microformats, including drafts, will encourage more developers to create tools that take advantage of the machine-readable metadata. And I want to be ready when those tools become available.

This notion of early adoption is nothing new in the web industry. Ever heard of CSS 3 and HTML5?

Not to mention, these elemental microformats are ridiculously easy to implement.

And if you are a developer, I hope that you can see the tremendous value of working with standardized, structured data. It makes it easier to develop things like aggregation services, which, in turn, make it easier for users to access information.

That's All She Wrote

Well, not quite, since I'm still writing, but that's all I've got for microformats that describe link relationships. Once again, I feel rather confident in saying that was easy.

Next on the list, we'll be taking `rel` to a new level with XFN, which describes human social relationships via links.

Chapter 4

Defining Relationships: XFN

In the last chapter, we examined how to define links using `rel`-based micro-formats and VoteLinks, which uses the `rev` attribute. Now we will focus on using the `rel` attribute for links in order to define social relationships.

What Is XFN?

XFN (XHTML Friends Network) is another elemental microformat—it uses just one attribute-value pair—that defines link relationships. But unlike the `rel`-based microformats, which describe relationships of `href` destinations to pages, XFN describes social relationships among people.

Developed by the Global Multimedia Protocols Group (GMPG), XFN evolved in response to the **blogroll** trend, where content authors publish links to other sites they recommend. Often these blogrolls are links to personal sites and blogs (hence the name) that are representative of the people behind them. In effect, these URLs are part of people's online identities.

XFN was created in order to represent these online identities through links, using the `rel` attribute and a standard set of keywords (values) that describe the relationships you, as the content author, have with the people whose sites you link to. Such relationships include whether you have physi-cally met that person, if that person is a friend or colleague, even if that person is a family member or significant other.

Benefits of the social web

As much as I detest the term *Web 2.0* (I think I just threw up in my mouth a little), it has come to represent, in part, the emergence of online social media. This includes everything from user-generated content to popular social networks like Facebook and Twitter.

XFN, too, is a part of this social web. Because it is used to describe human relationships, it supports the creation and extension of social networks. Web tools can crawl the web, searching for XFN links, and discover the social relationships among people, such as the following:

- Dick and Jane have `met` and they are `friends`

- Brad and Angelina are `spouses`

- A Blog Not Limited and @emilylewis are the same person

Let's consider the Google Social Graph API (Application Programming Interface), which drives Google's My Connections service. With My

Connections, you enter a few of your own URLs (such as that for your blog, your portfolio, and your Twitter profile page), and it uses the Social Graph API to gather links from other people with whom you've indicated a social relationship (via XFN). It also returns information about the people who have indicated, via XFN, relationships with you, including reciprocal relationships (**Figure 4.1**).

Figure 4.1
Google's My Connections displays my XFN social connections gathered from my blog, Twitter profile, and design portfolio.

Even better, you can use this Social Graph API to create your own social network without having to code your own application, access other APIs, or scrape sites for data. Google's Social Graph API has already indexed the sites and relationships.

And XFN is already widely used. The majority of social networking sites use XFN to describe the relationships between friends and followers using the XFN `contact` or `friend` values (assigned to links as `rel="contact"` and `rel="friend"`, respectively).

Benefits of identity consolidation

Nowadays, particularly with the emergence of social networks, people exist on many different and disparate sites. You may have a blog, a Twitter profile, a Facebook page, and more. With all of these distributed sites, a user may want a way to indicate that each site represents the same person. This is known as **identity consolidation**, and XFN supports it.

One of the values for XFN is `me` (assigned to links as `rel="me"`). By assigning this value to the links to all of your online "identities," you are indicating that each site represents you, effectively consolidating your identity without having to centrally maintain that information.

The key to identity consolidation with `rel="me"` is that each site in your online identity must have this XFN value applied. The logic is where any site claims another site, the identity between the two is consolidated.

This isn't too difficult. On your own sites, you control the content and can add `rel="me"` where relevant. And already, many sites and services apply `rel="me"` to links to their users' profile pages to support identity consolidation, including Flickr, Twitter, LinkedIn, Plaxo, and ClaimID. As such, web applications can gather all of your `rel="me"` links to create a single profile about you.

One social service that leverages the full power of identity consolidation via XFN is Huffduffer, the audio podcasting service. It utilizes Google's Social Graph API to gather reciprocal `rel="me"` links from a single URL (namely, your own blog or site) in order to generate a list of "elsewhere" links (such as Twitter and Flickr) on users' profiles.

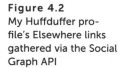

Figure 4.2
My Huffduffer profile's Elsewhere links gathered via the Social Graph API

So, when you create an account at Huffduffer, you enter a URL for one of your websites, and the Social Graph API then returns a list of all other sites that belong to you, based on the presence of the XFN `rel="me"`.

The beauty of this is that instead of editing your profile manually to include links for yourself, Huffduffer does it for you automatically, saving time and ensuring you don't have to maintain that data within the application (**Figure 4.2**).

Everything has challenges

Of course, despite these powerful benefits, XFN faces some challenges:

- There are 18 XFN values; however, the two most commonly used are `friend` and `contact`, making some folks question the semantic value of the other 16 values.

- Some people believe there isn't enough semantic distinction between `friend` and `contact`.

- Others suggest more values are needed to indicate narrower professional relationships beyond `co-worker` and `colleague`, such as "manager" or "subordinate."

- There isn't a way to indicate how a relationship may change over time, such as an "ex-friend."

Regarding the first point, I truly believe that as more people adopt XFN, the use of those remaining 16 values will increase and, with it, more tools will parse and extract information for those types of relationships. Kind of a "build it and they will come" perspective.

For the other concerns, I believe people are missing the point about microformats in general: they are intended to be simple and address the majority of use-cases, *not all*.

Adding more values to XFN, in my opinion, would convolute the microformat and go against simplicity. In the case of professional relationships, managers are co-workers, just as subordinates are; co-worker is a global value that encompasses both managers and subordinates. I don't see the need to get any more specific. Plus, XFN doesn't prohibit you from assigning to your rel attribute a value of "manager," which you can then use to customize your own web application to extract that particular data.

Finally, in the case of changed relationships, I believe that because XFN is assigned to links at a given point in time, the indicated relationship is relevant at the time the link was created. If the relationship changes over time, the XFN values assigned to links can change, thus suggesting that changed relationship.

Now that we've covered the good and the (not really) bad, let's take a look at XFN in detail, starting with the profile.

Profile

XFN has its own profile that you should reference in the `<head>` of your documents:

```
<head profile="http://gmpg.org/xfn/11">
```

Syntax

The XFN syntax should be very familiar to you, since it is identical to that of the rel-based microformats. You simply add the rel attribute to links referencing other people, and apply the appropriate XFN value to indicate your relationships with those people.

Table 4.1

XFN Values

Identity	Friendship (one value)	Professional (one or both values)	Family (one value)	Romantic (any or all values)	Physical	Geographic (one value)
me	contact	colleague	kin	muse	met	neighbor
	acquaintance	co-worker	spouse	crush		co-resident
	friend		child	date		
			parent	sweetheart		
			sibling			

For example, I often include links on my blog to my friends' sites, and I apply `rel="friend"` to those links:

```
<a href="http://twitter.com/cdharrison" rel="friend">Chris
Harrison</a>
```

Most of the time, though, I have more than one XFN relationship with those friends. For those cases, I can list more than one value, each separated in my markup with a space:

```
<a href="http://twitter.com/cdharrison" rel="friend met
colleague">Chris Harrison</a>
```

This compound XFN statement says:

- Chris is a `friend` of mine.
- I have `met` Chris.
- Chris is my `colleague`.

It is worth noting that for these compound XFN statements, the order of the values is irrelevant. Just be sure to separate each with a space so that all of the values can be parsed correctly.

Understanding the values

The XFN values are listed in Table 4.1 above, but their meaning may not be entirely clear to you, so let me explain them.

Identity The only value that falls under the identity category is `me`, which I've discussed in reference to identity consolidation. You apply it to links that reference URLs about you: your blog, your tumblelog, your design portfolio, or any site about you.

The one XFN value that should exist on its own is me. Yes, by some lines of thinking you have met yourself and you may even be a friend to yourself. However, these values are pretty much assumed. But hey, two thumbs up for good self-esteem and being your own friend!

Friendship   Of the three values in the friendship category, you can use only one:

- contact is the least intimate of the friendship relationships. It is basically someone for whom you have basic contact information, such as their name and, maybe, a URL to their site.

- acquaintance indicates someone with whom you are familiar and who is familiar with you. It's just a step above contact in terms of intimacy.

- friend is the most intimate friendship value, but it is largely defined by personal parameters. For me, it includes people I've known for years, as well as those I know more casually but who are more than just contacts or acquaintances.

Professional   You can use either one or both of the values in the professional category:

- colleague is a professional peer, someone with whom you share professional skills and/or interests.

- co-worker is someone you work with for the same employer.

Family   From the five family XFN values, you can use only one:

- kin is any relative, whether by blood, marriage, or adoption.

- spouse is someone to whom you are married. However, it does not require *legal* marriage. It can also be someone to whom you *feel* you are married, such as gay couples who aren't legally allowed to marry or folks in common-law marriages.

- child is anyone you parent, and applies to both biological and adoptive children.

- parent is someone—again, either biological or adoptive—who parented you.

- sibling is someone with whom you share a parent, either through biology, marriage, or adoption.

Romantic   You can use any one or all of the values in the romantic category:

- `muse` is someone who inspires you. Now I admit that, at the outset, it seems strange to categorize this as romantic. However, the value falls under the comparative definition of *romantic* with *rational,* the thinking being that inspiration isn't rational, so it must be romantic.

- `crush` is someone to whom you are attracted but doesn't return the feeling. And, in my case, someone who doesn't even know you are alive (ah, Hugh Jackman).

- `date` is someone you date on a regular basis, where there isn't (yet?) a commitment to the relationship.

- `sweetheart` is someone to whom you are committed and are physically and/or emotionally intimate.

Physical   The only physical value is `met`, and it refers to people you have actually met in person (so that would *not* be the guy in the chat room you just met online).

Geographic   Of the two geographic values, you can use only one:

- `neighbor` is someone who lives near you, but not at the same street address. This value has broad definitions: you may consider someone who lives in your condo building a `neighbor`, as well as someone who lives several blocks away.

- `co-resident` is someone with whom you share a street address, such as a roommate.

Another thing worth noting is that XFN doesn't require reciprocity. If you reference a person as a `date` and they reference you as a `friend`, it has no impact on the ability for machines to work with XFN. However, it may be time to have a "where are we in this relationship" conversation with that person.

Practical Markup

Since XFN describes social relationships via links, the markup is always a link (`<a>`). But it is still worthwhile to see some examples of how these links might appear in content.

Blogroll using `<ul>`

I mentioned that the blogroll trend was, in part, inspiration for the genesis of XFN, so let's see how it looks in action using an excerpt from my own blogroll:

```
<ul>
    <li><a href="http://cdharrison.com/">Chris Harrison</a>
</li>
    <li><a href="http://www.iso-100.com/">Ian Pitts</a></li>
    <li><a href="http://www.webteacher.ws/">Virginia
DeBolt</a></li>
</ul>
```

`rel="met"`

Each of the links in this example is to a site about a person I have met in real life, so I will add the `rel` attribute to each of my links and assign the value `met`:

```
<ul>
    <li><a href="http://cdharrison.com/" rel="met">Chris
Harrison</a></li>
    <li><a href="http://www.iso-100.com/" rel="met">Ian
Pitts</a></li>
    <li><a href="http://www.webteacher.ws/"
rel="met">Virginia DeBolt</a></li>
</ul>
```

`rel="friend"`

Additionally, each of these folks is someone I consider a `friend`, so I will also add that XFN value to my `rel` attribute, making sure to separate the multiple values with a space:

```
<ul>
    <li><a href="http://cdharrison.com/" rel="met friend">
Chris Harrison</a></li>
    <li><a href="http://www.iso-100.com/" rel="met friend">
Ian Pitts</a></li>
    <li><a href="http://www.webteacher.ws/" rel="met
friend">Virginia DeBolt</a></li>
</ul>
```

rel="co-worker"

One of the links is to my boss, so for his link I will also add the co-worker value:

```
<a href="http://www.iso-100.com/" rel="met friend
co-worker">Ian Pitts</a>
```

rel="colleague"

Another link is to someone who is my professional peer with similar interests and skills, so in goes the colleague value:

```
<a href="http://cdharrison.com/" rel="met friend colleague">
Chris Harrison</a>
```

rel="muse"

Finally, the last link is to someone whom I admire and who inspires me on a regular basis—a muse:

```
<a href="http://www.webteacher.ws/" rel="met friend muse">
Virginia DeBolt</a>
```

The end result

Now I have a nice blogroll that also indicates my social relationships:

```
<ul>
    <li><a href="http://cdharrison.com/" rel="met friend
colleague">Chris Harrison</a></li>
    <li><a href="http://www.iso-100.com/" rel="met friend
co-worker">Ian Pitts</a></li>
    <li><a href="http://www.webteacher.ws/" rel="met friend
muse">Virginia DeBolt</a></li>
</ul>
```

I would use this same markup structure (an unordered list) for lists of followers/friends in a social network, such as Twitter. Sadly, while Twitter embraces the semantics of XFN, it does not embrace POSH, instead using a bunch of completely nonsemantic <span> elements (tsk, tsk, but I still love you, Twitter).

The logic behind the markup

There's not much to the logic for a blogroll. It is a list of links to blogs/ sites that I read and recommend. So a link element makes POSH sense. And because there is no sequence to these links, an unordered list (`<ul>`) is appropriate.

However, if you wanted to have a blogroll with a bit more information than just a link, such as a brief description of the site/blog, you could use a definition list (`<dl>`). In this case, you would contain your XFN link in a `<dt>`, followed by your brief description contained in a `<dd>`, like so:

```
<dl>
    <dt><a href="http://www.webteacher.ws/" rel="met friend
muse">Virginia DeBolt</a></dt>
    <dd>Tips, web design book reviews, resources and
observations for teaching and learning web development.</dd>
</dl>
```

Note that I only included one link and description in this example for brevity's sake (I already suspect I've killed a few trees and this book isn't even halfway finished). I would *not* encourage a definition list with a single item. From my semantic perspective, lists should be for two or more items.

XFN in natural language

Links, by their nature, are commonly included in natural language. That is, you can put links in language that appears in natural sentences, as opposed to chunking the content in list elements as I've done in the previous examples.

So let's take a look at applying XFN to links that appear naturally in sentences of a paragraph that might be in one of my blog posts:

```
<p>At SXSWi, I attended an excellent session on the future
of web education, along with my friends Chris Harrison and
Virginia DeBolt.</p>
```

Adding the links

Whenever I reference a person on my blog (or any site I maintain, for that matter) and that person has a site, I always give them a little link-love:

```
<p>At SXSWi, I attended an excellent session on the future
of web education, along with my friends <a href="http://
```

(continues on next page)

```
cdharrison.com/">Chris Harrison</a> and <a href="http://
www.webteacher.ws/">Virginia DeBolt</a>.</p>
```

Adding the XFN

Once the links are in place, I just drop in the appropriate XFN values for each person's link:

This rel-friend markup is styled with CSS in Chapter 12 (page 273).

```
<p>At SXSWi, I attended an excellent session on the future
of web education, along with my friends <a href="http://
cdharrison.com/" rel="met friend colleague">Chris Harrison
</a> and <a href="http://www.webteacher.ws/" rel="met friend
muse">Virginia DeBolt</a>.</p>
```

Authoring Tools

I'm the first to admit that I'm a bit of a snob about hand-coding. But I realize that is my own issue, not yours. So you should be aware of a few tools available to help you author XFN:

- GPMG offers the XFN 1.1 Creator (www.gmpg.org/xfn/creator) to generate links containing XFN values.

- Accessify's XFN Link Creator (www.accessify.com/tools-and-wizards/developer-tools/xfn/default.php) also creates XFN links.

- Rel-lint (http://tools.microformatic.com/help/xhtml/rel-lint/) is a browser bookmark that validates your XFN (as well as the other `rel`-based microformats).

Bye-bye Elementals, Hello Compounds

So now you know how to add semantic richness to your social links with XFN. *And* you know all the elemental microformats: `rel`-based, VoteLinks, and XFN. Remember, these are microformats that rely on a single attribute-value pair.

From this point forward, all of the microformats we'll be covering are compound microformats, comprised of properties and subproperties. But don't fret! The elemental microformats are often used *within* compounds, so you'll be seeing them again.

Now get ready to learn how to add semantics to bookmarks with xFolk.

Chapter 5

Defining Bookmarks: xFolk

In Chapter 3, I covered the use of rel-tag for defining links that indicate what a web page—or part of the web page—is about. I also mentioned this is commonly used for tagging articles and blog posts, providing links to keywords, or tags, that tell what the content is about.

This concept of tagging can be extended beyond links, to keywords for an article or a blog post. Tagging can also be used in bookmarking—that is, how users save and share links to web pages and sites.

Modern browsers support bookmarks. In Mozilla Firefox, Apple Safari (**Figure 5.1**), Opera, and Google Chrome, users can save links to favorite URLs via the Bookmarks menu, and they can tag these links with keywords.

Figure 5.1
The Bookmarks menu in the Apple Safari browser

In Microsoft Internet Explorer versions 6 through 8, you save links via the Favorites tool, although you cannot tag the bookmarks (**Figure 5.2**).

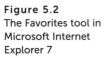

Figure 5.2
The Favorites tool in Microsoft Internet Explorer 7

This method of bookmarking, however, has limited use. The bookmarks are only available from the browser in which the links were saved.

Enter Social Bookmarking

Social bookmarking takes the notion of saving links beyond the browser by allowing users to save (and share) bookmarks using web-based services such as Delicious, Digg, Diigo, Newsvine, Reddit, StumbleUpon, and many others.

With these services, users can do much more than just save and share bookmarks, however. Social bookmarking services let users manage, organize, and search their saved links, primarily by assigning metadata like tags.

In social bookmarking parlance, tagging is assigning keywords to saved links (much like what the tagging feature does for bookmarks in browsers other than IE). But with *social tagging,* the keywords can be aggregated from keywords that other users of the service have used.

This collaborative/collective tagging creates what has been termed a **folksonomy** that ultimately categorizes the content according to these tags, thus making it easier to search, share, and organize.

It is this notion of a folksonomy that is the focus of our next microformat: xFolk, from *xFolksonomy.*

What Is xFolk?

xFolk is a draft microformat that is used for adding semantic value and structure to published bookmark collections.

xFolk is the first compound microformat we are covering (remember, compounds have properties and subproperties, as opposed to a single attribute-value pair in elementals), *and* it incorporates the rel-tag microformat we discussed in Chapter 2.

And the benefits?

xFolk provides an open standard for bookmarking that offers two primary benefits:

1. The aforementioned social bookmarking services can offer data in a format that is easily manipulated by third-party applications (machines!).

2. Users aren't restricted to social bookmarking services for their shared links.

By implementing xFolk, social bookmarking services extend functionality beyond the basic service, enabling their data to be extracted and rearranged for use in other services like search engines.

But the even greater benefit (at least as I see it) of xFolk is decentralized tagging. Folks who don't care to use a social bookmarking service, but who do care to publish collections of bookmarks, can utilize xFolk and automatically make their data extensible to machines.

And there are a couple of browser tools that expose xFolk on websites. Both the Operator (**Figure 5.3**) and Tails Export (**Figure 5.4**) add-ons for Firefox detect xFolk and let the user directly access bookmark links.

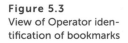

Figure 5.3
View of Operator identification of bookmarks

Bookmarks (20) ▾	Resources ▾
A Blog Not Limited ~ Created by Emily Lewis	▸
Emily P. Lewis	Design Portfolio	▸
Emily Lewis on iLike	▸
Emily Lewis on Last.fm	▸
Emily Lewis on Pandora	▸
Emily Lewis on Flickr	▸
Emily Lewis on Twitter	▸
Emily Lewis on Pownce	▸
Emily Lewis' Bookmarks on Delicious	▸
Emily Lewis' Bookmarks on Ma.gnolia	▸
Emily Lewis on Digg	▸
Emily Lewis on Design Float	▸
Emily Lewis on StumbleUpon	▸
Emily Lewis on Reddit	▸
Emily Lewis on LinkedIn	▸
Emily Lewis on Facebook	▸
Emily Lewis on MySpace	▸
Emily Lewis on Duke City Fix	▸
Emily Lewis on Bowie the 20715	▸
Emily Lewis on Technorati	▸

Figure 5.4
View of Tails Export identification of bookmarks

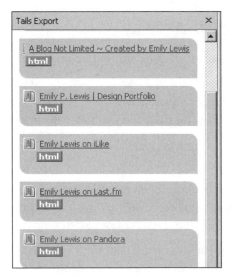

THE MA.GNOLIA LESSON

The shutdown of the popular social-bookmarking service Ma.gnolia left many users frustrated (to say the least) and pissed (putting it nicely) that their data had been lost.

But this lost data also revealed a benefit of microformats in the recovery of data. And not an unexpected benefit. One of the founders of microformats, Tantek Çelik, had anticipated that microformats would be a key to ensuring longevity of data. And he was right.

Ma.gnolia used xFolk (along with other microformats) in its markup. This alone does nothing for data recovery. However, if you can retrieve the data via a public archive, you can take advantage of tools that extract the xFolk-structured data and convert it into a format you can then import into another social bookmarking service.

In fact, Ma.gnolia crafted its recovery tools using a combination of RSS and xFolk extractors.

The sad truth, though, is that even crafty tools that extract xFolk from an archive or RSS or whatever can't (or don't) recover all the data. xFolk simply provides the "hook" a tool can use to extract the information. If all the data isn't archived, all the data can't be recovered.

Yet it does illustrate that microformats, because they offer a standard structure for data, can play an important part in ensuring data longevity.

Still, learn the Ma.gnolia lesson: back up your data!

Profile

The profile for xFolk, as for all microformats, is recommended (not required). Since it is so easy, go ahead and drop it into your `<head>` element:

```
<head profile="http://microformats.org/profile/xfolk>
```

Syntax

Now let's get into the meat of xFolk with a discussion of its syntax. As I mentioned, xFolk is the first compound microformat I'm covering. So let's take a look at its properties:

- `xfolkentry` is the root property of xFolk. It is applied (as a value of the `class` attribute) to the element that contains all relevant xFolk content. And remember, root properties can't be combined with any sub-properties.

- `taggedentry` is the property assigned to the link element (`<a>`) for the bookmark, again as a `class` attribute value. This property indicates the title or name of the bookmark. By default, the content contained by the link is used as the title. However, you can override the default and indicate the title of the bookmark via the link's `title` attribute.

- `description` is the property assigned to the element (also as a `class` attribute value) that contains a summary or brief description of the bookmark.

- `tag` is the property assigned to tags (keywords) describing the link via the rel-tag microformat.

Of these four properties, only `xfolkentry` and `taggedentry` are required. The other two are optional.

Additionally, you can have an unlimited number of tags per entry, as well as multiple instances of `description`.

Practical Markup

Now, as with most microformats, the markup used is largely irrelevant as long as it is POSH. The exceptions are the elements for `taggedentry` and `tag`, which must be links.

Other than that, the markup is your call. Let's take a look at some practical examples, starting with the most straightforward.

Simple bookmark list using `<ul>`

Like many bloggers, I import my Delicious feed into my blog so I can share my bookmarks with my readers:

```
<ul>
    <li><a href="http://radar.oreilly.com/2009/05/google
-announces-support-for-m.html">Google Announces Support for
Microformats and RDFa - O'Reilly Radar</a></li>
    <li><a href="http://googlewebmastercentral.blogspot.
com/2009/05/introducing-rich-snippets.html">Official Google
Webmaster Central Blog: Introducing Rich Snippets</a></li>
    <li><a href="https://addons.mozilla.org/en-US/firefox/
addon/11905/">Firefinder for Firebug :: Firefox Add-ons
</a></li>
    <li><a href="http://microformats.org/blog/2009/05/12/
value-class-pattern/">Microformats | weblog | Value Class
Pattern</a></li>
```

```
    <li><a href="http://ajaxian.com/archives/hixie
-discusses-the-addition-of-html5-microdata">Ajaxian » Hixie
discusses the addition of HTML5 "microdata"</a></li>
</ul>
```

As you can see, it is just an unordered list of links. No descriptions. No tags.

Now that we have some basic markup in place, let's apply xFolk.

Required root property: `xfolkentry`

First, I add the `xfolkentry` property to each of my list items, because those `<li>`s contain my bookmark information.

```
<li class="xfolkentry"><a href="http://radar.oreilly.
com/2009/05/google-announces-support-for-m.html">Google
Announces Support for Microformats and RDFa - O'Reilly
Radar</a></li>
```

Note that I'm *not* applying the `xfolkentry` property to the containing `<ul>` element because my list has *multiple* bookmarks, each of which is contained by an `<li>`.

Required property: `taggedentry`

Next, I just add the `taggedentry` property to all of my bookmark links:

```
<li class="xfolkentry"><a href="http://radar.oreilly.
com/2009/05/google-announces-support-for-m.html"
class="taggedentry">Google Announces Support for
Microformats and RDFa - O'Reilly Radar</a></li>
```

As I mentioned earlier, the content contained by my link element is, by default, the title or name of the bookmark.

```
<li class="xfolkentry"><a href="http://ajaxian.com/
archives/hixie-discusses-the-addition-of-html5-microdata"
class="taggedentry">Ajaxian » Hixie discusses the addition
of HTML5 "microdata"</a></li>
```

If I wanted to assign a different name or title, I would do that via the link's `title` attribute:

```
<li class="xfolkentry"><a href="http://ajaxian.com/
archives/hixie-discusses-the-addition-of-html5-microdata"
class="taggedentry" title="HTML5 Microdata">Ajaxian » Hixie
discusses the addition of HTML5 "microdata"</a></li>
```

The end result

```
<ul>
    <li class="xfolkentry"><a href="http://radar.oreilly.
com/2009/05/google-announces-support-for-m.html"
class="taggedentry">Google Announces Support for
Microformats and RDFa - O'Reilly Radar</a></li>
    <li class="xfolkentry"><a href="http://
googlewebmastercentral.blogspot.com/2009/05/introducing-
rich-snippets.html" class="taggedentry">Official Google
Webmaster Central Blog: Introducing Rich Snippets</a></li>
    <li class="xfolkentry"><a href="https://addons.mozilla.
org/en-US/firefox/addon/11905/" class="taggedentry">
Firefinder for Firebug :: Firefox Add-ons</a></li>
    <li class="xfolkentry"><a href="http://microformats.org/
blog/2009/05/12/value-class-pattern/" class="taggedentry">
Microformats | weblog | Value Class Pattern</a></li>
    <li class="xfolkentry"><a href="http://ajaxian.com/
archives/hixie-discusses-the-addition-of-html5-microdata"
class="taggedentry">Ajaxian » Hixie discusses the addition
of HTML5 "microdata"</a></li>
</ul>
```

And that's it. xFolk applied to a simple list of bookmarks. Now let's get a bit more detailed with our content, adding descriptions and tags.

Bookmark list using nested `<ul>`s

In this next example, I use nested unordered lists for my bookmarks so that I can provide additional information. I've shortened my list to just two bookmarks. You know, save the trees and all.

So let's take a gander at the markup before xFolk comes into the picture:

```
<ul>
    <li><a href="http://radar.oreilly.com/2009/05/google
-announces-support-for-m.html">Google Announces Support for
Microformats and RDFa - O'Reilly Radar</a>
        <ul>
            <li>Google introduces Rich Snippets which
utilize microformats and/or RDFa to generate more meaningful
snippets in search engine results.</li>
            <li><a href="http://technorati.com/tag/
microformats/">microformats</a></li>
            <li><a href=" http://technorati.com/tag/
rdfa/">RDFa</a></li>
            <li><a href=" http://technorati.com/tag/
google/">Google</a></li>
        </ul>
    </li>
    <li><a href="http://googlewebmastercentral.blogspot.
com/2009/05/introducing-rich-snippets.html">Official Google
Webmaster Central Blog: Introducing Rich Snippets</a></li>
        <ul>
            <li>Details from Google Webmaster Central on how
to apply microformats and/or RDFa to your Web content to
support the newly-released Rich Snippets.</li>
            <li><a href=" http://technorati.com/tag/
microformats/">microformats</a></li>
            <li><a href=" http://technorati.com/tag/rdfa/">
RDFa</a></li>
            <li><a href=" http://technorati.com/tag/
google/">Google</a></li>
        </ul>
    </li>
</ul>
```

You can see that I've nested a `<ul>` in each of my bookmark `<li>`s. This nested unordered list contains items for the bookmark description and tags. Now for the xFolk.

Required properties: `xfolkentry` and `taggedentry`

I repeat the application of the `xfolkentry` property to my container `<li>` and `taggedentry` to the bookmark link, as I did in the previous example:

```
<li class="xfolkentry"><a href="http://radar.oreilly.
com/2009/05/google-announces-support-for-m.html"
class="taggedentry">Google Announces Support for
Microformats and RDFa - O'Reilly Radar</a>
    <ul>
        <li>Google introduces Rich Snippets which utilize
microformats and/or RDFa to generate more meaningful
snippets in search engine results.</li>
        <li><a href=" http://technorati.com/tag/
microformats/">microformats</a></li>
        <li><a href=" http://technorati.com/tag/
rdfa/">RDFa</a></li>
        <li><a href=" http://technorati.com/tag/
google/">Google</a></li>
    </ul>
</li>
```

Optional property: `description`

Next I assign the optional `description` property to the nested `<li>`s
containing my bookmark descriptions:

```
<li class="xfolkentry"><a href="http://radar.oreilly.com/
2009/05/google-announces-support-for-m.html" class=
"taggedentry">Google Announces Support for Microformats and
RDFa - O'Reilly Radar</a>
    <ul>
        <li class="description">Google introduces Rich
Snippets which utilize microformats and/or RDFa to generate
more meaningful snippets in search engine results.</li>
        <li><a href=" http://technorati.com/tag/
microformats/">microformats</a></li>
        <li><a href=" http://technorati.com/tag/
rdfa/">RDFa</a></li>
        <li><a href=" http://technorati.com/tag/
google/">Google</a></li>
    </ul>
</li>
```

Optional: `rel-tag`

Lastly, I apply the rel-tag microformat to each of my tag links:

```
<li class="xfolkentry"><a href="http://radar.oreilly.com/
2009/05/google-announces-support-for-m.html" class=
"taggedentry">Google Announces Support for Microformats and
RDFa - O'Reilly Radar</a>
    <ul>
        <li class="description">Google introduces Rich
Snippets which utilize microformats and/or RDFa to generate
more meaningful snippets in search engine results.</li>
        <li><a href="http://technorati.com/tag/
microformats/" rel="tag">microformats</a></li>
        <li><a href="http://technorati.com/tag/rdfa/"
rel="tag">RDFa</a></li>
        <li><a href="http://technorati.com/tag/google/"
rel="tag">Google</a></li>
    </ul>
</li>
```

Regarding the use of rel-tag, be sure that the destination `href` of your tag link is a tag space. Remember, a tag space is a logical URL with the final segment being the actual tag content, as in my examples:

```
<a href="http://technorati.com/tag/google/" rel="tag">
Google</a>
```

The end result

And once again, that is it. Extremely simple.

```
<ul>
    <li class="xfolkentry"><a href="http://radar.oreilly.
com/2009/05/google-announces-support-for-m.html" class=
"taggedentry">Google Announces Support for Microformats and
RDFa - O'Reilly Radar</a>
        <ul>
            <li class="description">Google introduces Rich
Snippets which utilize microformats and/or RDFa to generate
more meaningful snippets in search engine results.</li>
            <li><a href=" http://technorati.com/tag/
microformats/" rel="tag">microformats</a></li>
```

(continues on next page)

```
                    <li><a href=" http://technorati.com/tag/rdfa/"
rel="tag">RDFa</a></li>
                    <li><a href=" http://technorati.com/tag/google/"
rel="tag">Google</a></li>
            </ul>
        </li>
        <li class="xfolkentry"><a href="http://
googlewebmastercentral.blogspot.com/2009/05/introducing-
rich-snippets.html" class="taggedentry">Official Google
Webmaster Central Blog: Introducing Rich Snippets</a></li>
            <ul>
                <li class="description">Details from Google
Webmaster Central on how to apply microformats and/or RDFa
to your Web content to support the newly-released Rich
Snippets.</li>
                <li><a href=" http://technorati.com/tag/
microformats/" rel="tag">microformats</a></li>
                <li><a href=" http://technorati.com/tag/rdfa/"
rel="tag">RDFa</a></li>
                <li><a href=" http://technorati.com/tag/google/"
rel="tag">Google</a></li>
            </ul>
        </li>
</ul>
```

The logic behind the markup

After looking at my example of nested unordered lists, you may be wondering why I didn't use a definition list (<dl>). It is a good semantic element for content that has a term and definition, or for content where list items have a direct relationship with each other—both of which could apply to my bookmark list with descriptions and tags.

However, to use xFolk correctly, you need a container element for each xfolkentry. With a <dl>, the only element to which I could apply the root xfolkentry property is the containing <dl>.

This would necessitate a single <dl> for each bookmark (xfolkentry), which goes against the notion of a true list: there would be only one bookmark in each <dl>. To me, this is not semantic. Furthermore, xFolk is for a *collection* of bookmarks. So, I'm going with nested unordered lists.

xFolk in natural language

Based on my two examples, you may be assuming that your bookmarks need to be structured in some sort of list element. But you'd be wrong. Remember, when you assume, you make an ass out of u and me.

As I've said from the beginning, markup doesn't matter with microformats (the exception being XOXO, which requires list elements, and the `rel-` and `rev`-based microformats, which are applied to links). If your markup is POSH (semantic and valid), then you are golden.

This means you can implement xFolk (and other microformats) in natural language—that is, language appearing in natural sentences, as opposed to chunking the content in list elements.

I could see taking this approach if you had a few bookmarks contained in the body of a blog post. So let's do that.

Google recently announced that it is rolling out a new feature, Rich Snippets, which takes advantage of microformats and RDFa for reviews and contact information. Sounds like a perfect blog post in which I might include some useful bookmarks.

And since a blog post is mostly just a series of paragraphs, let's drop xFolk into the natural language. Here's the basic markup and content:

```
<p>I'm uber excited about <a href="http://technorati.com/
tag/google/">Google</a>'s latest support of <a href="http://
technorati.com/tag/microformats/">microformats</a> and
<a href="http://technorati.com/tag/rdfa/">RDFa</a>: <a
href=" http://radar.oreilly.com/2009/05/google-announces
-support-for-m.html">Rich Snippets</a>. This new feature
leverages both microformats and RDFa encoding to provide
more contextually rich search results.</p>


<p>To take advantage of Rich Snippets, <a href="http://
technorati.com/tag/google/">Google</a> has provided some
<a href="http://googlewebmastercentral.blogspot.com/2009/05/
introducing-rich-snippets.html">basic instructions</a>
for implementing <a href="http://technorati.com/tag/
microformats/">microformats</a> and <a href="http://
technorati.com/tag/rdfa/">RDFa</a>. With these simple markup
guidelines, content authors can take advantage of semantics
and the added search benefit of Rich Snippets.</p>
```

There's the markup. Now let's turn to xFolk, focusing on just one of the paragraphs in the above example.

Required root property: `xfolkentry`

First I apply the root `xfolkentry` to my containing paragraph element:

```
<p class="xfolkentry">I'm uber excited about <a
href="http://technorati.com/tag/google/">Google</a>'s
latest support of <a href="http://technorati.com/tag/
microformats/">microformats</a> and <a href="http://
technorati.com/tag/rdfa/">RDFa</a>: <a href=" http://
radar.oreilly.com/2009/05/google-announces-support-for-m.
html">Rich Snippets</a>. This new feature leverages both
microformats and RDFa encoding to provide more contextually
rich search results.</p>
```

Required property: `taggedentry` (with `title`)

Then I assign the required `taggedentry` property to my bookmark link. And because I'm using natural language, the content contained by my link isn't the ideal title for the bookmark, so I'll add that via the `title` attribute:

```
<p class="xfolkentry">I'm uber excited about <a
href="http://technorati.com/tag/google/">Google</a>'s
latest support of <a href="http://technorati.com/tag/
microformats/">microformats</a> and <a href="http://
technorati.com/tag/rdfa/">RDFa</a>: <a href=" http://radar.
oreilly.com/2009/05/google-announces-support-for-m.html"
class="taggedentry" title="Google Announces Support for
Microformats and RDFa">Rich Snippets</a>. This new feature
leverages both microformats and RDFa encoding to provide
more contextually rich search results.</p>
```

Optional property: `description`

My natural language includes a decent description for the bookmark within the paragraph already, so I just want to assign the optional `description` property to that content. However, I don't currently have a containing element to which I can apply description. So I add a `<span>`.

Yes, I know. It's not semantic, but I told you at the beginning, being a purist with your semantic markup isn't always realistic. You need the `<span>` for a container, so just use it.

```
<p class="xfolkentry">I'm uber excited about <a href="http:
//technorati.com/tag/google/">Google</a>'s latest support
of <a href="http://technorati.com/tag/microformats/">
microformats</a> and <a href="http://technorati.com/tag/
rdfa/">RDFa</a>: <a href=" http://radar.oreilly.com/2009/05/
google-announces-support-for-m.html" class="taggedentry"
title="Google Announces Support for Microformats and
RDFa">Rich Snippets</a>. <span class="description">This new
feature leverages both microformats and RDFa encoding to
provide more contextually rich search results.</span></p>
```

Optional: rel-tag

Last, I assign rel-tag to the tag links I've included in my content. Remember, these are keywords describing the bookmark and the destination href is a tag space:

```
<p class="xfolkentry">I'm uber excited about <a
href="http://technorati.com/tag/google/" rel="tag">Google
</a>'s latest support of <a href="http://technorati.com/
tag/microformats/" rel="tag">microformats</a> and <a
href="http://technorati.com/tag/rdfa/">RDFa</a>: <a href="
http://radar.oreilly.com/2009/05/google announces-support-
for-m.html" class="taggedentry" title="Google Announces
Support for Microformats and RDFa">Rich Snippets</a>.
<span class="description">This new feature leverages both
microformats and RDFa encoding to provide more contextually
rich search results.</span></p>
```

The end result

The steps applied to both paragraphs, each of which contains a bookmark, result in the following:

```
<p class="xfolkentry">I'm uber excited about <a href="http:
//technorati.com/tag/google/" rel="tag">Google</a>'s latest
support of <a href="http://technorati.com/tag/microformats/"
rel="tag">microformats</a> and <a href="http://technorati
```

(continues on next page)

```
.com/tag/rdfa/" rel="tag">RDFa</a>: <a href=" http://
radar.oreilly.com/2009/05/google-announces-support-
for-m.html" class="taggedentry" title="Google Announces
Support for Microformats and RDFa">Rich Snippets</a>.
<span class="description">This new feature leverages both
microformats and RDFa encoding to provide more contextually
rich search results.</span></p>

<p class="xfolkentry">To take advantage of Rich Snippets,
<a href="http://technorati.com/tag/google/" rel="tag">Google
</a> has provided some <a href="http://googlewebmaster
central.blogspot.com/2009/05/introducing-rich-snippets.
html" class="taggedentry" title="Google's instructions for
implementing Rich Snippets">basic instructions</a>
for implementing <a href="http://technorati.com/tag/
microformats/" rel="tag">microformats</a> and <a href="http:
//technorati.com/tag/rdfa/" rel="tag">RDFa</a>. <span
class="description">With these simple markup guidelines,
content authors can take advantage of semantics and the
added search benefit of Rich Snippets.</span></p>
```

Combining Microformats: xFolk and VoteLinks

I've talked about combining microformats several times already, and I'm going to talk about it again. Because it's a good thing—where it makes contextual sense.

And since we are dealing with links in xFolk, combining it with VoteLinks makes sense. So let's apply VoteLinks to my basic unordered list of book-marks that already has xFolk applied:

```
<ul>
    <li class="xfolkentry"><a href="http://radar.
oreilly.com/2009/05/google-announces-support-for-m.
html" class="taggedentry">Google Announces Support for
Microformats and RDFa - O'Reilly Radar</a></li>
    <li class="xfolkentry"><a href="http://
googlewebmastercentral.blogspot.com/2009/05/introducing-
rich-snippets.html" class="taggedentry">Official Google
Webmaster Central Blog: Introducing Rich Snippets</a></li>
```

```
    <li class="xfolkentry"><a href="https://addons.mozilla.
org/en-US/firefox/addon/11905/" class="taggedentry">
Firefinder for Firebug :: Firefox Add-ons</a></li>
    <li class="xfolkentry"><a href="http://microformats.org/
blog/2009/05/12/value-class-pattern/" class="taggedentry">
Microformats | weblog | Value Class Pattern</a></li>
    <li class="xfolkentry"><a href="http://ajaxian.com/
archives/hixie-discusses-the-addition-of-html5-microdata"
class="taggedentry">Ajaxian » Hixie discusses the addition
of HTML5 "microdata"</a></li>
</ul>
```

Adding VoteLinks

As a reminder, because VoteLinks was covered way back in Chapter 3, this microformat indicates support, lack of support, or neutrality for a link destination via the `rev` attribute.

For most of the bookmarks in my example, I want to indicate support, so I would add `rev="vote-for"` to those link elements. However, there is one that I feel rather *meh* about, so that one will get `rev="vote-abstain"`. And if I had any that I really didn't want to support, I would assign `rev="vote-against"`.

All that applied to my xFolk list of bookmarks results in this:

```
<ul>
    <li class="xfolkentry"><a href="http://radar.oreilly.
com/2009/05/google-announces-support-for-m.html" class=
"taggedentry" rev="vote-for">Google Announces Support for
Microformats and RDFa - O'Reilly Radar</a></li>
    <li class="xfolkentry"><a href="http://googlewebmaster
central.blogspot.com/2009/05/introducing-rich-snippets.html"
class="taggedentry" rev="vote-for">Official Google Webmaster
Central Blog: Introducing Rich Snippets</a></li>
    <li class="xfolkentry"><a href="https://addons.mozilla.
org/en-US/firefox/addon/11905/" class="taggedentry"
rev="vote-abstain">Firefinder for Firebug :: Firefox Add-ons
</a></li>
```

(continues on next page)

```
    <li class="xfolkentry"><a href="http://microformats.org/
blog/2009/05/12/value-class-pattern/" class="taggedentry"
rev="vote-for">Microformats | weblog | Value Class Pattern
</a></li>
    <li class="xfolkentry"><a href="http://ajaxian.com/
archives/hixie-discusses-the-addition-of-html5-microdata"
class="taggedentry" rev="vote-for">Ajaxian » Hixie discusses
the addition of HTML5 "microdata"</a></li>
</ul>
```

It's your choice

Now, it is not required that you use these two microformats together. Neither depends on the other, and you may simply not see a need for xFolk and VoteLinks in reference to your own content.

But I believe it is important to know about potential use cases, so that's why I'm telling you. Evaluate your content and needs, then decide on the appropriate implementation for you.

Which Brings Us to the End

So now you know your first compound microformat. Proud? I am. You are already becoming my favorite person.

And now you know the basics:

- You know about the elemental microformats, which are used alone and as building blocks for the compound microformats.

- You know about compound microformats, which have properties and subproperties.

- You know about combining microformats.

I feel confident in saying that you are well prepared to dive into more detailed microformats. So let's do just that and take a look at hCard, which is used to describe people, places, and organizations.

Chapter 6

Defining People, Organizations and Places: hCard

The web is filled with oodles of content—about anything and everything. But one of the most common types of content that you can find on virtually every site is that which describes people, organizations, and even places.

Most often this content is in the form of contact information, such as a company's address and phone number. And it is for this type of content that the hCard microformat was developed.

What Is hCard?

hCard, which I introduced by way of example in Chapter 1, is a formal microformat specification that you apply to contact information for people, places, and organizations and companies, including the following:

- Names
- Addresses
- Phone numbers
- Email addresses
- Logos
- Birthdays

Electronic business cards

hCard was developed based on **vCard,** the standard for electronic business cards (.vcf) that are used to populate electronic address books, including Microsoft Outlook and Apple's Address Book.

In fact, hCard is based on a 1:1 representation of standard vCard properties and values, so every `class` name in hCard corresponds to a vCard property. This mapping helps machines extract hCard information from a web page and transform it into a .vcf that users can then add to their electronic address book. With hCard, users don't have to enter new contacts manually, they can just import .vcfs constructed from web pages with hCard.

There are a bunch of tools that do this hCard-to-vCard conversion, such as Technorati's Contacts Feed Service (**Figure 6.1**), which extracts hCard content from a submitted URL and generates a downloadable .vcf.

Figure 6.1
Technorati's Contacts
Feed Service

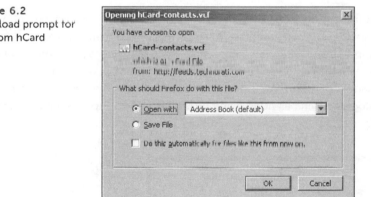

You can even let users download the .vcf directly from your site by providing a link to the page containing hCard and prepending the `href` value with the Technorati's Contact Feeds URL:

```
<a href="http://feeds.technorati.com/contact/http://www.
ablognotlimited.com/about/" title="Download vCard">Add to
Address Book</a>
```

When users select this link, the hCard is transformed into a .vcf, and users can download it directly to their computer (**Figure 6.2**). And the service recognizes multiple hCards on a page (such as you might find associated with a blogroll) and generates .vcfs for each.

Figure 6.2
Download prompt for
.vcf from hCard

There are also some add-ons for Firefox that provide .vcf export from hCard information, including Tails Export (**Figure 6.3** on the next page) and Operator. These, too, can identify multiple hCards and generate individual .vcfs.

Figure 6.3
The Tails Export 0.3.5 add-on for Mozilla Firefox identifies multiple hCards and provides .vcf export options for each.

One of the nice features of the Operator add-on is that it gives users even more functionality than an electronic business card. Operator also lets users search for hCard contacts in Google Maps, Yahoo! Maps, and MapQuest, and provides a direct import into Yahoo! Contacts (**Figure 6.4**).

Figure 6.4
The Operator 0.9.3 Firefox add-on provides search options for hCard, as well as electronic business card download.

But these tools aren't limited to Firefox. Left Logic's bookmarklet (http://leftlogic.com/lounge/articles/microformats_bookmarklet/) works in Apple Safari, Microsoft Internet Explorer (6 and 7), and Firefox. Like any bookmarklet, you drag it to your browser's bookmark toolbar and, when you are on a page with hCard, you select the bookmarklet. It then generates a modal dialog displaying all hCards and providing links to export each into .vcfs (**Figure 6.5**).

Figure 6.5
Microformats bookmarklet provides hCard-to-vCard conversion on any browser.

Also, the Oomph Microformats Toolkit provides a browser-independent microformat detector via a jQuery overlay that you add to your website. Once the jQuery is in place, Oomph detects hCard (as well as hCalendar) on the page and displays a glowing icon in the upper-left corner that users can select to see hCard detail and access a variety of search and export options (**Figure 6.6**).

Figure 6.6
Oomph jQuery overlay displays hCard details and provides both .vcf export and search options.

Oomph is a giant leap forward in furthering the consumption of micro formats by people who don't even know what they are. Users don't have to have a special browser or add-on. The site owner simply makes sure the jQuery overlay is in place, and Oomph instantly provides users with information and tools to make the most of hCard content.

Wide adoption

hCard is one of the more commonly used microformats today. This is primarily because, as I mentioned at the outset, contact information is virtually everywhere on the web. But I also think the wide range of tools to help users consume hCard information has encouraged its widespread use:

- Both Google Maps and Yahoo! Local mark up results with hCard.

- Google Profiles are published with hCard.

- Yahoo! Placemaker extracts adr and geo (hCard properties) content from web pages to help with geographic discovery and aggregation.

- Social networks Twitter, Facebook, and Last.fm apply hCard to their users' profile pages; Twitter even uses hCard for following and follower lists.

- Dozens of other popular online services provide hCard profiles, including Flickr, Cork'd, LinkedIn, Upcoming, Vimeo, Plaxo, Digg, ClaimID, Technorati, and many, many others. As a result, hCard is the most widely adopted social network profile format on the web.

- Hundreds (maybe thousands or even hundreds of thousands) of blogs and personal and corporate websites mark up their contact information with hCard.

Search and SEO

As hCard has grown in popularity and use, its benefits have grown beyond electronic business cards into search. Like all microformats, hCard provides a standardized way to add meaning (particularly for machines) to content.

This is well suited for search, as search engines can more easily identify specific types of content via the use of those standard `class` values. With hCard, for example, the `class` values tell search engines which bit of content is the person's or organization's name, address, phone number, and more.

Currently, there are two microformat-specific search engines:

- Technorati's Microformats Search (http://kitchen.technorati.com/search/)

- Virel (http://virel.de/)

These engines index submitted sites for microformats (hCard, hCalendar, and hReview) and generate results about contacts, events, and reviews. These results are published using microformats, enabling users to download, for example, .vcf from search results about a person.

For many years, major search engines like Yahoo! and Google were simply publishing their search results with hCard (and other microformats). They weren't consuming hCard in their spidering algorithms.

Until now.

Supporting my theory that "if you build it, they will come," Google developed Rich Snippets, a feature that indexes hCard- and hReview-microformatted content to provide summary information (snippets) in search results.

Since we're talking about hCard, let's focus on that for now. With Rich Snippets, users who search for people in Google will receive results with additional information (a Rich Snippet) that can help them distinguish between people with, perhaps, the same name.

More context leads to more meaningful search results and, potentially, more click-throughs. And, particularly for businesses, more click-through can mean more profit.

All content authors need to do to take advantage of Google's Rich Snippets is mark up their content with hCard. That's it. Google takes it from there.

As of this writing, Rich Snippets is still being rolled out gradually. But the simple fact that Google is now consuming microformats (rather than just publishing them) signals an important shift toward structure and markup with meaning—the core of microformats.

Google isn't the only major search player that sees the benefit of microformats to support search results. Yahoo! SearchMonkey is an open search platform that has supported numerous microformats, such as hCard, since early 2008. And Yahoo! Search uses microformats to provide more meaningful and visually appealing search results.

These latest developments in search demonstrate the power and simplicity of microformats. Search engines recognize the value of structured data so that they can give their users more relevant search results. And because microformats are so simple to implement, any content author can get in the game.

If you haven't yet joined the Microformats Are Way F'n' Cool Club by now, these new search benefits leave you no excuse. How can you argue against adding a few class values (and maybe a bit of markup) to get better search results?

Profile

Once again, you want to start your hCard journey with the profile in your document <head>:

```
<head profile="http://microformats.org/profile/hcard">
```

As I mentioned back in Chapter 1, you can list multiple profiles in your <head>. So if you are using both hCard and XFN, for example, you can declare both profiles together:

```
<head profile=" http://microformats.org/profile/hcard
http://gmpg.org/xfn/11">
```

Also, as I mentioned in Chapter 1, a combined profile for all formal microformat specifications is in development. Once completed, it will provide a more efficient profile declaration.

For example, since hCard and XFN are formal specifications, you will be able to just declare the single combined profile, rather than each microformat's profile.

Be sure to check http://microformats.org/profile/ for information about this forthcoming combined profile.

Syntax

hCard is a compound microformat that comprises many properties and subproperties.

The root property of hCard is `vcard` (remember the 1:1 representation with vCard properties?). All contact information must be contained by an element (any element) that is assigned `class="vcard"`. And as the root property, this value cannot be combined with any other hCard property values.

`fn` is the *only* required property for hCard (other than the root `vcard`). This is assigned to content that is a person's (or organization's or place's) formatted name.

What is a formatted name? Basically it is a string (more than one word) equivalent to a person's name as it would appear on a nameplate or label. This could be *Ms. Emily P. Lewis* or *Lewis, Emily* or, in the case of an organization, *Badass Tattoo Company.* Here is a simple example of a person hCard using only the required `fn` property:

```
<p class="vcard"><span class="fn">Emily Lewis</span></p>
```

Information about people

There are a number of properties and subproperties specific to people.

Names   The n property represents a person's structured name, and you use it to indicate that content contained by an element assigned `class="n"` represents parts of a person's name, such as first, middle, and last.

When you specify the n property, you must also specify its relevant subproperties:

- `given-name` is applied to content representing a person's first name.

- `additional-name` is commonly used for a person's middle name, but can be used more than once for people with many parts to their names.

- `family-name` indicates a person's last name.

- `honorific-prefix` indicates honorific name prefixes, such as *Mr.* or *Dr.* This subproperty can be used more than once.

- `honorific-suffix` is applied to content for honorific name suffixes such as *PhD* or *Esq.* This, too, can be used more than once.

If your content doesn't have name components for all of these n subproperties, don't worry. They are optional. Use only what you need for your content.

The n property is often used alongside fn, since the content is, typically, the same:

```
<p class="vcard"><span class="fn n"><span class="given-name">Emily</span> <span class="family-name">Lewis</span></span></p>
```

However, if the content is strictly two words representing first and last name, the n value is implied; it isn't necessary to specify it or its subproperties:

```
<p class="vcard"><span class="fn">Emily Lewis</span></p>
```

On the other hand, if the content is more than first and last name, you do need to specify n, along with its relevant subproperties.

Also, a reminder from Chapter 1: you cannot combine subproperty values with the parent property value. As such, `class="n given-name"` would be invalid.

The other name-related property for people hCards is `nickname`, which (can you guess?) indicates a person's nickname. This might be the affectionate name your family calls you (though my sister still insists "Rugrat" was not that affectionate), or it may even be something like your Twitter handle.

Organization/employment   If a person's contact information includes references to employment or association with an organization, there are several properties you can use.

The `org` property indicates the name of the person's employer or organization with which they are affiliated. You simply contain that organization name with an element assigned `class="org"`.

`org` has a few subproperties:

- `organization-name` indicates the full name of the organization. This subproperty, however, can be implied (that is, left out of your implementation) when the content contained by the parent `org` is just the organization's name:

```
<p class="org">Pitney Bowes Business Insight</p>
```

- `organization-unit` indicates the department (division, unit) a person works in or is affiliated with. In my case, that would be Marketing. So if you wanted to include department information in your `org` content, you would contain it in an element assigned `class="organization-unit"`.

In this case, you would also have to specify the `organization-name` subproperty so that machines could properly parse the name as separate from the department:

```
<p class="org"><span class="organization-name">Pitney
Bowes Business Insight</span> <span class="organization
-unit">Marketing</span></p>
```

If your hCard content is even more specific, you can implement these additional organization-related properties:

- `title` specifies a person's official job title, such as *Executive Vice President*.

- `role` specifies a person's role in relation to an organization or company. For example, *goalie* is a role on a sports team.

- The `agent` property is applied to content indicating another person who can act on behalf of the individual, such as an assistant. This property is most often assigned to a link (`<a>`) with an `href` value of the other person's (the agent's) own hCard.

- `logo` is a property that indicates the logo associated with the person's organization. It is applied to either an `<img>` or `<object>` element whose `href` value is a URL to a graphic of the organization's logo.

Other personal identification

Finally, here are the last personally identifying properties for hCard:

- The `photo` property is applied to either an `<img>` or `<object>` element whose `href` value is a URL to a photo of the person.

- `bday` indicates a person's date of birth. And remember, when dealing with dates, the machine-readable data is specified as an ISO 8601 value.

Information specific to organizations (and places)

So, I've covered the properties for people. And unbeknownst to you, I've also covered the properties for organizations, which are the same properties and subproperties for an individual's contact information related to their employment or organizational affiliation:

* `org` property
* `organization-unit` subproperty of `org`
* `organization-name` subproperty of `org`
* `logo` property

When marking up an hCard for an organization, the syntax is slightly different than that for people. Remember the required `fn` property? This is also applied to an organization's formatted name. But since the formatted name is most often the same as `org`, you combine the two values:

```
<p class="fn org">The Washington Post</p>
```

You would use this same `class="fn org"` syntax if you were also indicating content for the `org` subproperties:

```
<p class="fn org">
    <span class="organization-name">The Washington Post
</span>
    <span class="organization-unit">Circulation</span>
</p>
```

You may now be wondering about places (since I so cleverly included that in the previous subheading). And I'm here to tell you that hCard syntax for named places is, essentially, the same as that for organization hCards.

Named places are more like organizations than they are like people. They have a name, an address, perhaps even a website and logo. But they don't have family names, birthdays, or job titles. So in the markup for a named place, hCard uses the same name syntax I describe above for organizations:

```
<p class="fn org">The Washington Monument</p>
```

All the rest

The remaining hCard properties and subproperties can be applied, as needed and relevant, to information about people, organizations, and places.

Addresses   The `adr` property specifies address information, and it can be used multiple times in an hCard, such as to provide both home and work addresses.

Content contained by an `adr` element is broken up into components that are assigned various subproperties via the `class` attribute:

- `post-office-box` indicates PO Box information.

- `extended-address` is applied to content for apartment or suite numbers/letters.

- `street-address` indicates the street address.

- `locality` is for city information.

- `region` is applied to state and province content.

- `country-name` indicates country information.

- `postal-code` indicates the ZIP Code.

The last `adr` subproperty is `type`. This is not a component of the address, but rather the type of address, such as `work` or `home`. The only accepted values for `type` are as follows:

- `home`

- `work`

- `postal` indicates it is a postal mailing address.

- `parcel` indicates it is a parcel/package delivery address.

- `intl` indicates it is an international address.

- `dom` indicates it is a domestic address.

- `pref` indicates it is the preferred address if you have more than one `adr` for your hCard.

To indicate these values, you specify an element with `class="type"` and the inner text equivalent to one of the values:

```
<p class="adr"><span class="type">Home</span> ...</p>
```

In case you were wondering, these `type` values are case insensitive. So don't be concerned about the casing for the inner text.

Also you can use multiple `type` values where they make sense. So if you have a home address, which is also your preferred address and a domestic delivery address, you can use all three values, separated with a comma:

```
<p class="adr"><span class="type">Home, Dom, Pref</span>
...</p>
```

But what if you don't care to display these actual values to your users? You want to give the machines extra semantic yumminess, but you would prefer users to see something more human-friendly. Your solution is the value-title subset of the value class pattern.

If you recall from Chapter 1, you can use an empty `<span>` assigned `class="value-title"` to indicate the machine data is specified in the element's `title` attribute. Just contain this empty `<span>` within your `type` subproperty, making sure it immediately follows its parent element:

```
<p class="adr"><span class="type"><span class="value-title"
title="home dom pref"> </span>My preferred residential
address:</span> ...</p>
```

Notice that the multiple `type` values are separated by spaces in the `title` attribute, and that the more human-friendly text immediately follows the empty `<span>`.

If you do not specify a `type` value, machines default the `type` values to `intl`, `postal`, `parcel` and `work`. Translated into English: the address is an international work address for both postal and parcel deliveries.

`label` is the other property you can use for address information, but this is an address you *do not* care to break up into its various components (adr subproperties). It is primarily intended for content that specifies an actual delivery address label that you might, for example, print for shipping.

Like `adr`, `label` has an optional subproperty of `type` and the values are the same (home, work, `postal`, `parcel`, `intl`, `dom`, and `pref`). Also, as with adr, if you don't define a `type` for `label`, the default `type` values are `intl`, `postal`, `parcel` and `work`.

And finally, you can use `adr` and `label` together if you care to specify your address information with all of its components *and* indicate it is content appropriate for a delivery label:

```
<p class="adr label">
    <span class="street-address">1234 Microformats Way
</span>,
    <span class="locality">Albuquerque</span>,
    <abbr class="region" title="New Mexico">NM</abbr>
    <span class="postal-code">87106</span>
</p>
```

ADR ON ITS OWN

I've discussed `adr` as a property of hCard, but adr is also its very own draft microformat that is used when content authors provide address information that isn't associated with any named person, place, or organization.

Before you decide to use the adr microformat, make sure that hCard doesn't make more sense. If your address information can be tied to a person, place, or organization, hCard is the way to go.

To use the adr microformat, you should first start with the profile, which, like those for all microformats, is optional but recommended. Yet adr does not have its own profile. You just use the one for hCard:

`<head profile=" http://microformats.org/profile/hcard">`

And the properties for `adr` are already familiar to you:

* `post-office-box`
* `extended-address`
* `street-address`
* `locality`
* `region`
* `country-name`
* `postal-code`

You may have noticed that I didn't include `type` as a property. That's because it isn't. Without the context of who or what the address is associated with, `type` has no relevance. So it isn't part of the draft.

What might be some examples of using adr on its own? Maybe a blog post or article where you describe visiting a city—not a specific person or place, but just a city in general:

```
<p class="adr">I was in the mood for a road trip, so I headed
south to <span class="locality">El Paso</span>, <abbr class=
"region" title="Texas">TX</abbr>, <abbr class="country-name"
title="United States of America">USA</abbr>.</p>
```

Note that my root element is assigned `class="adr"` and contains all the relevant subproperties for city (`locality`), state (`region`), and country (`country-name`). Also note I would never willingly travel to El Paso for just a road trip.

Email and websites

The `email` property of hCard indicates email information and can be used multiple times in an hCard if you care to specify more than one email address. You should apply `email` (via the `class` attribute) to hyperlinks that specify an email address:

```
<a class="email" href="mailto:emily@ablognotlimited.com">
email me</a>
```

Machines extract the email address data from the `href` value, after removing the `"mailto:"` prefix.

You may also want to indicate what kind of email addresses your hCard contains with the `type` subproperty. Similar to `type` for `adr`, you create a `class="type"` element and use it to contain the accepted values (case insensitive):

- `internet` says that it is an Internet email address.

- `x400` says that it is an X.400 address.

- `pref` indicates it is the preferred address.

- Any registered IANA (Internet Assigned Numbers Authority) address value

In order to indicate type, though, your email property cannot be applied to the `<a>` element, because `type` is a subproperty and needs to be contained by the `email` element.

For these situations, you use the `type` property along with the `value` property (the value class pattern) assigned to the email link

```
<p class="email">
    <span class="type">Internet</span> email: <a
class="value" href="mailto:emily@ablognotlimited.com">emily@
ablognotlimited.com</a>
</p>
```

Once again, if you don't care to display these `type` values as content to your users, you can use the value-title subset of the value class pattern to provide machine data via the `title` attribute of an empty `<span class="value-title">`.

Another option is to use the abbr design pattern to display appropriate information to your users and give machines the data they want via the `<abbr>` `title` attribute:

```
<p class="email">
    <abbr class="type" title="internet pref">Email</abbr>
me at <a class="value" href="mailto:emily@ablognotlimited.
com">emily@ablognotlimited.com</a>
</p>
```

In this example, note how the `<abbr>` is assigned the `type` subproperty, and the actual values (yes, you can specify more than one) are in the `title` attribute.

Of course, keep in mind that the abbr design pattern results in a browser tooltip with the `title` values and the potential for screen readers to expand the `title`. If you have any concerns that this may cause accessibility or usability problems for your audience, consider the value-title subset of the value class pattern instead.

In addition to email addresses, you can indicate what type of email software a person (or place or organization) uses via the `mailer` property. There aren't any specified values for this property. You simply contain the name of the email software (for example, *Microsoft Outlook*) with an element assigned `class="mailer"`.

Finally, to specify website information for a person, place, or organization, you use the `url` property of hCard. The best semantic markup for this content is, obviously, a hyperlink (`<a>`):

```
<a class="url" href="http://www.ablognotlimited.com">my
blog</a>
```

Telephone numbers   You use the `tel` property to indicate telephone numbers, and it can be used multiple times in an hCard:

```
<span class="tel">505-123-4567</span>
```

And like `adr` and `email`, you can use the `type` subproperty to specify the type of phone number based on these values:

- home

- work

- voice

- fax

- cell

- pager

- modem

- msg indicates the number has an answering machine.

- video indicates the number is for a videoconferencing system.

- bbs indicates the number is for a bulletin-board system.

- isdn indicates it is an ISDN (integrated services digital network) number.

- pcs indicates it is a PCS (Personal Communications System) number.

- car indicates it is a number for a car phone.

- pref indicates the number is preferred over any other numbers you provide in your hCard.

When no type is specified, machines default to voice.

```
<p class="tel"><span class="type">Home</span> <span
class="value">505-123-4567</span></p>
```

Notice in this example that in addition to `<span class="type">`, I have a `<span class="value">` containing the actual number information. This is just another example of the value class pattern to differentiate the type from the actual number data.

But you don't even have to use the value property. If your tel property only contains the type information and the number, machines recognize that whatever *isn't* contained by class="type" is the number data:

```
<p class="tel"><span class="type">Home</span> 505-123-4567
</p>
```

Geographical information
With the tz property, you can specify the time zone where a person is currently located (or an organization or a place exists). Common implementations of tz utilize the abbr design pattern, where the `<abbr>` element is assigned class="tz" and the value for time zone is specified in the title attribute:

```
<p>I live in the <abbr class="tz" title="-7:00">Mountain
Time</span> time zone.</p>
```

Note that the time zone value is specified in UTC-offset, which is the Coordinated Universal Time offset by the number of hours (in this example, seven) the specified time zone differs.

Also keep in mind the accessibility and usability issues related to the abbr design pattern. If you are concerned that the -7:00 value will be read aloud to screen-reader users or display in a browser tooltip, the value-title subset of the value class pattern can also be used for time zones:

```
<p>I live in the <span class="tz"><span class="value-title"
title="-7:00"> </span>Mountain Time</span> timezone.</p>
```

You can provide even more geographic information in your hCard with the geo property, which indicates the global position of a person, organization, or place.

geo has two subproperties:

• latitude for locations north and south of the equator

• longitude for locations east and west of the prime meridian

The values for these two subproperties must be specified as decimals and to six decimal spaces for accurate GPS (Global Positioning System) locations:

```
<p>The University of New Mexico's GPS location is
    <span class="geo">
        <span class="latitude">35.089612</span>,
        <span class="longitude">-106.618318</span>
    </span>.
</p>
```

Realistically, there aren't going to be a lot of instances where you would want to display this latitude/longitude information to your users. But I can see a very valuable use of this information for machines, such as mapping and GPS applications.

You can choose to use the abbr design pattern, taking into account usability and accessibility needs:

```
<abbr class="geo" title="35.089612;-106.618318">GPS location
</abbr>
```

Note that with this design pattern, your latitude and longitude are listed together as the <abbr> title value, respectively, separated by a semicolon.

And yet again, if you are concerned about the usability and accessibility of the coordinate data, you can use the value-title subset of the value class pattern for geo coordinates.

GEO ON ITS OWN

geo is not only a property of hCard, it is also a separate draft microformat for geographic coordinates independent of a person, place, or organization. A popular example of geo in the wild is how Flickr marks up all geotagged photos with the geo microformat, which helps drive its map application.

So, if you wanted to do the same (or something similar), you would first add the profile to your pages. Yes, yes, I realize this is optional; I just think it is good practice.

With geo, you use the hCard profile (which includes geo):

```
<head profile=" http://microformats.org/profile/hcard">
```

Then you simply implement geo as you would in hCard:

1. Contain your coordinates with an element (any element) assigned `class="geo"`.

2. Specify the `latitude` value.

3. Specify the `longitude` value.

Before you implement geo on its own, though, be certain that the coordinates you are marking up are *not* tied to a named person, place, or organization. For that content, you must use geo as part of hCard.

The kitchen sink   The remaining hCard properties cover the rest of the fields in vCard (again, remember that whole 1:1 representation I mentioned?):

- The `category` property is used to indicate keywords that describe the contact information. For example, a `category` value for my contact information is "web design."

  These categories can be thought of as tags and, as such, you could use the rel-tag microformat along with the `category` property:

  ```
  <a class="category" rel="tag" href="http://www.technorati/
  tag/webdesign">web design</a>
  ```

  And `category` can be repeated, as needed, to describe your hCard.

- `class` indicates the access classification of the hCard information, whether it is *public*, *private*, or *confidential*. In practice, this property is little used, as there are better methods of providing access restrictions on the web.

- key specifies the public key or authentication certificate for the contact.

- You use note when you have supplemental information (a note, duh, or a comment) for your hCard; it can be used multiple times, if needed. Machines combine multiple instances of note into a single note value.

- rev is applied as a class value for date-time information indicating the last revision of the hCard information. Don't confuse this with the rev attribute for hyperlinks, as used with VoteLinks. In hCard, rev appears as class="rev" applied to an element containing date-time information.

- sort-string indicates how the name information should be sorted by machines. For example, if you wanted an application to extract the information and sort it based on last name, you would apply the sort-string property to the family-name:

```
<p class="fn n">
    <span class="given-name">Emily</span>
    <span class="additional-name">Paige</span>
    <span class="family-name sort-string">Lewis</span>
</p>
```

- sound indicates the hCard contains audio content to supplement the content. Most frequently, this is a sound file that provides the proper pronunciation of the name.

- uid specifies a unique global identifier for the contact, typically an IANA format. In practice, publishers have used uid to specify which url of an hCard is the primary or uniquely identifying URL.

The syntax for these properties is the same as the others: the property name is assigned to an element via the class attribute.

What to use?

Because of hCard's 1:1 relationship with vCard, there are a lot of properties (if you didn't already notice). Where vCard has a field, hCard has a property.

And all of these properties and subproperties may seem completely over-whelming to you. I have to admit, you aren't alone. In fact, I've only person-ally used about a third (or less) of these hCard properties for my own hCards. My content just hasn't (yet) required agent or geo or sort-string.

Just do me a favor: don't actually get overwhelmed. Instead, focus on your content. What hCard properties/subproperties are relevant? Once you know those, craft your hCard to suit your content's needs.

And, if it makes you feel any better, the majority of the tools supporting hCard don't use every single one of these properties. For the most part, hCard applications support the properties for the most common of contact information: name, address, telephone, email, website, organization.

That doesn't mean you shouldn't use any of these hCard properties. If you have the content that can benefit from the extra semantic value, apply the relevant properties. You can always create your own tools, and you never know when someone else will come up with some amazing application that uses the entirety of hCard.

Practical Markup for People

So far, I've shown you a bunch of disparate code snippets just to give you a flavor for the properties, subproperties, and syntax. Now it is time to look at some practical hCard examples using good ol' POSH.

hCard in natural language

One of the simplest ways to apply hCard is in natural language. We've already taken a look at this during our exploration into XFN. I mentioned that I often reference my friends' and colleagues' names in my blog posts, and I always give them some link-love.

```
<p>At SXSWi, I attended an excellent session on the future
of web education, along with my friend <a href="http://www.
webteacher.ws/">Virginia DeBolt</a>.</p>
```

In Chapter 4, we looked at applying the `rel` attribute to those links, but hCard is a good fit too, since I have the person's name (the only content required for hCard) and a website.

Required root property: `vcard`

First step, add the `vcard` root property to my parent element:

```
<p class="vcard">At SXSWi, I attended an excellent session
on the future of web education, along with my friend <a
href="http://www.webteacher.ws/">Virginia DeBolt</a>.</p>
```

Required property: `fn`

Next, I need to assign the required fn property to the element containing my friend's name:

```
<p class="vcard">At SXSWi, I attended an excellent session
on the future of web education, along with my friend <a
href="http://www.webteacher.ws/" class="fn">Virginia
DeBolt</a>.</p>
```

Remember, because the inner text of my fn element is exactly two words representing first and last name, the n property is implied and I do not have to use any subproperties.

Optional property: `url`

As it turns out in this example, the element containing the name also happens to be a link to the contact's website. So I can add the url property right alongside fn:

```
<p class="vcard">At SXSWi, I attended an excellent session
on the future of web education, along with my friend <a
href="http://www.webteacher.ws/" class="fn url">Virginia
DeBolt</a>.</p>
```

Combining XFN and hCard

I hope it has already occurred to you by this point: the hCard content can be further extended with XFN.

The person in this example content is a friend, I have met her, and she is a muse, so I add those values to the rel attribute of the hyperlink:

```
<p class="vcard">At SXSWi, I attended an excellent session
on the future of web education, along with my friend <a
href="http://www.webteacher.ws/" class="fn url" rel="friend
met muse">Virginia DeBolt</a>.</p>
```

The end result

And with just a few `class` values and the `rel` attribute, you have hCard and XFN in one:

```
<p class="vcard">At SXSWi, I attended an excellent session
on the future of web education, along with my friend <a
href="http://www.webteacher.ws/" class="fn url" rel="friend
met muse">Virginia DeBolt</a>.</p>
```

Personal site/blog contact information

On almost every single personal site and blog on the web, you will find contact information for the person who maintains it. Most times, this information is "chunked" in a fashion you would see in an address book entry, with name, email, website, address, and maybe even a photo:

```
<p><a href="mailto:emily@ablognotlimited.com">Emily Lewis
</a></p>
<img src="EmilyLewis.jpg" alt="Emily Lewis" />
<p><a href="http://www.ablognotlimited.com">A Blog Not
Limited</a></p>
<p>Albuquerque, <abbr title="New Mexico">NM</abbr></p>
```

Required root property: `vcard`

You will note that the content for this example is broken up into block elements (<p>), and I want to keep that structure in this case. But I need to contain everything with the root `vcard` property. Therefore, I add a containing element to my markup:

```
<div class="vcard">
    <p><a href="mailto:emily@ablognotlimited.com">Emily
Lewis</a></p>
    <img src="EmilyLewis.jpg" alt="Emily Lewis" />
    <p><a href="http://www.ablognotlimited.com">A Blog Not
Limited</a></p>
    <p>Albuquerque, <abbr title="New Mexico">NM</abbr></p>
</div>
```

Required property: `fn`

Next, I apply the `fn` property to the element containing the content of my first and last name. Once again, I don't have to include the `n` property:

```
<div class="vcard">
    <p><a href="mailto:emily@ablognotlimited.com"
class="fn">Emily Lewis</a></p>
    <img src="EmilyLewis.jpg" alt="Emily Lewis" />
    <p><a href="http://www.ablognotlimited.com">A Blog Not
Limited</a></p>
    <p>Albuquerque, <abbr title="New Mexico">NM</abbr></p>
</div>
```

Optional property: `email`

The name information is contained by an email link, so I can also add the `email` property:

```
<div class="vcard">
    <p><a href="mailto:emily@ablognotlimited.com" class=
"fn email">Emily Lewis</a></p>
    <img src="EmilyLewis.jpg" alt="Emily Lewis" />
    <p><a href="http://www.ablognotlimited.com">A Blog Not
Limited</a></p>
    <p>Albuquerque, <abbr title="New Mexico">NM</abbr></p>
</div>
```

Optional property: `photo`

The `<img />` in this example is to a `photo` of the contact (me in this example, because I'm incredibly vain):

```
<div class="vcard">
    <p><a href="mailto:emily@ablognotlimited.com" class=
"fn email">Emily Lewis</a></p>
    <img src="EmilyLewis.jpg" alt="Emily Lewis"
class="photo" />
    <p><a href="http://www.ablognotlimited.com"
class="url">A Blog Not Limited</a></p>
    <p>Albuquerque, <abbr title="New Mexico">NM</abbr></p>
</div>
```

Optional property: `url`

This example includes website information, so I also add the `url` property:

```
<div class="vcard">
    <p><a href="mailto:emily@ablognotlimited.com" class=
"fn email">Emily Lewis</a></p>
    <img src="EmilyLewis.jpg" alt="Emily Lewis" class=
"photo" />
    <p><a href="http://www.ablognotlimited.com" class="url">
A Blog Not Limited</a></p>
    <p>Albuquerque, <abbr title="New Mexico">NM</abbr></p>
</div>
```

Optional property: `adr`

Finally, for the address information, I add the `adr` property, along with the relevant subproperties for city and state:

```
<div class="vcard">
    <p><a href="mailto:emily@ablognotlimited.com" class=
"fn email">Emily Lewis</a></p>
    <img src="EmilyLewis.jpg" alt="Emily Lewis" class=
"photo" />
    <p><a href="http://www.ablognotlimited.com" class="url">
A Blog Not Limited</a></p>
    <p class="adr"><span class="locality">Albuquerque</
span>, <abbr title="New Mexico" class="region">NM</abbr></p>
</div>
```

Notice I had to add a nonsemantic `<span>` for my `locality` property because that content didn't have the element "hook" I assign the microformat `class` name.

Combining XFN and hCard

Yes, once again, we are going to add XFN to our hCard (this is quickly going to become familiar to you). Because we are dealing with hCards for people in these examples, it makes perfect sense to include XFN (which describes relationships among people).

In this particular example, I'm describing myself. So what XFN value would we use? You got it: me.

```
<div class="vcard">
    <p><a href="mailto:emily@ablognotlimited.com" class=
"fn email">Emily Lewis</a></p>
    <img src="EmilyLewis.jpg" alt="Emily Lewis" class=
"photo" />
    <p><a href="http://www.ablognotlimited.com" class="url"
rel="me">A Blog Not Limited</a></p>
    <p class="adr"><span class="locality">Albuquerque</
span>, <abbr title="New Mexico" class="region">NM</abbr></p>
</div>
```

Just as a reminder, the `rel` attribute is assigned to the link containing the URL to my site, and the value `me` indicates the site is part of my online identity.

Combining rel-home and hCard

But we aren't restricted to just XFN in combination with hCard. Because the content in this example includes a link to my site and this is content that appears on my site, I could also add rel-home:

```
<div class="vcard">
    <p><a href="mailto:emily@ablognotlimited.com" class=
"fn email">Emily Lewis</a></p>
    <img src="EmilyLewis.jpg" alt="Emily Lewis" class=
"photo" />
    <p><a href="http://www.ablognotlimited.com" class="url"
rel="me home">A Blog Not Limited</a></p>
    <p class="adr"><span class="locality">Albuquerque</
span>, <abbr title="New Mexico" class="region">NM</abbr></p>
</div>
```

If you recall from Chapter 3, the rel-home microformat indicates that the destination of the specified link is the site's home page.

The end result

Once again, a dash of new markup, a sprinkling of `classes`, a few `rel` attributes, and we have three microformats applied to a single set of content:

```
<div class="vcard">
    <p><a href="mailto:emily@ablognotlimited.com" class=
"fn email">Emily Lewis</a></p>
```

```
    <img src="EmilyLewis.jpg" alt="Emily Lewis" class=
"photo" />
    <p><a href="http://www.ablognotlimited.com" class="url"
rel="me home">A Blog Not Limited</a></p>
    <p class="adr"><span class="locality">Albuquerque</span>,
<abbr title="New Mexico" class="region">NM</abbr></p>
</div>
```

The logic behind the markup

In this example, I chose to use <p> block elements to contain my data, which required the addition of the nonsemantic <div> to serve as my root element. This is a personal choice, as the markup isn't relevant to the hCard. And I wanted to use block elements to help with the display of the content.

There are other options. I could put all this information in a list, with a <ul> serving as the root element, and <li>s containing the content. I could even use a <dl>. Hell, I could use a bunch of <span>s.

Another element that might be appropriate is <address>, which is used to contain the contact information for the site or page. In this example, that is exactly the type of content we are dealing with. So this might be the most semantic option:

```
<address class="vcard">
    <a href="mailto:emily@ablognotlimited.com" class=
"fn email">Emily Lewis</a>
    <img src="EmilyLewis.jpg" alt="Emily Lewis" class=
"photo" />
    <a href="http://www.ablognotlimited.com" class="url"
rel="me home">A Blog Not Limited</a>
    <span class="adr"><span class="locality">Albuquerque
</span>, <abbr title="New Mexico" class="region">NM</abbr>
</span>
</address>
```

So why didn't I choose this markup? First, <address> can't contain block-level elements (like <p>), and I did want that particular markup structure in this example.

But that's a fairly lame justification because display/presentation is easily controlled with CSS, and I could apply display:block to any of my classes. What it really comes down to is personal preference.

As for you, go with the structure that makes semantic sense for your content. If you use the `<address>` element, though, be certain you are using it correctly. It is only for contact information for a document (a site or a page), not necessarily the author of the document (though the two can be the same). Just remember, `<address>` shouldn't be used for just any hCard.

Blog comments using `<ol>`

Another type of content for which you might want to apply hCard is blog comments. When someone submits a comment, bloggers typically capture name and website, sometimes a photo.

Let's take a look at the basic markup for a couple of blog comments:

```
<ol>
    <li>
        <h5><a href="http://dontpanic.com">Arthur Dent</a>
</h5>
        <img src="ArthurDent.jpg" alt="Arthur Dent" />
        <p>Love the post on towels. I know how much I need
mine, but I keep forgetting it.</p>
    </li>
    <li>
        <h5><a href="http://nearbetelgeuse.com">Ford
Prefect</a></h5>
        <img src="FordPrefect.jpg" alt="Ford Prefect" />
        <p>I never leave home without my towel.</p>
    </li>
</ol>
```

Required root property: `vcard`

Because my list contains comments from multiple people, I do not want to apply the root vcard to the root `<ol>`. Instead, vcard is applied to each `<li>`, which contains the contact information for each person:

```
<ol>
    <li class="vcard">
        <h5><a href="http://dontpanic.com">Arthur Dent</a>
</h5>
        <img src="ArthurDent.jpg" alt="Arthur Dent" />
```

```
        <p>Love the post on towels. I know how much I need
mine, but I keep forgetting it.</p>
    </li>
    <li class="vcard">
        <h5><a href="http://nearbetelgeuse.com">Ford
Prefect</a></h5>
        <img src="FordPrefect.jpg" alt="Ford Prefect" />
        <p>I never leave home without my towel.</p>
    </li>
</ol>
```

Required property: `fn`

Next, apply the fn property to the element containing each person's name:

```
<ol>
    <li class="vcard">
        <h5><a href="http://dontpanic.com" class="fn">Arthur
Dent</a></h5>
        <img src="ArthurDent.jpg" alt="Arthur Dent" />
        <p>Love the post on towels. I know how much I need
mine, but I keep forgetting it.</p>
    </li>
    <li class="vcard">
        <h5><a href="http://nearbetelgeuse.com" class="fn">
Ford Prefect</a></h5>
        <img src="FordPrefect.jpg" alt="Ford Prefect" />
        <p>I never leave home without my towel.</p>
    </li>
</ol>
```

Optional property: `url`

The element containing the name also happens to be a link to the person's website, so I also add the url property:

```
<ol>
    <li class="vcard">
        <h5><a href="http://dontpanic.com" class="fn url">
Arthur Dent</a></h5>
        <img src="ArthurDent.jpg" alt="Arthur Dent" />
        <p>Love the post on towels. I know how much I need
mine, but I keep forgetting it.</p>
```

```
    </li>
    <li class="vcard">
        <h5><a href="http://nearbetelgeuse.com" class=
"fn url">Ford Prefect</a></h5>
        <img src="FordPrefect.jpg" alt="Ford Prefect" />
        <p>I never leave home without my towel.</p>
    </li>
</ol>
```

Optional property: `photo`

The last bit of contact information we have for each person is a photo:

```
<ol>
    <li class="vcard">
        <h5><a href="http://dontpanic.com" class="fn url">
Arthur Dent</a></h5>
        <img src="ArthurDent.jpg" alt="Arthur Dent"
class="photo" />
        <p>Love the post on towels. I know how much I need
mine, but I keep forgetting it.</p>
    </li>
    <li class="vcard">
        <h5><a href="http://nearbetelgeuse.com" class=
"fn url">Ford Prefect</a></h5>
        <img src="FordPrefect.jpg" alt="Ford Prefect"
class="photo" />
        <p>I never leave home without my towel.</p>
    </li>
</ol>
```

The end result

After applying all the properties, the final markup is:

```
<ol>
    <li class="vcard">
        <h5><a href="http://dontpanic.com" class="fn url">
Arthur Dent</a></h5>
        <img src="ArthurDent.jpg" alt="Arthur Dent" class=
"photo" />
        <p>Love the post on towels. I know how much I need
mine, but I keep forgetting it.</p>
```

```
    </li>
    <li class="vcard">
        <h5><a href="http://nearbetelgeuse.com" class=
"fn url">Ford Prefect</a></h5>
        <img src="FordPrefect.jpg" alt="Ford Prefect"
class="photo" />
        <p>I never leave home without my towel.</p>
    </li>
</ol>
```

The logic behind the markup

As with any content, there are dozens of approaches to markup. And let me say it again (because repetition is the spice of life): hCard doesn't care what your markup is. So why an ordered list in this example?

From my perspective, an ordered list is a great semantic element for blog post comments. People submit comments at different times, so I like the sequential properties of <ol> to indicate which comment was first, second, and so on.

Additionally, <li>s can contain almost every markup element. So I can nest headings, images, paragraphs, even lists to accommodate not only the commenter's contact information but also their actual comment.

Simple as that.

Employee directory using <ol>

So far, the examples for people-based hCards have been simple, with just name and basic contact info. How about we add some more hCard properties to the mix?

One example of content that would include additional contact information is that which you might see in a corporate employee directory:

```
<ol>
    <li>
        <h5><a href="mailto:ansel@artinc.com">Ansel Easton
Adams</a></h5>
        <img src="AnselAdams.jpg" alt="Ansel Adams" />
        <p>Artistry Incorporated, Photography</p>
        <p>Art Director, Lead Photographer</p>
```

(continues on next page)

```
    <ul>
        <li>Phone: 555-678-9012</li>
        <li>Fax: 555-678-9212</li>
    </ul>
    <p>Birthday: February 20</p>
    </li>
<li>
        <h5><a href="mailto:charlese@artinc.com">Charles
Warren Eaton</a></h5>
        <img src="CharlesEaton.jpg" alt="Charles Eaton" />
        <p>Artistry Incorporated, Painting</p>
        <p>Painter, Landscape Artist</p>
        <ul>
            <li>Phone: 555-678-9019</li>
            <li>Fax: 555-678-9219</li>
        </ul>
        <p>Birthday: January 1</p>
    </li>
</ol>
```

Required root property: `vcard`

First I apply the root `vcard` to the element (`<li>`) containing each contact's information:

```
<ol>
    <li class="vcard">
        <h5><a href="mailto:ansel@artinc.com">Ansel Easton
Adams</a></h5>
        <img src="AnselAdams.jpg" alt="Ansel Adams" />
        <p>Artistry Incorporated, Photography</p>
        <p>Art Director, Lead Photographer</p>
        <ul>
            <li>Phone: 555-678-9012</li>
            <li>Fax: 555-678-9212</li>
        </ul>
        <p>Birthday: February 20</p>
    </li>
    <li class="vcard">
        <h5><a href="mailto:charlese@artinc.com">Charles
Warren Eaton</a></h5>
```

```
        <img src="CharlesEaton.jpg" alt="Charles Eaton" />
        <p>Artistry Incorporated, Painting</p>
        <p>Painter, Landscape Artist</p>
        <ul>
            <li>Phone. 555 678 9019</li>
            <li>Fax: 555-678-9219</li>
        </ul>
        <p>Birthday: January 1</p>
    </li>
</ol>
```

Required property: fn

Next I apply the fn property to indicate each contact's formatted name:

```
<ol>
    <li class="vcard">
        <h5><a href="mailto:ansel@artinc.com"
class="fn">Ansel Easton Adams</a></h5>
        <img src="AnselAdams.jpg" alt="Ansel Adams" />
        <p>Artistry Incorporated, Photography</p>
        <p>Art Director, Lead Photographer</p>
        <ul>
            <li>Phone: 555-678-9012</li>
            <li>Fax: 555-678-9212</li>
        </ul>
        <p>Birthday: February 20</p>
    </li>
    <li class="vcard">
        <h5><a href="mailto:charlese@artinc.com"
class="fn">Charles Warren Eaton</a></h5>
        <img src="CharlesEaton.jpg" alt="Charles Eaton" />
        <p>Artistry Incorporated, Painting</p>
        <p>Painter, Landscape Artist</p>
        <ul>
            <li>Phone: 555-678-9019</li>
            <li>Fax: 555-678-9219</li>
        </ul>
        <p>Birthday: January 1</p>
    </li>
</ol>
```

Required property: n

Because the names in this example are more than two words representing first and last names, I must use the n property along with the appropriate subproperties for given-name, additional-name, and family-name:

```
<ol>
    <li class="vcard">
        <h5><a href="mailto:ansel@artinc.com" class="fn n">
<span class="given-name">Ansel</span> <span class=
"additional-name">Easton</span> <span class="family-
name">Adams</span></a></h5>
        <img src="AnselAdams.jpg" alt="Ansel Adams" />
        <p>Artistry Incorporated, Photography</p>
        <p>Art Director, Lead Photographer</p>
        <ul>
            <li>Phone: 555-678-9012</li>
            <li>Fax: 555-678-9212</li>
        </ul>
        <p>Birthday: February 20</p>
    </li>
    <li class="vcard">
        <h5><a href="mailto:charlese@artinc.com" class=
"fn n"><span class="given-name">Charles</span> <span
class="additional-name">Warren</span> <span class="family
-name">Eaton</span></a></h5>
        <img src="CharlesEaton.jpg" alt="Charles Eaton" />
        <p>Artistry Incorporated, Painting</p>
        <p>Painter, Landscape Artist</p>
        <ul>
            <li>Phone: 555-678-9019</li>
            <li>Fax: 555-678-9219</li>
        </ul>
        <p>Birthday: January 1</p>
    </li>
</ol>
```

Note that in order to apply the n subproperties, I had to add nonsemantic <span>s to contain the relevant content.

Optional property: `email`

I apply the `email` property to the link containing each contact's email address:

```
<ol>
    <li class="vcard">
        <h5><a href="mailto:ansel@artinc.com" class="fn n
email"><span class="given-name">Ansel</span> <span
class="additional-name">Easton</span> <span class="family
-name">Adams</span></a></h5>
        <img src="AnselAdams.jpg" alt="Ansel Adams" />
        <p>Artistry Incorporated, Photography</p>
        <p>Art Director, Lead Photographer</p>
        <ul>
            <li>Phone: 555-678-9012</li>
            <li>Fax: 555-678-9212</li>
        </ul>
        <p>Birthday: February 20</p>
    </li>
    <li class="vcard">
        <h5><a href="mailto:charlese@artinc.com" class=
"fn n email"><span class="given-name">Charles</span> <span
class="additional-name">Warren</span> <span class="family
-name">Eaton</span></a></h5>
        <img src="CharlesEaton.jpg" alt="Charles Eaton" />
        <p>Artistry Incorporated, Painting</p>
        <p>Painter, Landscape Artist</p>
        <ul>
            <li>Phone: 555-678-9019</li>
            <li>Fax: 555-678-9219</li>
        </ul>
        <p>Birthday: January 1</p>
    </li>
</ol>
```

Optional property: `photo`

The contacts in this example each have a photo, so the `photo` property is applied to each `<img />`:

```
<ol>
    <li class="vcard">
        <h5><a href="mailto:ansel@artinc.com" class="fn
n email"><span class="given-name">Ansel</span> <span
class="additional-name">Easton</span> <span class="family
-name">Adams</span></a></h5>
        <img src="AnselAdams.jpg" alt="Ansel Adams"
class="photo" />
        <p>Artistry Incorporated, Photography</p>
        <p>Art Director, Lead Photographer</p>
        <ul>
            <li>Phone: 555-678-9012</li>
            <li>Fax: 555-678-9212</li>
        </ul>
        <p>Birthday: February 20</p>
    </li>
    <li class="vcard">
        <h5><a href="mailto:charlese@artinc.com" class=
"fn n email"><span class="given-name">Charles</span> <span
class="additional-name">Warren</span> <span class="family
-name">Eaton</span></a></h5>
        <img src="CharlesEaton.jpg" alt="Charles Eaton"
class="photo" />
        <p>Artistry Incorporated, Painting</p>
        <p>Painter, Landscape Artist</p>
        <ul>
            <li>Phone: 555-678-9019</li>
            <li>Fax: 555-678-9219</li>
        </ul>
        <p>Birthday: January 1</p>
    </li>
</ol>
```

Optional property: `org`

This example includes organizational information for the contacts' employer, so I need to add the `org` property. And because the organization content includes not only the organization name, but also the department, I need to add the subproperties `organization-name` and `organization-unit`:

```
<ol>
    <li class="vcard">
        <h5><a href="mailto:ansel@artinc.com" class=
"fn n email"><span class="given-name">Ansel</span> <span
class="additional-name">Easton</span> <span class="family
-name">Adams</span></a></h5>
        <img src="AnselAdams.jpg" alt="Ansel Adams"
class="photo" />
        <p class="org"><span class="organization-
name">Artistry Incorporated</span>, <span
class="organization-unit">Photography</span></p>
        <p>Art Director, Lead Photographer</p>
        <ul>
            <li>Phone: 555-678-9012</li>
            <li>Fax: 555-678-9212</li>
        </ul>
        <p>Birthday: February 20</p>
    </li>
    <li class="vcard">
        <h5><a href="mailto:charles@artinc.com" class=
"fn n email"><span class="given-name">Charles</span> <span
class="additional-name">Warren</span> <span class="family
-name">Eaton</span></a></h5>
        <img src="CharlesEaton.jpg" alt="Charles Eaton"
class="photo" />
        <p class="org"><span class="organization-
name">Artistry Incorporated</span>, <span
class="organization-unit">Painting</span></p>
        <p>Painter, Landscape Artist</p>
        <ul>
            <li>Phone: 555-678-9019</li>
            <li>Fax: 555-678-9219</li>
        </ul>
        <p>Birthday: January 1</p>
    </li>
</ol>
```

Once again, note that I added <span>s to contain the org subproperties.

NESTING HCARDS

Having looked at some content for an individual that also references an organization, now might be the time to talk about nesting hCards.

It is exactly what it sounds like: you can contain hCards within other hCards. Crazy, I know. That's just how us microformats geeks roll.

So let's see how this would look using one of the hCards from the employee directory example (slightly modified to save the trees):

```
<li class="vcard">
    <h5><a href="mailto:charlese@artinc.com" class="fn email">Charles Eaton</h5>
    <p class="org">Artistry Incorporated</p>
</li>
```

The content for this contact includes that person's organization, so why not also mark up an hCard for that organization—within the individual's hCard. To start, add another root `vcard` property to the element that contains the organization info:

```
<li class="vcard">
    <h5><a href="mailto:charlese@artinc.com" class="fn email">Charles Eaton</h5>
    <p class="org vcard">Artistry Incorporated</p>
</li>
```

Next you need the required `fn` property and, because we are talking about an organization, you need to accompany `fn` with `org`:

```
<li class="vcard">
    <h5><a href="mailto:charlese@artinc.com" class="fn email">Charles Eaton</h5>
    <p class="org vcard"><span class="fn org">Artistry Incorporated</span></p>
</li>
```

Note that I added a `<span>` to contain my `class="fn org"` content, but I'm willing to bet that a lot of companies have website information you could include. If that's the case, change the `<span>` to an `<a>`:

```
<li class="vcard">
    <h5><a href="mailto:charlese@artinc.com" class="fn email">Charles Eaton</h5>
    <p class="org vcard"><a href="http://artinc.com" class="fn org">Artistry
Incorporated</a></p>
```

And now that we have a website referenced, add in the `url` property:

```
<li class="vcard">
    <h5><a href="mailto:charlese@artinc.com" class="fn email">Charles Eaton</h5>
    <p class="org vcard"><a href="http://artinc.com" class="fn org url">Artistry
Incorporated</a></p>
```

And that's all there is to it. You can add more properties to the nested organization hCard as you care to. Just be sure all the relevant content is contained by the nested `vcard` property.

Optional properties: `title` and `role`

The content for each of these contacts also includes their job `title` and `role`:

```
<ol>
    <li class="vcard">
        <h5><a href="mailto:ansel@artinc.com" class=
"fn n email"><span class="given-name">Ansel</span> <span
class="additional-name">Easton</span> <span class="family
-name">Adams</span></a></h5>
        <img src="AnselAdams.jpg" alt="Ansel Adams"
width="32px height="32px" class="photo" />
        <p class="org"><span class="organization-name">
Artistry Incorporated</span>, <span class="organization
-unit">Photography</span></p>
        <p><span class="title">Art Director</span>, <span
class="role">Lead Photographer</span></p>
        <ul>
            <li>Phone: 555-678-9012</li>
            <li>Fax: 555-678-9212</li>
        </ul>
        <p>Birthday: February 20</p>
    </li>
    <li class="vcard">
        <h5><a href="mailto:charlese@artinc.com" class=
"fn n email"><span class="given-name">Charles</span> <span
class="additional-name">Warren</span> <span class="family
-name">Eaton</span></a></h5>
        <img src="CharlesEaton.jpg" alt="Charles Eaton"
class="photo" />
        <p class="org"><span class="organization-name">
Artistry Incorporated</span>, <span class="organization
-unit">Painting</span></p>
        <p><span class="title">Painter</span>, <span class=
"role">Landscape Artist</span></p>
        <ul>
            <li>Phone: 555-678-9019</li>
            <li>Fax: 555-678-9219</li>
        </ul>
        <p>Birthday: January 1</p>
    </li>
</ol>
```

Optional property: `tel`

Each contact also has multiple telephone numbers listed, so I include the `tel` property, as well as the `type` subproperty to differentiate the two different numbers:

```
<ol>
    <li class="vcard">
        <h5><a href="mailto:ansel@artinc.com" class=
"fn n email"><span class="given-name">Ansel</span> <span
class="additional-name">Easton</span> <span class="family
-name">Adams</span></a></h5>
        <img src="AnselAdams.jpg" alt="Ansel Adams" class=
"photo" />
        <p class="org"><span class="organization-
name">Artistry Incorporated</span>, <span
class="organization-unit">Photography</span></p>
        <p><span class="title">Art Director</span>, <span
class="role">Lead Photographer</span></p>
        <ul>
            <li class="tel"><em class="type">Phone</em>:
555-678-9012</li>
            <li class="tel"><em class="type">Fax</em>:
555-678-9212</li>
        </ul>
        <p>Birthday: February 20</p>
    </li>
    <li class="vcard">
        <h5><a href="mailto:charlese@artinc.com" class=
"fn n email"><span class="given-name">Charles</span> <span
class="additional-name">Warren</span> <span class="family
-name">Eaton</span></a></h5>
        <img src="CharlesEaton.jpg" alt="Charles Eaton"
class="photo" />
        <p class="org"><span class="organization-name">
Artistry Incorporated</span>, <span class="organization
-unit">Painting</span></p>
        <p><span class="title">Painter</span>, <span class=
"role">Landscape Artist</span></p>
        <ul>
            <li class="tel"><em class="type">Phone</em>:
555-678-9019</li>
```

```
        <li class="tel"><em class="type">Fax</em>:
555-678-9219</li>
      </ul>
      <p>Birthday: January 1</p>
   </li>
</ol>
```

You may notice that for the `type` subproperty, I added `<em>`s instead of `<span>`s to contain the content. That's because, in this content, I think `<em>` is a good semantic element as it offers a bit of emphasis to the content that is describing the type of telephone number.

Optional property: `bday`

I also assign the `bday` property to each contact's date of birth, using the value class pattern to indicate my ISO 8601 machine data:

```
<ol>
   <li class="vcard">
      <h5><a href="mailto:ansel@artinc.com" class=
"fn n email"><span class="given-name">Ansel</span> <span
class="additional-name">Easton</span> <span class="family
-name">Adams</span></a></h5>
      <img src="AnselAdams.jpg" alt="Ansel Adams"
class="photo" />
      <p class="org"><span class="organization-name">
Artistry Incorporated</span>, <span class="organization
-unit">Photography</span></p>
      <p><span class="title">Art Director</span>, <span
class="role">Lead Photographer</span></p>
      <ul>
         <li class="tel"><em class="type">Phone</em>:
555-678-9012</li>
         <li class="tel"><em class="type">Fax</em>:
555-678-9212</li>
      </ul>
      <p>Birthday: <span class="bday"><span class="value
-title" title="1902-02-20"> </span>February 20</span></p>
   </li>
   <li class="vcard">
```

(continues on next page)

```
        <h5><a href="mailto:charlese@artinc.com" class=
"fn n email"><span class="given-name">Charles</span> <span
class="additional-name">Warren</span> <span class="family
-name">Eaton</span></a></h5>
        <img src="CharlesEaton.jpg" alt="Charles Eaton"
class="photo" />
        <p class="org"><span class="organization-name">
Artistry Incorporated</span>, <span class="organization
-unit">Painting</span></p>
        <p><span class="title">Painter</span>, <span class=
"role">Landscape Artist</span></p>
        <ul>
            <li class="tel"><em class="type">Phone</em>:
555-678-9019</li>
            <li class="tel"><em class="type">Fax</em>:
555-678-9219</li>
        </ul>
        <p>Birthday: <span class="bday"><span class="value
-title" title="1857-01-01"> </span>January 1</span></p>
    </li>
</ol>
```

For the birthday content, I used the value-title subset of the value class pattern to indicate my date information. This is to eliminate potential issues with screen readers and browser tooltips.

However, because the `bday` value is only the date (not date and time), you can also use `<abbr>` with the value class pattern:

```
<p>Birthday: <abbr class="bday" title="1857-01-01">January
1</abbr></p>
```

This implementation still results in a browser tooltip and potential screen reader expansion, but the value class pattern allows for this method of separately indicating ISO 8601 machine information for date and time.

It is only the use of `<abbr>` with a combined date-time value (AKA, the datetime design pattern) that is deprecated.

The end result

And after all of the relevant properties and subproperties have been assigned, we get this final markup:

```
<ol>
    <li class="vcard">
        <h5><a href="mailto:ansel@artinc.com" class=
"fn n email"><span class="given-name">Ansel</span> <span
class="additional-name">Easton</span> <span class="family
-name">Adams</span></a></h5>
        <img src="AnselAdams.jpg" alt="Ansel Adams"
class="photo" />
        <p class="org"><span class="organization-name">
Artistry Incorporated</span>, <span class="organization
-unit">Photography</span></p>
        <p><span class="title">Art Director</span>, <span
class="role">Lead Photographer</span></p>
        <ul>
            <li class="tel"><em class="type">Phone</em>:
555-678-9012</li>
            <li class="tel"><em class="type">Fax</em>:
555-678-9212</li>
        </ul>
        <p>Birthday: <span class="bday"><span class="value
-title" title="1902-02-20"> </span>February 20</span></p>
    </li>
    <li class="vcard">
        <h5><a href="mailto:charlese@artinc.com" class=
"fn n email"><span class="given-name">Charles</span> <span
class="additional-name">Warren</span> <span class="family
-name">Eaton</span></a></h5>
        <img src="CharlesEaton.jpg" alt="Charles Eaton"
class="photo" />
        <p class="org"><span class="organization-name">
Artistry Incorporated</span>, <span class="organization
-unit">Painting</span></p>
        <p><span class="title">Painter</span>, <span class=
"role">Landscape Artist</span></p>
        <ul>
            <li class="tel"><em class="type">Phone</em>:
555-678-9019</li>
            <li class="tel"><em class="type">Fax</em>:
555-678-9219</li>
        </ul>
```

(continues on next page)

```
        <p>Birthday: <span class="bday"><span class="value
-title" title="1857-01-01"> </span>January 1</span></p>
    </li>
</ol>
```

The logic behind the markup

Typically, directories are listed in alphabetical order, so once again, I chose an unordered list due to its inherent sequential nature. I like that I can nest block-level elements in the <li>s for all of the contact information, particularly <h5>s for each person's name, which can help with search engine optimization.

But I could've done it differently using a definition list within each <li> for the contact information:

```
<li class="vcard">
    <dl>
        <dt><a href="mailto:charlese@artinc.com" class=
"fn n email"><span class="given-name">Charles</span> <span
class="additional-name">Warren</span> <span class="family
-name">Eaton</span></a></dt>
        <dd><img src="CharlesEaton.jpg" alt="Charles Eaton"
class="photo" /></dd>
        <dd class="org"><span class="organization-name">
Artistry Incorporated</span>, <span class="organization
-unit">Painting</span></dd>
        <dd><span class="title">Painter</span>, <span class=
"role">Landscape Artist</span></dd>
        <dd class="tel"><em class="type">Phone</em>: 555-
678-9019</dd>
        <dd class="tel"><em class="type">Fax</em>: 555-678-
9219</dd>
        <dd>Birthday: <span class="bday"><span class="value
-title" title="1857-01-01"> </span>January 1</span></dd>
    </dl>
</li>
```

In this approach, the <dt> contains the person's name information, and all the subsequent <dd>s contain information that describes the person in fuller detail. This is an acceptable use of a definition list. I could even move the root vcard from the containing <li> to the <dl>. Don't you love having so many options?

DEFINITION LISTS

I've mentioned definition lists a couple of times already. It is about time I give you the background on this element.

There are two schools of thought on the appropriate use of definition lists:

- Only for terms (<dt>) and definitions (<dd>)

- For any items that have a direct relationship with each other, so that the <dd> content relates to that of the <dt>

Personally, I agree with that second notion, which is also supported by the W3C specification.

That said, <dt>s can't contain block-level elements, such as <h3>. So if you want to achieve heading importance for content contained by a <dt>, you can't. And search engines do index heading-based content differently (usually with higher priority) than content in a <dl>.

So if heading-based keyword exposure is a priority for your content, reconsider the use of a <dl>. If not, experiment and see where <dl> may be a good fit for your content.

Practical Markup for Organizations (and Places)

The following examples focus on hCards for organizations and places. A lot of what you'll see will be familiar, because the syntax is almost the same as it is for people hCards.

Corporate-site contact information using <dl>

Any corporate site provides contact information for the organization. Or at least sites for companies with content authors who aren't idiots do.

The approach is the same as in the example I provided for contact information on a personal site, but this time I'm going to use a definition list as the markup container:

```
<dl>
    <dt><a href="http://badasstattoo.com">Badass Tattoo
Company</a></dt>
    <dd><img src="BadAss.png" alt="Badass Tattoo Company" />
</dd>
    <dd>
        <ul>
            <li>567 Main Street</li>
            <li>Albuquerque, <abbr title="New Mexico">NM
</abbr> 87110</li>
        </ul>
    </dd>
    <dd>
        <ul>
            <li>PO Box 3456</li>
            <li>Albuquerque, <abbr title="New Mexico">NM
</abbr> 87110</li>
        </ul>
    </dd>
    <dd><a href="mailto:info@badasstattoo.com">info@
badasstattoo.com</a></dd>
    <dd>Phone: 505-456-1234</dd>
    <dd>Fax: 505-456-2234</dd>
</dl>
```

Required root property: `vcard`

Because this example is for just one organization, I apply the root vcard to the containing <dl>:

```
<dl class="vcard">
    <dt><a href="http://badasstattoo.com">Badass Tattoo
Company</a></dt>
    <dd><img src="BadAss.png" alt="Badass Tattoo Company" />
</dd>
    <dd>
        <ul>
            <li>567 Main Street</li>
            <li>Albuquerque, <abbr title="New Mexico">NM
</abbr> 87110</li>
        </ul>
```

```
    </dd>
    <dd>
        <ul>
            <li>PO Box 3456</li>
            <li>Albuquerque, <abbr title="New Mexico">NM
</abbr> 87110</li>
        </ul>
    </dd>
    <dd><a href="mailto:info@badasstattoo.com">info@
badasstattoo.com</a></dd>
    <dd>Phone: 505-456-1234</dd>
    <dd>Fax: 505-456-2234</dd>
</dl>
```

Required properties: `fn` and `org`

Next, I assign the required fn and org properties:

```
<dl class="vcard">
    <dt><a href="http://badasstattoo.com" class="fn org">
Badass Tattoo Company</a></dt>
    <dd><img src="BadAss.png" alt="Badass Tattoo Company" />
</dd>
    <dd>
        <ul>
            <li>567 Main Street</li>
            <li>Albuquerque, <abbr title="New Mexico">NM
</abbr> 87110</li>
        </ul>
    </dd>
    <dd>
        <ul>
            <li>PO Box 3456</li>
            <li>Albuquerque, <abbr title="New Mexico">NM
</abbr> 87110</li>
        </ul>
    </dd>
    <dd><a href="mailto:info@badasstattoo.com">info@
badasstattoo.com</a></dd>
    <dd>Phone: 505-456-1234</dd>
    <dd>Fax: 505-456-2234</dd>
</dl>
```

Optional property: `logo`

This example includes a logo for the organization, so the `logo` property is applied to the `<img>`:

```
<dl class="vcard">
    <dt><a href="http://badasstattoo.com" class="fn org">
Badass Tattoo Company</a></dt>
    <dd><img src="BadAss.png" alt="Badass Tattoo Company"
class="logo" /></dd>
    <dd>
        <ul>
            <li>567 Main Street</li>
            <li>Albuquerque, <abbr title="New Mexico">NM
</abbr> 87110</li>
        </ul>
    </dd>
    <dd>
        <ul>
            <li>PO Box 3456</li>
            <li>Albuquerque, <abbr title="New Mexico">NM
</abbr> 87110</li>
        </ul>
    </dd>
    <dd><a href="mailto:info@badasstattoo.com">info@
badasstattoo.com</a></dd>
    <dd>Phone: 505-456-1234</dd>
    <dd>Fax: 505-456-2234</dd>
</dl>
```

Optional property: `adr`

This example includes two addresses: one for the street address and one for mailing (postal). As such, I want to assign the `adr` property to each, and be sure to differentiate the two addresses with the `type` subproperty.

And because I'm using `adr`, I also need to assign the various subproperties to the address components:

```
<dl class="vcard">
    <dt><a href="http://badasstattoo.com" class="fn org">
Badass Tattoo Company</a></dt>
```

```
        <dd><img src="BadAss.png" alt="Badass Tattoo Company"
class="logo" /></dd>
        <dd class="adr">
            <span class="type"><span class="value-title"
title="work pref"> </span></span>
            <ul>
                <li class="street-address">567 Main Street</li>
                <li><span class="locality">Albuquerque</span>,
<abbr title="New Mexico" class="region">NM</abbr> <span
class="postal-code">87110</span></li>
            </ul>
        </dd>
        <dd class="adr">
            <span class="type"><span class="value-title" title=
"work parcel dom"> </span></span>
            <ul>
                <li class="post-office-box">PO Box 3456</li>
                <li><span class="locality">Albuquerque</span>,
<abbr title="New Mexico" class="region">NM</abbr> <span
class="postal-code">87110</span></li>
            </ul>
        </dd>
        <dd><a href="mailto:info@badasstattoo.com">info@
badasstattoo.com</a></dd>
        <dd>Phone: 505-456-1234</dd>
        <dd>Fax: 505-456-2234</dd>
</dl>
```

Once again, for the address components that need an element hook to assign the subproperties, I've added <span>s.

Also note that for the type subproperty, I am using the value-title subset of the value class pattern to provide machines the type data, but not to display that information to my users.

Optional property: label

Because this example includes a PO Box that is indicated as the mailing delivery address (via parcel), it may also make sense to add the label property to that address:

```
<dl class="vcard">
    <dt><a href="http://badasstattoo.com" class="fn org">
Badass Tattoo Company</a></dt>
    <dd><img src="BadAss.png" alt="Badass Tattoo Company"
class="logo" /></dd>
    <dd class="adr">
        <span class="type"><span class="value-title"
title="work pref"> </span></span>
        <ul>
            <li class="street-address">567 Main Street</li>
            <li><span class="locality">Albuquerque</span>,
<abbr title="New Mexico" class="region">NM</abbr> <span
class="postal-code">87110</span></li>
        </ul>
    </dd>
    <dd class="adr label">
        <span class="type"><span class="value-title"
title="work parcel dom"> </span></span>
        <ul>
            <li class="post-office-box">PO Box 3456</li>
            <li><span class="locality">Albuquerque</span>,
<abbr title="New Mexico" class="region">NM</abbr> <span
class="postal-code">87110</span></li>
        </ul>
    </dd>
    <dd><a href="mailto:info@badasstattoo.com">info@
badasstattoo.com</a></dd>
    <dd>Phone: 505-456-1234</dd>
    <dd>Fax: 505-456-2234</dd>
</dl>
```

Optional properties: `email` and `url`

This example includes links for the organization's website and email, so I
add the `url` and `email` properties:

```
<dl class="vcard">
    <dt><a href="http://badasstattoo.com" class="fn org url">
Badass Tattoo Company</a></dt>
    <dd><img src="BadAss.png" alt="Badass Tattoo Company"
class="logo" /></dd>
    <dd class="adr">
```

```
        <span class="type"><span class="value-title"
title="work pref"> </span></span>
        <ul>
            <li class="street-address">567 Main Street</li>
            <li><span class="locality">Albuquerque</span>,
<abbr title="New Mexico" class="region">NM</abbr> <span
class="postal-code">87110</span></li>
        </ul>
    </dd>
    <dd class="adr label">
        <span class="type"><span class="value-title" title=
"work parcel dom"> </span></span>
        <ul>
            <li class="post-office-box">PO Box 3456</li>
            <li><span class="locality">Albuquerque</span>,
<abbr title="New Mexico" class="region">NM</abbr> <span
class="postal-code">87110</span></li>
        </ul>
    </dd>
    <dd><a href="mailto:info@badasstattoo.com" class=
"email">info@badasstattoo.com</a></dd>
    <dd>Phone: 505-456-1234</dd>
    <dd>Fax: 505-456-2234</dd>
</dl>
```

Optional property: `tel`

I'm providing both phone and fax numbers in this example, so I want to be sure to specify not only the `tel` property for each, but also the `type` subproperty:

```
<dl class="vcard">
    <dt><a href="http://badasstattoo.com" class="fn org url">
Badass Tattoo Company</a></dt>
    <dd><img src="BadAss.png" alt="Badass Tattoo Company"
class="logo" /></dd>
    <dd class="adr">
        <span class="type"><span class="value-title" title=
"work pref"> </span></span>
        <ul>
            <li class="street-address">567 Main Street</li>
```

(continues on next page)

```
            <li><span class="locality">Albuquerque</span>,
<abbr title="New Mexico" class="region">NM</abbr> <span
class="postal-code">87110</span></li>
        </ul>
    </dd>
    <dd class="adr label">
        <span class="type"><span class="value-title" title=
"work parcel dom"> </span></span>
        <ul>
            <li class="post-office-box">PO Box 3456</li>
            <li><span class="locality">Albuquerque</span>,
<abbr title="New Mexico" class="region">NM</abbr> <span
class="postal-code">87110</span></li>
        </ul>
    </dd>
    <dd><a href="mailto:info@badasstattoo.com" class=
"email">info@badasstattoo.com</a></dd>
    <dd class="tel"><em class="type"><span class="value
-title" title="work"> </span>Phone</em>: 505-456-1234</dd>
    <dd class="tel"><em class="type">Fax</em>: 505-456-
2234</dd>
</dl>
```

Note that *Phone* is not a valid `type` value, so I'm using the value-title sub-set of the value class pattern to indicate a value of `work` for that number (via `title`). *Fax*, however, is a valid `type` value, so that content does not need the addition of the value class pattern.

Optional property: `geo`

My original content did not include geographical coordinates, but let's say you wanted to include those (perhaps to leverage Yahoo! Placemaker functionality).

You can include that information for machines and not display it to your users, if you like, using the value-title subset of the value class pattern:

```
<dl class="vcard">
    <dt><a href="http://badasstattoo.com" class="fn org url">
Badass Tattoo Company</a></dt>
    <dd><img src="BadAss.png" alt="Badass Tattoo Company"
class="logo" /></dd>
    <dd class="adr">
```

```
            <span class="geo"><span class="value-title" title=
"35.342166;-89.162347"> </span></span>
            <span class="type"><span class="value-title" title=
"work pref"> </span></span>
            <ul>
                <li class="street-address">567 Main Street</li>
                <li><span class="locality">Albuquerque</span>,
<abbr title="New Mexico" class="region">NM</abbr> <span
class="postal-code">87110</span></li>
            </ul>
        </dd>
        <dd class="adr label">
            <span class="type"><span class="value-title" title=
"work parcel dom"> </span></span>
            <ul>
                <li class="post-office-box">PO Box 3456</li>
                <li><span class="locality">Albuquerque</span>,
<abbr title="New Mexico" class="region">NM</abbr> <span
class="postal-code">87110</span></li>
            </ul>
        </dd>
        <dd><a href="mailto:info@badasstattoo.com"
class="email">info@badasstattoo.com</a></dd>
        <dd class="tel"><em class="type"><span class="value
-title" title="work"> </span>Phone</em>: 505-456-1234</dd>
        <dd class="tel"><em class="type">Fax</em>: 505-456-
2234</dd>
</dl>
```

Note that I applied the geo information (completely fictional, by the way)
to the street address, rather than the PO Box, as that is the content the geo
coordinates describe.

The end result

And our final markup looks like:

*This hCard markup
is styled with CSS in
Chapter 12 (page 274).*

```
<dl class="vcard">
    <dt><a href="http://badasstattoo.com" class="fn org">
Badass Tattoo Company</a></dt>
    <dd><img src="BadAss.png" alt="Badass Tattoo Company"
class="logo" /></dd>
```

(continues on next page)

```
    <dd class="adr">
        <span class="geo"><span class="value-title" title=
"35.342166;-89.162347"> </span></span>
        <span class="type"><span class="value-title"
title="work pref"> </span></span>
        <ul>
            <li class="street-address">567 Main Street</li>
            <li><span class="locality">Albuquerque</span>,
<abbr title="New Mexico" class="region">NM</abbr> <span
class="postal-code">87110</span></li>
        </ul>
    </dd>
    <dd class="adr label">
        <span class="type"><span class="value-title" title=
"work parcel dom"> </span></span>
        <ul>
            <li class="post-office-box">PO Box 3456</li>
            <li><span class="locality">Albuquerque</span>,
<abbr title="New Mexico" class="region">NM</abbr> <span
class="postal-code">87110</span></li>
        </ul>
    </dd>
    <dd><a href="mailto:info@badasstattoo.com" class=
"email">info@badasstattoo.com</a></dd>
    <dd class="tel"><em class="type"><span class="value
-title" title="work"> </span>Phone</em>: 505-456-1234</dd>
    <dd class="tel"><em class="type">Fax</em>: 505-456-
2234</dd>
</dl>
```

The logic behind the markup

The reason behind using a definition list for this content is that all of the contact information describes the company. So the company name and URL are contained by the <dt>, and all of the additional contact information appear within the <dd>s, which, from a semantic markup perspective, relate to that <dt>.

You may also have noticed that the address information is contained by unordered lists nested within <dd>s. Why? Well, I really think address information can be thought of, semantically, as list information.

Corporate directory for multiple branches using <dl>

Let's say you work for an organization that has branches in, perhaps, many different locations, and you are tasked with putting together an online directory that provides contact information for each:

```
<ol>
    <li>
        <h5><a href="http://helpinghands.org">Helping Hands
Community Outreach</a></h5>
        <ul>
            <li>678 Volunteer Way</li>
            <li>Suite A</li>
            <li>Alexandria, <abbr title="Virginia">VA</abbr>
22301</li>
        </ul>
        <ul>
            <li><a href="mailto:community@helpinghands.org">
Email</a></li>
            <li>Phone: 703-675-9932</li>
            <li>Fax: 703-675-0032</li>
        </ul>
    </li>
    <li>
        <h5><a href="http://helpinghands.org">Helping Hands
Training Center</a></h5>
        <ul>
            <li>678 Volunteer Way</li>
            <li>Vienna, <abbr title="Virginia">VA</abbr>
22027</li>
        </ul>
        <ul>
            <li><a href="mailto:training@helpinghands.org">
Email</a></li>
            <li>Phone: 703-784-5468</li>
            <li>Fax: 703-784-5400</li>
        </ul>
    </li>
</ol>
```

Required root property: `vcard`

Because my content contains multiple contacts (a different one for each branch), I need to assign the `vcard` root property to each:

```
<ol>
    <li class="vcard">
        <h5><a href="http://helpinghands.org">Helping Hands
Community Outreach</a></h5>
        <ul>
            <li>678 Volunteer Way</li>
            <li>Suite A</li>
            <li>Alexandria, <abbr title="Virginia">VA</abbr>
22301</li>
        </ul>
        <ul>
            <li><a href="mailto:community@helpinghands.org">
Email</a></li>
            <li>Phone: 703-675-9932</li>
            <li>Fax: 703-675-0032</li>
        </ul>
    </li>
    <li class="vcard">
        <h5><a href="http://helpinghands.org">Helping Hands
Training Center</a></h5>
        <ul>
            <li>678 Volunteer Way</li>
            <li>Vienna, <abbr title="Virginia">VA</abbr>
22027</li>
        </ul>
        <ul>
            <li><a href="mailto:training@helpinghands.org">
Email</a></li>
            <li>Phone: 703-784-5468</li>
            <li>Fax: 703-784-5400</li>
        </ul>
    </li>
</ol>
```

Required properties: `fn` and `org`

Not only do I need to include the required fn and org properties for each branch's name information, I also need to specify the org subproperties, so that I can differentiate between the branches (via `organization-unit`):

```
<ol>
    <li class="vcard">
        <h5><a href="http://helpinghands.org" class="fn
org"><span class="organization-name">Helping Hands</span>
<span class="organization-unit">Community Outreach</span></
a></h5>
        <ul>
            <li>678 Volunteer Way</li>
            <li>Suite A</li>
            <li>Alexandria, <abbr title="Virginia">VA</abbr>
22301</li>
        </ul>
        <ul>
            <li><a href="mailto:community@helpinghands.org">
Email</a></li>
            <li>Phone: 703-675-9932</li>
            <li>Fax: 703-675-0032</li>
        </ul>
    </li>
    <li class="vcard">
        <h5><a href="http://helpinghands.org" class="fn org">
<span class="organization-name">Helping Hands</span> <span
class="organization-unit">Training Center</span></a></h5>
        <ul>
            <li>678 Volunteer Way</li>
            <li>Vienna, <abbr title="Virginia">VA</abbr>
22027</li>
        </ul>
        <ul>
            <li><a href="mailto:training@helpinghands.org">
Email</a></li>
            <li>Phone: 703-784-5468</li>
            <li>Fax: 703-784-5400</li>
        </ul>
    </li>
</ol>
```

Depending on your presentational requirements, you may not want to display the main organization name (Helping Hands) for every single branch; you may want your users to see only the branch name.

But you need the organization name for machines to properly parse your hCards. What to do? Just use some clever CSS (`display:none`) for the `organization-name`.

I know, I know. Hiding content with CSS is generally frowned upon. But mostly that's when it's used for black hat SEO purposes. Still, I don't like to do it. Sometimes it may be necessary, though. Decide for yourself.

Optional property: `url`

The organization's website is included in this example, so we also include the `url` property on the link:

```
<ol>
    <li class="vcard">
        <h5><a href="http://helpinghands.org" class="fn org
url"><span class="organization-name">Helping Hands</span>
<span class="organization-unit">Community Outreach</span>
</a></h5>
        <ul>
            <li>678 Volunteer Way</li>
            <li>Suite A</li>
            <li>Alexandria, <abbr title="Virginia">VA</abbr>
22301</li>
        </ul>
        <ul>
            <li><a href="mailto:community@helpinghands.org">
Email</a></li>
            <li>Phone: 703-675-9932</li>
            <li>Fax: 703-675-0032</li>
        </ul>
    </li>
    <li class="vcard">
        <h5><a href="http://helpinghands.org" class="fn org
url"><span class="organization-name">Helping Hands</span>
<span class="organization-unit">Training Center</span></a>
</h5>
        <ul>
            <li>678 Volunteer Way</li>
```

```
            <li>Vienna, <abbr title="Virginia">VA</abbr>
22027</li>
        </ul>
        <ul>
            <li><a href="mailto:training@helpinghands.org">
Email</a></li>
            <li>Phone: 703-784-5468</li>
            <li>Fax: 703-784-5400</li>
        </ul>
    </li>
</ol>
```

Optional property: `adr`

Whenever you add the `adr` property, be sure to include the relevant sub-properties for all the address components:

```
<ol>
    <li class="vcard">
        <h5><a href="http://helpinghands.org" class="fn org
url"><span class="organization-name">Helping Hands</span>
<span class="organization-unit">Community Outreach</span>
</a></h5>
        <ul class="adr">
            <li class="street-address">678 Volunteer Way</li>
            <li class="extended-address">Suite A</li>
            <li><span class="locality">Alexandria</span>,
<abbr title="Virginia" class="region">VA</abbr> <span
class="postal-code">22301</span></li>
        </ul>
        <ul>
            <li><a href="mailto:community@helpinghands.
org">Email</a></li>
            <li>Phone: 703-675-9932</li>
            <li>Fax: 703-675-0032</li>
        </ul>
    </li>
    <li class="vcard">
        <h5><a href="http://helpinghands.org" class="fn org
url"><span class="organization-name">Helping Hands</span>
<span class="organization-unit">Training Center</span></a>
</h5>
```

(continues on next page)

```
    <ul class="adr">
        <li class="street-address">678 Volunteer Way</li>
        <li><span class="locality">Vienna</span>, <abbr
title="Virginia" class="region">VA</abbr> <span class=
"postal-code">22027</span></li>
    </ul>
    <ul>
        <li><a href="mailto:training@helpinghands.org">
Email</a></li>
        <li>Phone: 703-784-5468</li>
        <li>Fax: 703-784-5400</li>
    </ul>
    </li>
</ol>
```

Optional properties: `email` and `tel`

Last, I add the `email` and `tel` properties. And because I'm specifying more than one phone number for each branch, I also include the `type` subproperty:

```
<ol>
    <li class="vcard">
        <h5><a href="http://helpinghands.org" class="fn org
url"><span class="organization-name">Helping Hands</span>
<span class="organization-unit">Community Outreach</span>
</a></h5>
        <ul class="adr">
            <li class="street-address">678 Volunteer Way</li>
            <li class="extended-address">Suite A</li>
            <li><span class="locality">Alexandria</span>,
<abbr title="Virginia" class="region">VA</abbr> <span
class="postal-code">22301</span></li>
        </ul>
        <ul>
            <li><a href="mailto:community@helpinghands.org"
class="email">Email</a></li>
            <li class="tel"><em class="type"><span
class="value-title" title="work"> </span>Phone</em>: 703-
675-9932</li>
            <li class="tel"><em class="type">Fax</em>: 703-
675-0032</li>
```

```
            </ul>
        </li>
        <li class="vcard">
            <h5><a href="http://helpinghands.org" class="fn org
url"><span class="organization-name">Helping Hands</span>
<span class="organization-unit">Training Center</span></a>
</h5>
            <ul class="adr">
                <li class="street-address">678 Volunteer Way</li>
                <li><span class="locality">Vienna</span>,
<abbr title="Virginia" class="region">VA</abbr> <span
class="postal-code">22027</span></li>
            </ul>
            <ul>
                <li><a href="mailto:training@helpinghands.org"
class="email">Email</a></li>
                <li class="tel"><em class="type"><span
class="value-title" title="work"> </span>Phone</em>: 703-
784-5468</li>
                <li class="tel"><em class="type">Fax</em>: 703-
784-5400</li>
            </ul>
        </li>
</ol>
```

Once again, make note of the value-title subset of the value class pattern for the *Phone* tel type. I'm indicating a valid value with the inclusion of an empty <span class="value-title"> that has work in the title.

The end result

All of the properties and subproperties results in this final markup:

```
<ol>
    <li class="vcard">
        <h5><a href="http://helpinghands.org" class="fn org
url"><span class="organization-name">Helping Hands</span>
<span class="organization-unit">Community Outreach</span>
</a></h5>
            <ul class="adr">
                <li class="street-address">678 Volunteer Way</li>
                <li class="extended-address">Suite A</li>
```

(continues on next page)

```
        <li><span class="locality">Alexandria</span>,
<abbr title="Virginia" class="region">VA</abbr> <span
class="postal-code">22301</span></li>
        </ul>
        <ul>
        <li><a href="mailto:community@helpinghands.org"
class="email">Email</a></li>
        <li class="tel"><em class="type"><span
class="value-title" title="work"> </span>Phone</em>: 703-
675-9932</li>
        <li class="tel"><em class="type">Fax</em>: 703-
675-0032</li>
        </ul>
    </li>
    <li class="vcard">
        <h5><a href="http://helpinghands.org" class="fn org
url"><span class="organization-name">Helping Hands</span>
<span class="organization-unit">Training Center</span></a>
</h5>
        <ul class="adr">
        <li class="street-address">678 Volunteer Way</li>
        <li><span class="locality">Vienna</span>,
<abbr title="Virginia" class="region">VA</abbr> <span
class="postal-code">22027</span></li>
        </ul>
        <ul>
        <li><a href="mailto:training@helpinghands.org"
class="email">Email</a></li>
        <li class="tel"><em class="type"><span
class="value-title" title="work"> </span>Phone</em>: 703-
784-5468</li>
        <li class="tel"><em class="type">Fax</em>: 703-
784-5400</li>
        </ul>
    </li>
</ol>
```

The logic behind the markup

I'm hoping it is already obvious to you why I chose the markup for this example, because it is very similar to the other examples I've described:

- The `<ol>` is appropriate for the sequential (alphabetical) nature of the listing, and each `<li>` can contain the block-level content I wish to use for my contact information.

- The nested `<ul>`s for address information suit my semantic perspective that such content is really just a list.

- The same logic applies to the nested `<ul>`s containing email and telephone information: list content.

Alternately, I could've used a `<dl>` nested in each `<li>` for my contact information; however, I wanted the extra "SEO power" of the `<h5>` for each branch.

It's really up to you. Think about your content and consider the markup structure that is most semantic and appropriate for your needs.

Natural language for a named place

Last, but certainly not least, let's look at an example of an hCard for a named place. As I said, it is essentially the same as an hCard for an organization:

```
<p>One of the best road trips I have ever taken was to
Graceland in Memphis, Tennessee.</p>
```

Required root property: `vcard`

First, we start with the required root property:

```
<p class="vcard">One of the best road trips I have ever
taken was to Graceland in Memphis, Tennessee.</p>
```

Required properties: `fn` and `org`

Because this example is for a named place, not a person, you use the `org` subproperty to indicate the place's name, along with `fn`:

```
<p class="vcard">One of the best road trips I have ever
taken was to <span class="fn org">Graceland</span> in
Memphis, Tennessee.</p>
```

Because my example did not have an element I could use as a hook for these two properties, I added a `<span>` to contain *Graceland*.

Optional property: `adr`

Once again, I add `<span>`s to provide the containing elements needed to assign `adr` and its relevant subproperties.

```
<p class="vcard">One of the best road trips I have ever
taken was to <span class="fn org">Graceland</span> in <span
class="adr"><span class="locality">Memphis</span>, <span
class="region">Tennessee</span></span>.</p>
```

Optional property: `geo`

Finally, it seems this particular hCard would benefit from some geographical coordinates. But, as with my other examples, I don't care to display that content to my users, so I will use the value-title subset of the value class pattern:

```
<p class="vcard">One of the best road trips I have ever
taken was to <span class="fn org"><span class="geo">
<span class="value-title" title="35.046862,-90.023239">
</span>Graceland</span></span> in <span class="adr">
<span class="locality">Memphis</span>, <span class="region">
Tennessee</span></span>.</p>
```

Notice that in this instance, I've applied `geo` to the name content rather than the address content. That is because the coordinates describe the named place (*Graceland*), rather than the city and state.

The end result

That handful of properties and subproperties we added gives us:

```
<p class="vcard">One of the best road trips I have ever
taken was to <span class="fn org"><span class="geo">
<span class="value-title" title="35.046862,-90.023239">
</span>Graceland</span></span> in <span class="adr"><span
class="locality">Memphis</span>, <span class="region">
Tennessee</span></span>.</p>
```

Authoring Tools

Not a fan of hand-coding? I won't make fun of you (to your face, at least).

Seriously, though, hand-coding isn't for everyone and it is, arguably, inefficient at times. So here are a number of resources to help you author and validate your hCards:

- hCard creator: http://microformats.org/code/hcard/creator

- Optimus microformats transformer (for validation): http://microformatique.com/optimus/

- hCard microformat validator: http://hcard.geekhood.net/

- hCard cheat sheet: http://microformats.org/wiki/hcard-cheatsheet

Just the Beginning

As you may have noticed, hCard is one of the more detailed microformats. Lots of properties and subproperties to choose from. Lots of design pattern options for indicating enumerated values of the adr and tel type subproperties. Lots of choices when it comes to markup.

It seems like a lot because it is a lot. But in many ways, understanding the details of hCard gives you a great foundation for the microformats you'll be learning about in future chapters.

You are well prepared now to dive into the next microformat, hCalendar, which can be combined with hCard and also can utilize the geo property we've already covered.

Chapter 7

Defining Events:
hCalendar

Information about events is another one of the more common types of web content. It's everywhere. People publish details about their events to share information, encourage attendance, and even prompt users to save the event specifics to their calendars.

And the hCalendar microformat was developed for just such content. Concerts, parties, and conferences, oh my!

What Is hCalendar?

hCalendar is a formal microformat used to mark up content about events. Specifically, the type of event information you would find on a calendar, such as the following:

- Name/summary

- Location

- Start and end dates and times

- Longer description (than summary)

- Type of event

Electronic calendars

iCalendar, a standard for calendar data, is commonly used to share calendar information electronically, such as via email. iCalendar files with the universal calendar extension .ics can be added to users' electronic calendars such as Apple iCal.

hCalendar was developed based on a 1:1 representation of iCalendar properties, so that content authors can provide event information on their websites that users can then download (as .ics files) and save to their preferred electronic calendar application.

It functions much like the hCard-to-vCard conversion. Content marked up with hCalendar can be extracted from web pages and transformed into an .ics file (machines to the rescue, once again). This frees users from having to manually add event details to their electronic calendars. They just import the .ics file.

And, of course, there are tools available that handle this conversion. Let's start with Technorati's Events Feed Service. Users simply enter a URL for a web page containing microformats (**Figure 7.1**), and the service generates a downloadable .ics file (**Figure 7.2**). Users can also use this service to subscribe to a feed of all hCalendar events from the submitted URL.

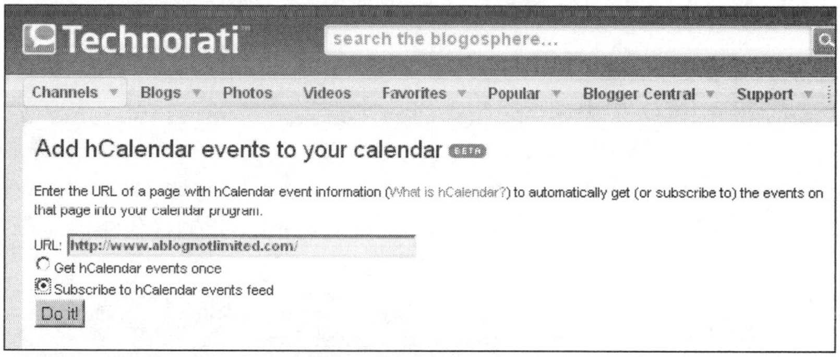

Figure 7.1
Technorati's Events
Feed Service

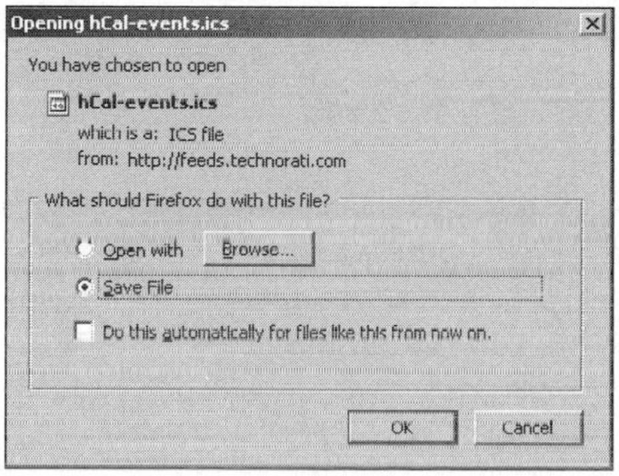

Figure 7.2
Technorati's Events
Feed Service generates an .ics file users can import into their electronic calendars.

You can also let users bypass the need to go to the Events Feed Service page by offering the hCalendar conversion directly on your site. Just provide a link to your page containing hCalendar events that has an `href` value prepended with the Technorati Events Feed Service URL:

```
<a href="http://technorati.com/events/http://www.
ablognotlimited.com/" title="Download iCalendar">Add to
Calendar</a>
```

And if your page contains more than one event marked up with hCalendar, all events are extracted and transformed.

You can also extract the electronic calendar files from your hCalendar events using browser-based tools. The Tails Export add-on for Mozilla Firefox identifies hCalendar events and provides options for viewing the containing HTML and exporting the .ics file (**Figure 7.3**).

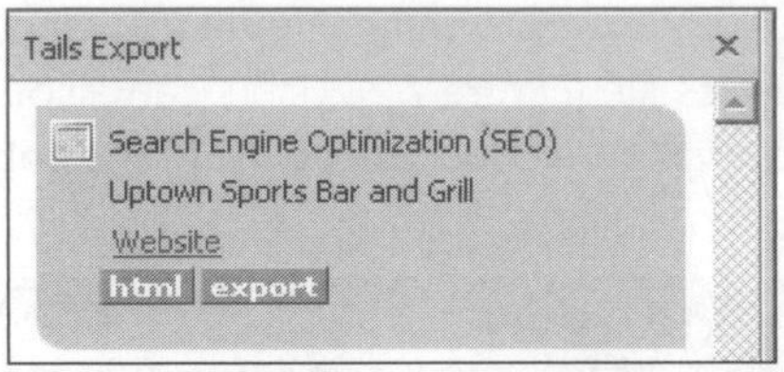

Figure 7.3
The Tails Export 0.3.5 Firefox add-on extracts and exports hCalendar events.

The Operator Firefox add-on provides the same functionality, transforming hCalendar into an .ics export. Operator also provides automatic functionality to import the .ics into several calendar applications, including 30 Boxes, Yahoo! Calendar, and Google Calendar (**Figure 7.4**).

Figure 7.4
The Operator 0.9.3 Firefox add-on provides automatic import into popular web-based calendars.

Left Logic's microformats bookmarklet also allows users to import .ics files of hCalendar events, but it isn't restricted to Firefox. If a user drags the bookmarklet to their browser bookmark toolbar (in Apple Safari, Camino, Firefox, and Microsoft Internet Explorer 6 and 7), they can then select that bookmarklet while on a page containing hCalendar and are prompted to download the .ics file (**Figure 7.5**).

Figure 7.5
Left Logic's microformats bookmarklet provides a modal overlay displaying hCalendar information and an option to export the resulting .ics file.

I mentioned the Oomph Microformats Toolkit in the previous chapter on hCard, but it is also useful for hCalendar. By adding the jQuery functionality of Oomph to your site, you provide a browser-independent means for your users to easily see and export hCalendar from your pages.

When Oomph detects hCalendar on a page, an icon (Gleam) appears in the upper left-hand corner (**Figure 7.6**). When users select the icon, a jQuery overlay on the page provides details about the event, as well as a number of export options (**Figure 7.7**).

Figure 7.6
The Oomph Microformats Toolkit Gleam icon

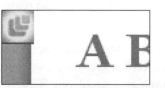

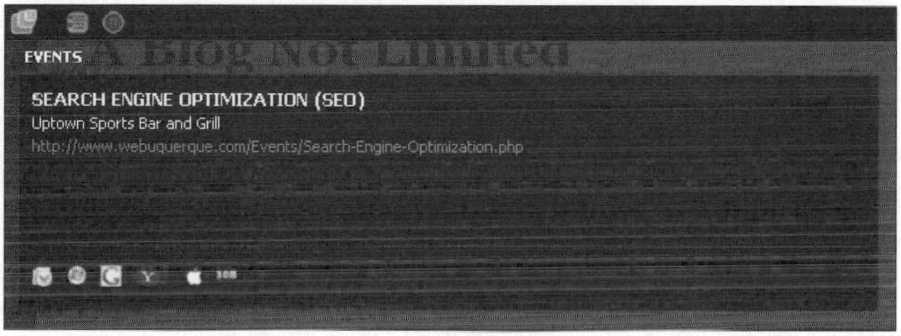

Figure 7.7
The Oomph overlay displays hCalendar details and options to export to Microsoft Outlook, Windows Live, Google Calendar, 30 Boxes, and Yahoo! Calendar.

Once again, I'll mention that Oomph is one of the first tools that broadens microformats consumption for everyday users. Folks don't need to have a special application or browser. They don't even need to know what microformats are. They just see the icon and can get all the goodness of hCalendar in a single click.

hCalendar, it's the new black

Like hCard, hCalendar is one of the more popular microformats. Content authors all over the web are using hCalendar to publish information such as the following:

- Yahoo! Upcoming and Local events

- MapQuest Local events

- TripIt itineraries

- Last.fm concerts

- Facebook events

And these are just some of the "big" names. Hundreds of corporate, per-sonal, and nonprofit sites are publishing their events with hCalendar.

Search implications

Aside from the electronic calendar feature of hCalendar (which no doubt enhances the user experience), I believe a big reason hCalendar enjoys its popularity is *search*.

There isn't much that hCalendar does for search *today*. There is Technorati's Microformats Search, which indexes and provides search results about hCalendar events. And Yahoo! SearchMonkey also provides the ability to search hCalendar events on the web.

The future implications of hCalendar (and other microformats) on search are potentially huge. The major search engines (Google, Yahoo!) are encouraging authors to publish structured content using microformats: just look at Google's Rich Snippets and Yahoo! SearchMonkey. These are rela-tively new developments in the search world that utilize microformats, and more could be coming.

Personally, I'd rather take the time now to implement microformats than rush to get them in place once some new search technology is unveiled.

Profile

Since I know you are just itching to be like the cool kids and implement hCalendar, let's get started with the recommended profile:

```
<head profile="http://microformats.org/profile/hcalendar">
```

If you are using more than one formal microformat in your content, such as hCalendar and hCard, you can add the relevant profiles together, sepa-rated by a space:

```
<head profile="http://microformats.org/profile/hcalendar
http://microformats.org/profile/hcard">
```

And once the combined profile I've mentioned is ready, you can use that for all formal microformats.

Syntax

As a compound microformat, hCalendar has a number of properties and subproperties, each of which correlates to an iCalendar field thanks to hCalendar's 1:1 representation with iCalendar.

The root property of hCalendar is `vcalendar`. It is unique from other microformats' root properties in that it is *optional*; `vcalendar` is required only on pages that contain more than one calendar of events. For pages that contain just one calendar of events, you can certainly use it, but it isn't required.

What's the difference? A "calendar of events" can be considered a grouping of events—by date, by topic, or however you may choose to group your events. For example, perhaps you want to provide a calendar of events for your organization and you want to group events by month. If you have a page that lists an entire year of events, you could contain each month's calendar with `vcalendar`, indicating that each month is a unique and separate calendar of events.

Conversely, if your page only listed a single month, you could skip the `vcalendar` property because it is assumed on the page itself. Similarly, if you don't care to group multiple events in any fashion or if you are only listing a single event, you can omit the `vcalendar` property.

Required properties

So, if you are listing a single event or a single calendar of events, the only required properties for hCalendar are these:

- `vevent` applies to the element containing all of a single event's information. In the case of multiple events on a page, each event must be contained by `vevent`.

- `summary` provides a short description of the event, but is commonly used to contain the name or title of the event.

- `dtstart` contains start date and/or time information for the event.

Once again, if you are providing multiple calendars of events on a single page, you must use the root `vcalendar` property to contain each calendar on the page.

Optional properties

The remaining properties and subproperties are optional. Use them if you have the content. Don't sweat it if you don't.

- `dtend` designates end date and/or time information.

- `duration` indicates the length of time an event spans. This can be seconds, minutes, hours, days—even weeks, months, and years.

We've discussed the datetime design pattern used for indicating date-time information in microformats via `<abbr>`, but this pattern is deprecated. So, for the examples in this chapter, I detail the more accessible and usable options for this type of information with the value class pattern.

In context with `duration`, you indicate the machine-readable data via the `title` attribute of the element, using the following syntax, where the ? is a digit representing time:

- `P?Y` indicates years, so `P3Y` = 3 years.

- `P?M` indicates months, so `P5M` = 5 months.

- `P?W` indicates weeks, so `P1W` = 1 week.

- `P?D` indicates days, so `P2D` = 2 days.

- `PT?H` indicates hours, so `PT6H` = 6 hours.

- `PT?M` indicates minutes, so `PT55M` = 55 minutes.

- `PT?S` indicates seconds, so `PT30S` = 30 seconds.

Note that once I get into hours, minutes, and seconds, the new T delimiter (for time) enters the picture. It always precedes hours, minutes, and seconds.

You can combine these duration values for more specific date-time information:

- `P2DT4H` = 2 days, 4 hours

- `P1W2DT3H` = 1 week, 2 days, 3 hours

Now, let's get back to the rest of the optional hCalendar properties:

- `url` specifies a link for the event.

- `location` indicates where the event is held.

- `category` defines what type of event it is. The type is up to you; there are no specified `category` values that you must use. However, some commonly used values are *meeting*, *expo*, *conference*, and *appointment*. But you can certainly use *party*, *concert*, *workshop*, or whatever category you think is appropriate for your event. And your event can belong to more than one category. As such, it can be used multiple times within a *vevent*.

- `description` is a longer (than the `summary`) description of the event and can be as long and detailed as your heart desires.

- `dtstamp` can be used to indicate the date and/or time the page containing the event was created.

- `last-modified` indicates the date and/or time the event information was last updated.

- `status` specifies whether an event is *cancelled*, *confirmed*, or *tentative*. And, yes, you smart little monkey, those are the three `status` values you can use.

- `class` is assigned to the access classification of the event, either *public*, *private*, or *confidential*. In practice this property is little used, as there are better methods of providing access restrictions on the web.

- `uid` specifies a unique global identifier for the contact, typically an IANA format. In practice, publishers have used `uid` to specify which `url` of an hCalendar is the primary or uniquely identifying URL.

- `geo` can be included to indicate the global position of the event in latitude and longitude.

Recurring events

Sometimes events are recurring. And there are a few optional hCalendar properties you can include for such events.

`rrule` indicates *regular* recurrence of an event. If you use `rrule`, you must also use its subproperty, `freq`, which indicates the frequency of occurrence.

When would you use this? What about for a meeting that occurs on the first of every month? In this example, you first apply `rrule` to the content indicating recurrence:

```
<p class="vevent">Our meetings are <span
class="rrule">monthly</span>.</p>
```

Next you indicate the frequency (*monthly*) by containing that content with the `freq` subproperty:

```
<p class="vevent">Our meetings are <span class="rrule"><span
class="freq">monthly</span></span>.</p>
```

Another approach for expressing the frequency of recurring events uses `<abbr>`:

```
<p class="vevent">Our meetings are <abbr class="rrule"
title="freq=monthly">monthly</abbr>.</p>
```

This method, however, results in a `title` value that is, arguably, not that human readable: `freq=monthly`. So, you can instead use the empty `<span>` value-title method of the value-class-pattern, which is useful when the `title` date-time information is *only* machine readable:

```
<p class="vevent">Our meetings are <span class="rrule"><span
class="value-title" title="freq=monthly"> </span>monthly
</span>.</p>
```

The standard values you can use for `freq` are as follows:

- `secondly`

- `minutely`

- `hourly`

- `daily`

- `monthly`

- `yearly`

You can further clarify your `freq` values with the `interval`, `count`, and `until` qualifiers:

- `interval` indicates the interval of frequency, such as every two weeks.

- `count` indicates how many events occur within the range of recurrence.

- `until` indicates the end date for the range of recurrence.

The `count` and `until` qualifiers are mutually exclusive. You can use one or the other, not both.

To specify these qualifiers, use the value class pattern empty `<span>` value-title method for `rrule`, and include the qualifier and value in the `title`, along with `freq`:

```
<p class="vevent">Our meetings are <span class="rrule">
<span class="value-title" title="freq=weekly;interval=2">
</span>every other week</span>.</p>
```

In English, the machine data contained in the `title` of this example says the event is every other week. I could be even more specific and indicate there will be, for example, nine events in this range of recurrence:

```
<p class="vevent">Our meetings are <span class="rrule"><span
class="value-title" title="freq=weekly;interval=2;count=9">
</span>every other week</span>.</p>
```

Or, instead of a specific count, I can indicate the end date of the recurrence:

```
<p class="vevent">Our meetings are <span class="rrule"><span
class="value-title" title="freq=weekly;interval=2;until
=2009-12-05"> </span>every other week</span>.</p>
```

Note that when using multiple qualifiers, each has a value preceded by an equal sign, and each is separated from the others by a semicolon.

And yet there are even more `freq` qualifiers you can use to get even more specific, each of which has a range of values (listed in parentheses below) you can assign:

- `bysecond` (0–59)
- `byminute` (0–59)
- `byhour` (0–23)
- `bymonthday` (1–31)
- `byyearday` (1–366, to account for leap years)
- `byweekno` (1–53)
- `bymonth` (1–23)
- `byday` (SU, MO, TU, WE, TH, FR, and SA are case insensitive)

You treat these `freq` qualifiers the same as `interval`, `count`, and `until`: apply the qualifier and its value to the `title`, separating it from other qualifiers with a semicolon.

So, here's what I would do if I wanted to indicate that an event recurs monthly, on the first Wednesday of the month:

```
<p class="vevent">Our meetings are <span class="rrule"><span
class="value-title" title="freq=monthly;byweekno=1;byday=w
e"> </span>on the first Wednesday of every month</span>.</p>
```

Of course, there are also those types of events that recur *irregularly*. For these, you can specify the `rdate` property, which allows you to enumerate the specific dates of recurrence in a comma-separated list of ISO 8601 dates.

```
<p class="vevent">Our meetings are <span class="rdate"><span
class="value-title" title="2009-02-04,2009-03-04,2009-04-
01,2009-05-05"> </span>on the first Wednesday of every
month</span>.</p>
```

Once again, you use the value class pattern empty `<span>` value-title method to contain the machine data in the `title` of `<span class="value-title">` immediately inside `<span class="rdate">`.

Practical Markup

Now that you know your property and subproperty options for hCalendar, let's see what some of your POSH options are.

Single-event listing

For this example, I want to demonstrate the markup I would use to detail a single event. Let's use one of my favorite events: SXSWi—the conference as a whole, in this case, not all of its sessions:

```
<h3><a href="http://sxsw.com/interactive/">SXSWi 2010</a>
</h3>
<ul>
    <li>March 12-16, 2010</li>
    <li>Austin, TX</li>
</ul>
<p>The SXSW Interactive Festival is a five-day conference
celebrating the creativity and passion behind the coolest
new media technologies.</p>
```

Optional root property: `vcalendar`

This example includes just one event. As such, I can omit the `vcalendar` root property because it is assumed on the page.

Required property: `vevent`

I do, however, need to add the `vevent` property to all event information. Because there is no containing element for all of the event details in this example, I add a `<div>`:

```
<div class="vevent">
    <h3><a href="http://sxsw.com/interactive/">SXSWi 2010
</a></h3>
    <ul>
        <li>March 12 16, 2010</li>
        <li>Austin, TX</li>
    </ul>
    <p>The SXSW Interactive Festival is ...</p>
</div>
```

Required property: `summary`

Since summary is most commonly the event name, I add that required property to the <a> element containing the name:

```
<div class="vevent">
    <h3><a href="http://sxsw.com/interactive/" class=
"summary">SXSWi 2010</a></h3>
    <ul>
        <li>March 12-16, 2010</li>
        <li>Austin, TX</li>
    </ul>
    <p>The SXSW Interactive Festival is ...</p>
</div>
```

Optional property: `url`

Indeed, this example contains a link to the event's website, so I can add the url property:

```
<div class="vevent">
    <h3><a href="http://sxsw.com/interactive/" class="
summary url">SXSWi 2010</a></h3>
    <ul>
        <li>March 12-16, 2010</li>
        <li>Austin, TX</li>
    </ul>
    <p>The SXSW Interactive Festival is ...</p>
</div>
```

Required property: `dtstart`

I add the other required property, `dtstart`, to the date information using the value-title subset of value class pattern:

```
<div class="vevent">
    <h3><a href="http://sxsw.com/interactive/" class=
"summary url">SXSWi 2010</a></h3>
    <ul>
        <li><span class="dtstart"><span class="value-title"
title="2010-03-12">March 12</span></span>-16, 2010</li>
        <li>Austin, TX</li>
    </ul>
    <p>The SXSW Interactive Festival is ...</p>
</div>
```

I could also use the empty `<span>` technique of the value-title subset for `dtstart`:

```
<li><span class="dtstart"><span class="value-title" title=
"2010-03-12"> </span>March 12</span>-16, 2010</li>
```

Or I could use `<abbr>` with the value class pattern, since I'm only specifying a date ISO 8601 value, rather than a date-time value:

```
<li><span class="dtstart"><abbr class="value" title="2010
-03-12">March 12</abbr></span>-16, 2010</li>
```

Just pick your preferred poison, taking into account your audience. Will browser tooltips of the ISO 8601 date confuse them? Do you have screen-reader users who will be confused by the expanded `<abbr>`? Or do you have world-wide readers for whom the ISO 8601 date may make sense in a tooltip or screen-reader expansion?

Optional property: `dtend`

The `dtend` property, for specifying the event's end date, is treated the same way as `dtstart`, using the value-title subset of the value class pattern:

```
<div class="vevent">
    <h3><a href="http://sxsw.com/interactive/" class=
"summary url">SXSWi 2010</a></h3>
    <ul>
        <li><span class="dtstart"><span class="value-title"
title="2010-03-12">March 12</span></span>-<span class=
```

```
"dtend"><span class="value-title" title="2010-03-16">16,
2010</span></span></li>
        <li>Austin, TX</li>
    </ul>
    <p>The SXSW Interactive Festival is    </p>
</div>
```

But again, you can use any of the methods I detailed for `dtstart`. Just be consistent and use the same method for both properties.

Optional property: `location`

As this example includes the location, the `location` property is added:

```
<div class="vevent">
    <h3><a href="http://sxsw.com/interactive/" class=
"summary url">SXSWi 2010</a></h3>
    <ul>
        <li><span class="dtstart"><span class="value-title"
title="2010-03-12">March 12</span></span>-<span class=
"dtend"><span class="value-title" title="2010-03-16">16,
2010</span></span></li>
        <li class="location">Austin, TX</li>
    </ul>
    <p>The SXSW Interactive Festival is ...</p>
</div>
```

Optional property: `description`

This example includes a somewhat detailed `description` of the event, so I can include that property:

```
<div class="vevent">
    <h3><a href="http://sxsw.com/interactive/" class=
"summary url">SXSWi 2010</a></h3>
    <ul>
        <li><span class="dtstart"><span class="value-title"
title="2010-03-12">March 12</span></span>-<span class=
"dtend"><span class="value-title" title="2010-03-16">16,
2010</span></span></li>
        <li class="location">Austin, TX</li>
    </ul>
```

(continues on next page)

```
    <p class="description">The SXSW Interactive Festival is
a five-day conference celebrating the creativity and passion
behind the coolest new media technologies.</p>
</div>
```

Optional property: `category`

The content in my `description` includes the `category` to which I would
like this event to be assigned:

```
<div class="vevent">
    <h3><a href="http://sxsw.com/interactive/" class=
"summary url">SXSWi 2010</a></h3>
    <ul>
        <li><span class="dtstart"><span class="value-title"
title="2010-03-12">March 12</span></span>-<span class=
"dtend"><span class="value-title" title="2010-03-16">16,
2010</span></span></li>
        <li class="location">Austin, TX</li>
    </ul>
    <p class="description">The SXSW Interactive Festival
is a five-day <span class="category">conference</span>
celebrating the creativity and passion behind the coolest
new media technologies.</p>
</div>
```

Optional property: `duration`

Finally, my `description` content also mentions the `duration` of the
conference:

```
<div class="vevent">
    <h3><a href="http://sxsw.com/interactive/" class=
"summary url">SXSWi 2010</a></h3>
    <ul>
        <li><span class="dtstart"><span class="value-title"
title="2010-03-12">March 12</span></span>-<span class=
"dtend"><span class="value-title" title="2010-03-16">16,
2010</span></span></li>
        <li class="location">Austin, TX</li>
    </ul>
```

```
    <p class="description">The SXSW Interactive Festival
is a <span class="duration"><span class="value-title"
title="P5D"> </span>five-day</span> <span class="category">
conference</span> celebrating the creativity and passion
behind the coolest new media technologies.</p>
</div>
```

Once again, because I'm dealing with date-time information, I'm using the value-title subset of the value class pattern for `duration`. And, once again, because the date-time information for duration is only machine readable, I'm using the empty `<span>` value-title technique.

The end result

Here's the complete code example, fully marked up with `hCalendar`:

```
<div class="vevent">
    <h3><a href="http://sxsw.com/interactive/" class=
"summary url">SXSWi 2010</a></h3>
    <ul>
        <li><span class="dtstart"><span class="value-title"
title="2010-03-12">March 12</span></span>-<span class=
"dtend"><span class="value-title" title="2010-03-16">16,
2010</span></span></li>
        <li class="location">Austin, TX</li>
    </ul>
    <p class="description">The SXSW Interactive Festival
is a <span class="duration"><span class="value-title"
title="P5D"> </span>five-day</span> <span class="category">
conference</span> celebrating the creativity and passion
behind the coolest new media technologies.</p>
</div>
```

The logic behind the markup

I chose a bunch of different elements for my event content in this example. The `<h3>` potentially offers some SEO for my event name, as many search engines give content contained by heading elements additional importance.

The date-time and location information, meanwhile, makes sense as a list. In fact, this could even be a `<dl>`, with `<dt>`s "introducing" the content:

```
<dl>
    <dt>When:</dt>
    <dd><span class="dtstart"><span class="value-title"
title="2010-03-12">March 12</span></span>-<span class=
"dtend"><span class="value-title" title="2010-03-16">16,
2010</span></span></dd>
    <dt>Where:</dt>
    <dd class="location">Austin, TX</dd>
</dl>
```

And finally, the description is most definitely a paragraph, so it makes sense to use <p>.

Single event using `<dl>`

The previous example required the addition of a nonsemantic `<div>` container, which isn't a bad thing (remember, reality over purity). But I could've also contained all of my event information in a definition list:

```
<dl>
    <dt><a href="http://sxsw.com/interactive/">SXSWi 2010
</a></dt>
    <dd>March 12-16, 2010</dd>
    <dd>Austin, TX</dd>
    <dd>The SXSW Interactive Festival is a five day
conference celebrating the creativity and passion behind the
coolest new media technologies.</dd>
</dl>
```

Required property: `vevent`

Note that since I've assigned `vevent` to the `<dl>`, I cannot include other events within this definition list. And I can't assign `vevent` to the `<dt>`, because it doesn't contain the `<dd>`s.

So if you have multiple events on your page, this implementation may not be ideal.

```
<dl class="vevent">
    <dt><a href="http://sxsw.com/interactive/">SXSWi 2010
</a></dt>
    <dd>March 12-16, 2010</dd>
    <dd>Austin, TX</dd>
```

```
    <dd>The SXSW Interactive Festival is ...</dd>
</dl>
```

Required property: `summary`

The `summary` property is most often used for the event name, so I apply it to the `<a>` element containing that content:

```
<dl class="vevent">
    <dt><a href="http://sxsw.com/interactive/" class=
"summary">SXSWi 2010</a></dt>
    <dd>March 12-16, 2010</dd>
    <dd>Austin, TX</dd>
    <dd>The SXSW Interactive Festival is ...</dd>
</dl>
```

Optional property: `url`

I also add the `url` property to the `<a>`, since it indicates the website for the event:

```
<dl class="vevent">
    <dt><a href="http://sxsw.com/interactive/" class=
"summary url">SXSWi 2010</a></dt>
    <dd>March 12-16, 2010</dd>
    <dd>Austin, TX</dd>
    <dd>The SXSW Interactive Festival is ...</dd>
</dl>
```

Required property: `dtstart`

For this example, I've decided to use the empty `<span>` method of the value-title subset in order to avoid any confusing browser tooltips or screen-reader expansions.

```
<dl class="vevent">
    <dt><a href="http://sxsw.com/interactive/" class=
"summary url">SXSWi 2010</a></dt>
    <dd><span class="dtstart"><span class="value-title"
title="2010-03-12"> </span>March 12</span>-16, 2010</dd>
    <dd>Austin, TX</dd>
    <dd>The SXSW Interactive Festival is ...</dd>
</dl>
```

Optional property: `dtend`

I use the same empty `<span>` method to indicate the event end date with `dtend`:

```
<dl class="vevent">
    <dt><a href="http://sxsw.com/interactive/" class=
"summary url">SXSWi 2010</a></dt>
    <dd><span class="dtstart"><span class="value-title"
title="2010-03-12"> </span>March 12</span>-<span class=
"dtend"><span class="value-title" title="2010-03-16">
</span>16, 2010</span></dd>
    <dd>Austin, TX</dd>
    <dd>The SXSW Interactive Festival is ...</dd>
</dl>
```

Optional property: `location`

Next, I assign the `location` property to the `<dd>` containing the city and state where the event takes place:

```
<dl class="vevent">
    <dt><a href="http://sxsw.com/interactive/" class=
"summary url">SXSWi 2010</a></dt>
    <dd><span class="dtstart"><span class="value-title"
title="2010-03-12"> </span>March 12</span>-<span class=
"dtend"><span class="value-title" title="2010-03-16">
</span>16, 2010</span></dd>
    <dd class="location">Austin, TX</dd>
    <dd>The SXSW Interactive Festival is ...</dd>
</dl>
```

Optional property: `description`

The `description` property is then assigned to the `<dd>` containing the event description:

```
<dl class="vevent">
    <dt><a href="http://sxsw.com/interactive/" class=
"summary url">SXSWi 2010</a></dt>
    <dd><span class="dtstart"><span class="value-title"
title="2010-03-12"> </span>March 12</span>-<span class=
```

```
"dtend"><span class="value-title" title="2010-03-16">
</span>16, 2010</span></dd>
    <dd class="location">Austin, TX</dd>
    <dd class="description">The SXSW Interactive Festival is
a five day conference celebrating the creativity and passion
behind the coolest new media technologies.</dd>
</dl>
```

Optional property: `category`

The description content includes a reference to the type of event (conference), so I apply the `category` property, but first have to create a `<span>` to contain the content:

```
<dl class="vevent">
    <dt><a href="http://sxsw.com/interactive/" class=
"summary url">SXSWi 2010</a></dt>
    <dd><span class="dtstart"><span class="value-title"
title="2010-03-12"> </span>March 12</span>-<span class=
"dtend"><span class="value-title" title="2010-03-16">
</span>16, 2010</span></dd>
    <dd class="location">Austin, TX</dd>
    <dd class="description">The SXSW Interactive Festival
is a five day <span class="category">conference</span>
celebrating the creativity and passion behind the coolest
new media technologies.</dd>
</dl>
```

Optional property: `duration`

The description also includes the length of the event, which is ideal for the `duration` property. Once again, I add a containing `<span>`, as well as an inner empty `<span>` to indicate the machine data for `duration` using the value class pattern:

```
<dl class="vevent">
    <dt><a href="http://sxsw.com/interactive/" class=
"summary url">SXSWi 2010</a></dt>
    <dd><span class="dtstart"><span class="value-title"
title="2010-03-12"> </span>March 12</span>-<span class=
"dtend"><span class="value-title" title="2010-03 16">
</span>16, 2010</span></dd>
```

(continues on next page)

```
    <dd class="location">Austin, TX</dd>
    <dd class="description">The SXSW Interactive Festival
is a <span class="duration"><span class="value-title"
title="P5D"> </span>five day</span> <span class="category">
conference</span> celebrating the creativity and passion
behind the coolest new media technologies.</dd>
</dl>
```

The end result

After all the relevant hCalendar properties and subproperties are added, the final markup appears as:

```
<dl class="vevent">
    <dt><a href="http://sxsw.com/interactive/" class=
"summary url">SXSWi 2010</a></dt>
    <dd><span class="dtstart"><span class="value-title"
title="2010-03-12"> </span>March 12</span>-<span class=
"dtend"><span class="value-title" title="2010-03-16">
</span>16, 2010</span></dd>
    <dd class="location">Austin, TX</dd>
    <dd class="description">The SXSW Interactive Festival
is a <span class="duration"><span class="value-title"
title="P5D"> </span>five day</span> <span class="category">
conference</span> celebrating the creativity and passion
behind the coolest new media technologies.</dd>
</dl>
```

The logic behind the markup

Personally, I'm not a huge fan of using list elements for just one item, in this case a single event. However, the <dl> does work nicely to contain all the event information. Further, the event name is contained in the <dt>, while all the related descriptive information is contained in <dd>s—an appropriate use of a definition list.

There is just one minor drawback to this implementation: a <dt> cannot contain block-level elements, so I lose the potential SEO the <h3> element (in the previous example) offers.

The point is, though, your markup options are far greater than you realize. Consider your content, consider semantics, and then experiment.

<ABBR> VS. <ACRONYM>

Throughout this book, I talk a fair amount about the abbr design pattern and I use the `<abbr>` element in my examples where relevant and/or necessary. I figured now might be a good time to explore this element further, particularly in reference to the `<acronym>` element.

Let's start with definitions. *The Associated Press Stylebook* (my favorite writing resource of all time, by the way) defines abbreviations as "the abbreviated form that may be used for a word in some contexts." Some examples the *AP Stylebook* lists are *Dr., Ph.D., Ave.,* and *U.S.*

Acronyms, meanwhile, are defined as "a word formed from the first letter or letters of a series of words," such as *laser* and *scuba*.

And then there are initialisms, which are defined as abbreviations of phrases consisting of the initial letter of each word in the phrase, but distinguishable from an acronym in that it is *not* pronounced as a single word, such as *ASAP*.

But these are just definitions relevant to the English language. What about the web? Let's see what the W3C says:

- `<abbr>` indicates an abbreviated form (WWW, HTTP, URI, Mass)

- `<acronym>` indicates an acronym (WAC, radar, FBI)

Seems OK, until you look closer. The W3C considers *FBI* an acronym, while I would argue it is an initialism and, therefore, an abbreviation.

But let's add yet another layer of complexity with accessibility and usability. Both `<abbr>` and `<acronym>` can be assigned `title` values that correspond with the expanded value of the content. For example, `<acronym title="Self-contained underwater breathing apparatus">scuba</acronym>`.

This helps with usability, as the `title` value of any element displays as a tooltip in most browsers. Furthermore, many screen readers can be set up to allow `<abbr>` and `<acronym>` `title` values to be read aloud to users. Good stuff, right?

Now, enter the lovely, joy-of-my-life browser, Internet Explorer 6. It doesn't display tooltips for `<abbr>`. Why? Because Internet Explorer for Windows didn't support `<abbr>` until version 7. And meanwhile, designers and developers started to accommodate this IE 6 deficiency by only using `<acronym>`, even if it wasn't the most semantic element to use.

What's the solution? I don't believe there is a silver bullet. Many people get caught up in the various definitions, which is fine but doesn't lead to any progress. For my two cents, I believe that every acronym is actually an abbreviation. As such, I prefer the `<abbr>` tag, despite the issues with IE 6.

Also, `<acronym>` is deprecated in the "forthcoming" HTML5 specification, while `<abbr>` remains supported. Not to mention, microformats have an *abbr* design pattern, not an *acronym* design pattern. So those points alone might make your decision for you.

But as always, semantics and HTML are open to interpretation. Do what you will; just be informed before you do it.

Multiple events using nested lists

In this next example, we're dealing with content for a date-based (monthly) calendar that includes multiple events, such as sessions for a two-day conference:

```
<ol>
    <li>September
        <ol>
            <li>1</li>
            <li>2</li>
            <li>3
                <ul>
                    <li>
                        <h3><a href="http://web12steps.com/
tables">Letting Go of Tables for Layout</a></h3>
                        <p>9:00-11:30 am</p>
                    </li>
                    <li>
                        <h3><a href="http://web12steps.com/
animated">Animated GIFs: They Aren't Your Friends</a></h3>
                        <p>1:00-:30 pm</p>
                    </li>
                </ul>
            </li>
            <li>4
                <ul>
                    <li>
                        <h3><a href="http://web12steps.com/
tagsoup">The Web Isn't a Kitchen. Eliminate Tag Soup</a>
</h3>
                        <p>9:00-1:30 am</p>
                    </li>
                    <li>
                        <h3><a href="http://web12steps.com/
ie6">How to Break Your Co-Dependent Relationship With IE 6
</a></h3>
                        <p>1:00-:30 pm</p>
                    </li>
                </ul>
            </li>
```

```
            </ol>
        </li>
</ol>
```

Optional root property: `vcalendar`

While I am listing multiple events in this example, I consider these events as part of one calendar. As such, I do not need to include the `vcalendar` root property.

If, however, this example included multiple calendars (such as one per month), then I would include `vcalendar` and apply it to the relevant elements containing each month (`<li>`s in this case).

Required property: `vevent`

If you have more than one event, you need more than one `vevent`. Add it to the containing element for all of each event's information, `<li>`s again in this case:

```
<ol>
    <li>September
        <ol>
            <li>1</li>
            <li>2</li>
            <li>3
                <ul>
                    <li class="vevent">
                        <h3><a href="http://web12steps.com/
tables">Letting Go of Tables for Layout</a></h3>
                        <p>9:00-11:30 am</p>
                    </li>
                    <li class="vevent">
                        <h3><a href="http://web12steps.com/
animated">Animated GIFs: They Aren't Your Friends</a></h3>
                        <p>1:00-3:30 pm</p>
                    </li>
                </ul>
            </li>
            <li>4
                <ul>
                    <li class="vevent">
```

(continues on next page)

```
                    <h3><a href="http://web12steps.com/
tagsoup">The Web Isn't a Kitchen. Eliminate Tag Soup</a>
</h3>
                        <p>9:00-11:30 am</p>
                </li>
                <li class="vevent">
                    <h3><a href="http://web12steps.com/
ie6">How to Break Your Co-Dependent Relationship With IE 6
</a></h3>
                        <p>1:00-3:30 pm</p>
                </li>
            </ul>
        </li>
    </ol>
  </li>
  ...
</ol>
```

Because all of the events in this example are essentially the same (name, link, start and end times), I'm going to focus on just one of the events for the rest of the properties. Now it's for more than the trees—my fingers are tired from typing.

Required property: `summary`

For each event name, I assign the `summary` property:

```
<li class="vevent">
    <h3><a href="http://web12steps.com/tables"
class="summary">Letting Go of Tables for Layout</a></h3>
    <p>9:00-11:30 am</p>
</li>
```

Optional property: `url`

I also indicate the website for the event by adding the `url` property to the `<a>`:

```
<li class="vevent">
    <h3><a href="http://web12steps.com/tables"
class="summary url">Letting Go of Tables for Layout</a></h3>
    <p>9:00-11:30 am</p>
</li>
```

Required property: `dtstart`

I'm using the empty `<span>` value-title method of the value class pattern for my date-time information in this example because only time is visible to humans, but I still want the full date-time machine information:

```
<li class="vevent">
    <h3><a href="http://web12steps.com/tables"
class="summary url">Letting Go of Tables for Layout</a></h3>
    <p><span class="dtstart"><span class="value-title" title=
"2009-09-03T09:00:00"> </span>9:00</span>-11:30 am</p>
</li>
```

Required property: `dtend`

And, because I like consistency within an implementation, I'm also using the empty `<span>` value-title method of the value class pattern for my end date-time:

```
<li class="vevent">
    <h3><a href="http://web12steps.com/tables"
class="summary url">Letting Go of Tables for Layout</a></h3>
    <p><span class="dtstart"><span class="value-title"
title="2009-09-03T09:00:00"> </span>9:00</span>-<span
class="dtend"><span class="value-title" title="2009-09-
03T11:30:00"> </span>11:30 am</span></p>
</li>
```

The end result

A few properties and subproperties later, our code example is completely marked up with hCalendar:

```
<ol>
    <li>September
        <ol>
            <li>1</li>
            <li>2</li>
            <li>3
                <ul>
                    <li class="vevent">
                        <h3><a href="http://web12steps.com/
tables" class="summary url">Letting Go of Tables for Layout
</a></h3>
```

(continues on next page)

```
                <p><span class="dtstart"><span
class="value-title" title="2009-09-03T09:00:00"> </span>
9:00</span>-<span class="dtend"><span class="value-title"
title="2009-09-03T11:30:00"> </span>11:30 am</span></p>
                </li>
                <li class="vevent">
                    <h3><a href="http://web12steps.com/
animated" class="summary url">Animated GIFs: They Aren't
Your Friends</a></h3>
                    <p><span class="dtstart"><span
class="value-title" title="2009-09-03T13:00:00"> </span>
1:00</span>-<span class="dtend"><span class="value-title"
title="2009-09-03T15:30:00"> </span>3:30 pm</span></p>
                </li>
            </ul>
        </li>
        <li>4
            <ul>
                <li class="vevent">
                    <h3><a href="http://web12steps.
com/tagsoup" class="summary url">The Web Isn't a Kitchen.
Eliminate Tag Soup</a></h3>
                    <p><span class="dtstart"><span
class="value-title" title="2009-09-04T09:00:00"> </span>
9:00</span>-<span class="dtend"><span class="value-title"
title="2009-09-04T11:30:00"> </span>11:30 am</span></p>
                </li>
                <li class="vevent">
                    <h3><a href="http://web12steps.com/
ie6" class="summary url">How to Break Your Co-Dependent
Relationship With IE 6</a></h3>
                    <p><span class="dtstart"><span
class="value-title" title="2009-09-04T13:00:00"> </span>
1:00</span>-<span class="dtend"><span class="value-title"
title="2009-09-04T15:30:00"> </span>3:30 pm</span></p>
                </li>
            </ul>
        </li>
    </ol>
  </li>
</ol>
```

The logic behind the markup

As you can see in this example, the outermost containing element is an ordered list, which contains the months (starting with September in this example). The days of the month are then nested within the `<li>`s as another ordered list. Can you guess why I used ordered lists? Yep, sequence. Gold star time!

Because each day features multiple events (two sessions each, one in the morning and one in the afternoon), each event is contained in an `<li>` of a nested `<ul>`. And because `<li>`s can contain block elements, I'm aiming for some SEO goodness with `<h3>`s on the names.

I definitely understand the argument that calendars naturally and semantically fit in an ordered list (due to its inherent sequential nature), which is why I included the last example.

But I also see a calendar as tabular data that would be well suited for a `<table>`.

Calendar using `<table>`

I'll be the first to admit that I'm not a fan of `<table>`s—for layout.

In fact, I hate, abhor, and despise them almost as much as I hate, abhor, and despise IE 6. And frankly, I don't think too highly of the "professionals" who choose to use them for layout.

But that is a discussion for a different day. The point is `<table>`s *do* have a place in web design—for *tabular data* like this calendar:

```
<table summary="September 2009 calendar of events">
    <caption>September 2009</caption>
    <tr>
        <th>Sunday</th>
        <th>Monday</th>
        <th>Tuesday</th>
        <th>Wednesday</th>
        <th>Thursday</th>
        <th>Friday</th>
        <th>Saturday</th>
    </tr>
    <tr>
        <td>1</td>
```

(continues on next page)

```
            <td>2</td>
            <td>3
                <h3><a href="http://web12steps.com/tables">
Letting Go of Tables for Layout</a></h3>
                <dl>
                    <dt>Status:</dt>
                    <dd>Confirmed</dd>
                    <dt>Access:</dt>
                    <dd>Private</dd>
                    <dt>Start:</dt>
                    <dd>9:00 am</dd>
                    <dt>End:</dt>
                    <dd>11:30 am</dd>
                </dl>

                <h3><a href="http://web12steps.com/animated">
Animated GIFs: They Aren't Your Friends</a></h3>
                <dl>
                    <dt>Status:</dt>
                    <dd>Cancelled</dd>
                    <dt>Access:</dt>
                    <dd>Private</dd>
                    <dt>Start:</dt>
                    <dd>1:00 pm</dd>
                    <dt>End:</dt>
                    <dd>3:30 pm</dd>
                </dl>
            </td>
            <td>4
                <h3><a href="http://web12steps.com/tagsoup">The
Web Isn't a Kitchen. Eliminate Tag Soup</a></h3>
                <dl>
                    <dt>Status:</dt>
                    <dd>Confirmed</dd>
                    <dt>Access:</dt>
                    <dd>Public</dd>
                    <dt>Start:</dt>
                    <dd>9:00 am</dd>
                    <dt>End:</dt>
                    <dd>11:30 am</dd>
                </dl>
```

```
        <h3><a href="http://web12steps.com/ie6">How to
Break Your Co-Dependent Relationship With IE 6</a></h3>
        <dl>
            <dt>Status:</dt>
            <dd>Tentative</dd>
            <dt>Access:</dt>
            <dd>Public</dd>
            <dt>Start:</dt>
            <dd>1:00 pm</dd>
            <dt>End:</dt>
            <dd>3:30 pm</dd>
        </dl>
        </td>
        <td>5</td>
        <td>6</td>
        <td>7</td>
    </tr>
    ...
</table>
```

<TABLE> ACCESSIBILITY

When you use a `<table>` *for data*, it is important to make use of the accessibility elements and attributes for `<table>`s so that screen-reader users can better understand and access the information.

Because our example is a comparatively simple data table, I've added the following to the `<table>` markup

- a `summary` attribute, which provides a detailed description of the table for screen-reader users

- a `<caption>` element, which provides a brief description of the table and is rendered visually in most browsers above the `<table>`

- `<th>` rather than `<td>` elements for my header cells which helps screen-reader users know to which header each data cell is related.

For more complex tables, there are many more elements and attributes to consider for optimal accessibility.

- `abbr` attribute assigned to `<th>`s, to provide abbreviated versions of long header names

- `scope="col"` property-value pair assigned to `<th>`s, and `scope="row"` assigned to `<td>`s, to associate headers to data cells

- `<thead>`, `<tfoot>`, and `<tbody>`, to group table rows.

- `<col>` and `<colgroup>`, to group table columns.

In addition to offering accessibility and usability benefits, these elements and attributes can give you more "hooks" for styling your table using these elements and attribute selectors.

Optional root property: `vcalendar`

This example is a single month of events, which I consider to be part of a single calendar, so we will exclude the `vcalendar` root. If I had included multiple months, I would assign `vcalendar` to each month's `<table>`. But I didn't, so let's move on.

Required property: `vevent`

Next we need to assign the required `vevent` to each event. In the last example, I contained event information in the `<li>`s of a nested `<ul>`. But in this example, I don't really want the list element involved.

So I will drop in some nonsemantic `<div>`s to contain each event, and then assign `vevent` to each:

```
<table summary="September 2009 calendar of events">
    <caption>September 2009</caption>
    <tr>
        <th>Sunday</th>
        <th>Monday</th>
        <th>Tuesday</th>
        <th>Wednesday</th>
        <th>Thursday</th>
        <th>Friday</th>
        <th>Saturday</th>
    </tr>
    <tr>
        <td>1</td>
        <td>2</td>
        <td>3
            <div class="vevent">
                <h3><a href="http://web12steps.com/tables">
Letting Go of Tables for Layout</a></h3>
                <dl>
                    <dt>Status:</dt>
                    <dd>Confirmed</dd>
                    <dt>Access:</dt>
                    <dd>Private</dd>
                    <dt>Start:</dt>
                    <dd>9:00 am</dd>
                    <dt>End:</dt>
```

```
                        <dd>11:30 am</dd>
                    </dl>
                </div>
                <div class="vevent">
                    <h3><a href="http://web2steps.com/
animated">Animated GIFs: They Aren't Your Friends</a></h3>
                    <dl>
                        <dt>Status:</dt>
                        <dd>Cancelled</dd>
                        <dt>Access:</dt>
                        <dd>Private</dd>
                        <dt>Start:</dt>
                        <dd>1:00 pm</dd>
                        <dt>End:</dt>
                        <dd>3:30 pm</dd>
                    </dl>
                </div>
            </td>
            <td>4
                <div class="vevent">
                    <h3><a href="http://web2steps.com/tagsoup">
The Web Isn't a Kitchen. Eliminate Tag Soup</a></h3>
                    <dl>
                        <dt>Status:</dt>
                        <dd>Confirmed</dd>
                        <dt>Access:</dt>
                        <dd>Public</dd>
                        <dt>Start:</dt>
                        <dd>9:00 am</dd>
                        <dt>End:</dt>
                        <dd>11:30 am</dd>
                    </dl>
                </div>
                <div class="vevent">
                    <h3><a href="http://web2steps.com/ie6">How
to Break Your Co-Dependent Relationship With IE 6</a></h3>
                    <dl>
                        <dt>Status:</dt>
                        <dd>Tentative</dd>
                        <dt>Access:</dt>
```

(continues on next page)

```
                        <dd>Public</dd>
                        <dt>Start:</dt>
                        <dd>1:00 pm</dd>
                        <dt>End:</dt>
                        <dd>3:30 pm</dd>
                    </dl>
                </div>
            </td>
            <td>5</td>
            <td>6</td>
            <td>7</td>
        </tr>
        ...
</table>
```

If the day of the month contained only a single event, rather than two, `vevent` could easily be assigned to the `<td>`.

As my fingers are tiring and trees everywhere are crying, I'm going to use just a single event to demonstrate the remaining properties.

Required property: `summary`

The `summary` property is added to the element containing the event name, in this example, the `<a>`:

```
<div class="vevent">
    <h3><a href="http://web12steps.com/ie6"
class="summary">How to Break Your Co-Dependent Relationship
With IE 6</a></h3>
    <dl>
        <dt>Status:</dt>
        <dd>Tentative</dd>
        <dt>Access:</dt>
        <dd>Public</dd>
        <dt>Start:</dt>
        <dd>1:00 pm</dd>
        <dt>End:</dt>
        <dd>3:30 pm</dd>
    </dl>
</div>
```

Required property: `dtstart`

Can you tell which method I used for my dstart date-time information? Take a close look:

```
<div class="vevent">
    <h3><a href="http://web12steps.com/ie6" class="summary">
How to Break Your Co-Dependent Relationship With IE 6</a>
</h3>
    <dl>
        <dt>Status:</dt>
        <dd>Tentative</dd>
        <dt>Access:</dt>
        <dd>Public</dd>
        <dt>Start:</dt>
        <dd class="dtstart"><span class="value-title" title=
"2009-09-04T13:00:00"> </span>1:00 pm</dd>
        <dt>End:</dt>
        <dd>3:30 pm</dd>
    </dl>
</div>
```

Notice the empty `<span class="value-title">`? Yeah, that's the value title subset of the value class pattern using a `<span>` containing a single space.

Oh, and you may notice I applied the dtstart property to the `<dd>`, rather than a `<span>` as I've done in previous examples. That's because (1) dtstart can be applied to *any* element, and (2) I didn't have a containing "hook" for the content in previous examples.

Because the `<dd>` serves as the container for my start time, it is the perfect element to assign dtstart. If you can avoid "spanitis," please do so.

Optional property: `url`

I apply the url property to the link for the event's website:

```
<div class="vevent">
    <h3><a href="http://web12steps.com/ie6" class="summary
url">How to Break Your Co-Dependent Relationship With IE 6
</a></h3>
    <dl>
```

(continues on next page)

```
        <dt>Status:</dt>
        <dd>Tentative</dd>
        <dt>Access:</dt>
        <dd>Public</dd>
        <dt>Start:</dt>
        <dd class="dtstart"><span class="value-title" title=
"2009-09-04T13:00:00"> </span>1:00 pm</dd>
        <dt>End:</dt>
        <dd>3:30 pm</dd>
    </dl>
</div>
```

Optional property: `status`

I described the `status` property when I was covering syntax, but this is the first example in which I use it. So, as a reminder, `status` indicates whether an event is *confirmed*, *cancelled*, or *tentative*:

```
<div class="vevent">
    <h3><a href="http://web12steps.com/ie6" class="summary
url">How to Break Your Co-Dependent Relationship With IE 6
</a></h3>
    <dl>
        <dt>Status:</dt>
        <dd class="status">Tentative</dd>
        <dt>Access:</dt>
        <dd>Public</dd>
        <dt>Start:</dt>
        <dd class="dtstart"><span class="value-title" title=
"2009-09-04T13:00:00"> </span>1:00 pm</dd>
        <dt>End:</dt>
        <dd>3:30 pm</dd>
    </dl>
</div>
```

Because these status values often occur in natural language, they are case insensitive.

Optional property: `class`

Next, because my content includes the information about whether the event is *public*, *private*, or *confidential*, I add the `class` property:

```html
<div class="vevent">
    <h3><a href="http://web12steps.com/ie6" class="summary
url">How to Break Your Co-Dependent Relationship With IE 6
</a></h3>
    <dl>
        <dt>Status:</dt>
        <dd class="status">Tentative</dd>
        <dt>Access:</dt>
        <dd class="class">Public</dd>
        <dt>Start:</dt>
        <dd class="dtstart"><span class="value-title"
title="2009-09-04T13:00:00"> </span>1:00 pm</dd>
        <dt>End:</dt>
        <dd>3:30 pm</dd>
    </dl>
</div>
```

The class values *private, public,* and *confidential* are also case insensitive.

Optional property: dtend

Lastly, I use the value class pattern with my dtend property:

```html
<div class="vevent">
    <h3><a href="http://web12steps.com/ie6" class="summary
url">How to Break Your Co-Dependent Relationship With IE 6
</a></h3>
    <dl>
        <dt>Status:</dt>
        <dd class="status">Tentative</dd>
        <dt>Access:</dt>
        <dd class="class">Public</dd>
        <dt>Start:</dt>
        <dd class="dtstart"><span class="value-title" title=
"2009-09-04T13:00:00"> </span>1:00 pm</dd>
        <dt>End:</dt>
        <dd class="dtend"><span class="value-title" title=
"2009-09-04T15:30:00"> </span>3:30 pm</dd>
    </dl>
</div>
```

The end result

And now our hCalendar `<table>` example is complete:

This hCalendar markup is styled with CSS in Chapter 12 (page 277).

```
<table summary="September 2009 calendar of events">
    <caption>September 2009</caption>
    <tr>
        <th>Sunday</th>
        <th>Monday</th>
        <th>Tuesday</th>
        <th>Wednesday</th>
        <th>Thursday</th>
        <th>Friday</th>
        <th>Saturday</th>
    </tr>
    <tr>
        <td>1</td>
        <td>2</td>
        <td>3
            <div class="vevent">
                <h3><a href="http://web12steps.com/tables"
class="summary url">Letting Go of Tables for Layout</a></h3>
                <dl>
                    <dt>Status:</dt>
                    <dd class="status">Confirmed</dd>
                    <dt>Access:</dt>
                    <dd class="class">Private</dd>
                    <dt>Start:</dt>
                    <dd class="dtstart"><span class="value-
title" title="2009-09-03T09:00:00"> </span>9:00 am</dd>
                    <dt>End:</dt>
                    <dd class="dtend"><span class="value-
title" title="2009-09-03T11:30:00"> </span>11:30 am</dd>
                </dl>
            </div>
            <div class="vevent">
                <h3><a href="http://web12steps.com/animated"
class="summary url">Animated GIFs: They Aren't Your Friends
</a></h3>
                <dl>
                    <dt>Status:</dt>
                    <dd class="status">Cancelled</dd>
                    <dt>Access:</dt>
```

```
                <dd class="class">Private</dd>
                <dt>Start:</dt>
                <dd class="dtstart"><span class="value-
title" title="2009-09-03T13:00:00"> </span>1:00 pm</dd>
                <dt>End:</dt>
                <dd class="dtend"><span class="value-
title" title="2009-09-03T15:30:00"> </span>3:30 pm</dd>
            </dl>
          </div>
        </td>
        <td>4
          <div class="vevent">
              <h3><a href="http://web12steps.com/tagsoup"
class="summary url">The Web Isn't a Kitchen. Eliminate Tag
Soup</a></h3>
              <dl>
                <dt>Status:</dt>
                <dd class="status">Confirmed</dd>
                <dt>Access:</dt>
                <dd class="class">Public</dd>
                <dt>Start:</dt>
                <dd class="dtstart"><span class="value-
title" title="2009-09-04T09:00:00"> </span>9:00 am</dd>
                <dt>End:</dt>
                <dd class="dtend"><span class="value-
title" title="2009-09-04T11:30:00"> </span>11:30 am</dd>
              </dl>
          </div>
          <div class="vevent">
              <h3><a href="http://web12steps.com/
ie6" class="summary url">How to Break Your Co-Dependent
Relationship With IE 6</a></h3>
              <dl>
                <dt>Status:</dt>
                <dd class="status">Tentative</dd>
                <dt>Access:</dt>
                <dd class="class">Public</dd>
                <dt>Start:</dt>
                <dd class="dtstart"><span class="value-
title" title="2009-09-04T13:00:00"> </span>1:00 pm</dd>
                <dt>End:</dt>
```

(continues on next page)

```
                         <dd class="dtend"><span class="value-
title" title="2009-09-04T15:30:00"> </span>3:30 pm</dd>
                  </dl>
            </div>
         </td>
         <td>5</td>
         <td>6</td>
         <td>7</td>
      </tr>
      ...
</table>
```

The logic behind the markup

Aside from the fact that I consider this calendar to be tabular data, another reason I like a `<table>` for this example is that if I wanted to style (via CSS) this content as a traditional calendar (you know, grid-like), then a `<table>` gives me a foundation for that structure.

If I were to use the nested `<ol>`s that I did in the first multiple-events example, there would be much more styling involved to result in a grid-type calendar. So when it comes to two different elements for which you could easily argue the semantic value, consider what may be required on the presentation level. That may help you make a decision.

hCalendar in natural language

While hCalendar is obviously well suited to a chunked presentation, as I've demonstrated in the previous examples, it works equally well in natural language. In fact, for my own blog I prefer natural-language hCalendar events. Here's an example:

```
<p>Webuquerque's next presentation, <a href="http://
webuquerque.com/Events/Search-Engine-Optimization.php">
Search Engine Optimization</a> is July 1, 2009 from 6:30-
7:30 pm at Uptown Sports Bar and Grill.</p>
```

Required property: `vevent`

First I add the `vevent` property to the root element containing all of my event information— `<p>` in this example:

```
<p class="vevent">Webuquerque's next presentation,
<a href="http://webuquerque.com/Events/Search-Engine-
Optimization.php">Search Engine Optimization</a> is July 1,
2009 from 6:30-7:30 pm at Uptown Sports Bar and Grill.</p>
```

Required property: `summary`

Next I assign the `summary` property, which, as I've mentioned several times, is often the name of the event:

```
<p class="vevent">Webuquerque's next presentation,
<a href="http://webuquerque.com/Events/Search-Engine-
Optimization.php" class="summary">Search Engine
Optimization</a> is July 1, 2009 from 6:30-7:30 pm at Uptown
Sports Bar and Grill.</p>
```

In this example, my name content is contained by a site link, so I use the `<a>` as the hook for my `summary` property

Required property: `dtstart`

For the event start time, I add the `dtstart` property and specify the date-time machine data using the value class pattern:

```
<p class="vevent">Webuquerque's next presentation, <a href=
"http://webuquerque.com/Events/Search-Engine-Optimization.
php" class="summary">Search Engine Optimization</a> is <span
class="dtstart"><span class="value-title" title="2009-07-
01T18:30:00">July 1, 2009 from 6:30</span></span>-7:30 pm at
Uptown Sports Bar and Grill.</p>
```

If I were concerned about browser tooltips (which display the `title` value of any element), I could've used the empty `<span>` technique for the value-title subset:

```
<span class="dtstart"><span class="value-title" title="2009-
07-01T18:30:00"> </span>July 1, 2009 from 6:30</span>
```

Tooltips not a concern? Or you happen to feel that separate date and time ISO 8601 values are more internationally appropriate? Then use the value class pattern with `<abbr>` to separately indicate date and time:

```
<span class="dtstart"><abbr class="value" title="2009-
07-01">July 1, 2009</abbr> from <abbr class="value"
title="18:30:00">6:30</abbr></span>
```

With this separated date and time information, machines know to combine the two `<abbr>` `title` values for the complete date-time information. Meanwhile, the resulting tooltips are much more human friendly.

I know I sound like a broken record, but you should avoid using the value class pattern with `<abbr>` for combined date-time information (known as the datetime design pattern, now deprecated) such as in this example:

```
<span class="dtstart"><abbr class="value" title="2009-07-
01T18:30:00">July 1, 2009 from 6:30</abbr></span>
```

Due to the readability and listenability issues with ISO 8601 date-times in the `title` attribute of `<abbr>` elements, such uses are discouraged.

Optional property: `url`

This example also includes a site link, so I add the `url` property to the `<a>`:

```
<p class="vevent">Webuquerque's next presentation, <a href=
"http://webuquerque.com/Events/Search-Engine-Optimization.
php" class="summary url">Search Engine Optimization</a> is
<span class="dtstart"><span class="value-title" title="2009-
07-01T18:30:00">July 1, 2009 from 6:30</span></span>-7:30 pm
at Uptown Sports Bar and Grill.</p>
```

Optional property: `location`

Once again, the location content in this example doesn't already have an HTML container, so I assign the `location` property to a `<span>`.

```
<p class="vevent">Webuquerque's next presentation, <a href=
"http://webuquerque.com/Events/Search-Engine-Optimization.
php" class="summary url">Search Engine Optimization</a> is
<span class="dtstart"><span class="value-title" title="2009-
07-01T18:30:00">July 1, 2009 from 6:30</span></span>-7:30 pm
at <span class="location">Uptown Sports Bar and Grill
</span>.</p>
```

The end result

After adding those properties, our example is now an hCalendar:

```
<p class="vevent">Webuquerque's next presentation, <a href=
"http://webuquerque.com/Events/Search-Engine-Optimization.
php" class="summary url">Search Engine Optimization</a> is
```

```
<span class="dtstart"><span class="value-title" title="2009-
07-01T18:30:00">July 1, 2009 from 6:30</span></span>-7:30 pm
at <span class="location">Uptown Sports Bar and Grill
</span>.</p>
```

Combining hCalendar and hCard

As you may have noticed in these examples and across the web, hCalendar events often reference a location. And more often than not, this is a named place, which means it's the perfect content for an hCard.

Required root property: `vcard`

Using the natural-language hCalendar example as a basis, let's add an hCard for the location, starting with the root `vcard` property:

```
<p class="vevent">Webuquerque's next presentation, <a href=
"http://webuquerque.com/Events/Search-Engine-Optimization.
php" class="summary url">Search Engine Optimization</a> is
<span class="dtstart"><span class="value-title" title="2009-
07-01T18:30:00">July 1, 2009 from 6:30</span></span>-7:30
pm at <span class="location vcard">Uptown Sports Bar and
Grill</span>.</p>
```

My content was already contained by a `<span>` assigned the hCalendar `location` property, so I just add `vcard` to that.

Required properties: `fn` and `org`

If you remember, the only required properties for place hCards are `fn` and `org`:

```
<p class="vevent">Webuquerque's next presentation, <a href=
"http://webuquerque.com/Events/Search-Engine-Optimization.
php" class="summary url">Search Engine Optimization</a> is
<span class="dtstart"><span class="value-title" title="2009-
07-01T18:30:00">July 1, 2009 from 6:30</span></span>-7:30 pm
at <span class="location vcard"><span class="fn org">Uptown
Sports Bar and Grill</span></span>.</p>
```

The end result

With just a few extra elements and some classes, I'm giving my users not only a downloadable event for their calendars, but an electronic business card as well. And I could've included even more information for the hCard, without any problems. Content dictates what properties and subproperties you should use.

```
<p class="vevent">Webuquerque's next presentation, <a href=
"http://webuquerque.com/Events/Search-Engine-Optimization.
php" class="summary url">Search Engine Optimization</a> is
<span class="dtstart"><span class="value-title" title="2009-
07-01T18:30:00">July 1, 2009 from 6:30</span></span>-7:30 pm
at <span class="location vcard"><span class="fn org">Uptown
Sports Bar and Grill</span></span>.</p>
```

Authoring Tools

Want to be efficient with your hCalendar implementations? Then make use of these tools to help you create and validate hCalendar:

- hCalendar Creator: http://microformats.org/code/hcalendar/creator
- Conference Schedule Creator: http://dmitry.baranovskiy.com/work/csc/
- hCalendar Cheatsheet: http://microformats.org/wiki/hcalendar -cheatsheet
- Optimus Microformats Transformer (for validation): http:// microformatique.com/optimus/
- For more hCalendar tools, see http://microformats.org/wiki/ hcalendar-implementations

What's Next?

The next microformat we'll be covering, hResume, is used for resume/CV (curriculum vitae) content. While, like all microformats, it has its own properties and subproperties, you'll be pleased to know that it leverages both the hCard and hCalendar microformats.

So not only will you learn a new microformat, you will also be practicing what you've already learned. Remember, folks: practice does, indeed, make a close approximation to perfect.

Defining Résumés: hResume

In today's economy and job market, a résumé or CV is like air. You need it. And in the web industry, having an online résumé is just as important.

If you are currently unemployed, you know what I'm talking about. You also know the joys of having to maintain your résumé on all the various job sites out there, like Monster and CareerBuilder.

What's even better is all of these job sites format their résumés differently. So you have to maintain information on multiple sites, often in different fashions. I've been there myself and it totally sucks … sucks time better spent actually looking for a job … sucks energy better spent improving the content of your résumé … sucks your will to live.

Can you imagine a world where this isn't the case? A world in which you have one résumé that you can share across any and all job sites? A world where being unemployed or seeking a job is made less horrible because your résumé is exactly that: yours?

I can. Because I know about hResume.

What Is hResume?

hResume is a draft microformat. At its core, it is just a design pattern that adds semantic richness to online résumés and curricula vitae (CVs), providing both humans and machines information about your job skills and experience.

The properties (`class` values) for hResume were developed based on existing résumé formats (Europass and HR-XML) and common "fields" seen in today's résumés:

- Education
- Work experience
- Specific skills
- Affiliations

One résumé to rule them all

Aside from its semantic yumminess, hResume was developed, in part, to provide a standard way for people to control their résumé data. Such standardization provides the foundation for résumé content to be created and maintained in one location, but made available to any application (the machines!) that needs résumé information.

This would mean an end to filling out all of those annoying résumé forms on all of the various employment sites. You would simply ping those sites and services when you had a new résumé or updated an existing one. And then those services would extract the data from your single résumé (which would, of course, be using hResume) and populate your account with the new information.

And because you would truly own your résumé in this context, you could present it in any fashion you cared to, rather than being tied to the often ugly, boring and homogenous résumés generated by services like Monster.

A standard for online résumés could also help connect employers and job seekers. Using standardized, structured data like hResume would help search tools better find candidates qualified for particular jobs.

As of today, however, all of this is pure potential that has yet to be realized. My guess is that the draft status of hResume may discourage implementation. But you and I, as founding members of the Microformats Are Way F'n Cool Club, know that is really no reason not to publish hResume.

Semantics are good. Standards are good. Microformats are good. And I believe in the "build it and they will come" philosophy, especially when "build it" is just a few class values.

Recognizing the potential

Of course, I'm not alone in this thinking. While hResume isn't one of the more popular microformats, it is in use:

- Emurse offers templates that publish hResume.

- LinkedIn generates hResume for all of its 9 million (and counting) public profiles.

- Resolio publishes all résumés in hResume format.

Electronic business cards and calendars

hResume incorporates hCard, hCalendar, and rel-tag into its format. hCard is applied to content about the résumé owner, as well as information about employers (organizations, companies). hCalendar, meanwhile, is applied to content about previous jobs and education, both of which can be thought of as date-time—based events. And rel-tag is applied to links containing skill information.

So, with hResume you get all the benefits of hCard, hCalendar, and rel-tag. Four microformats in one!

Profile

Let's start with the hResume profile that you can add to your document `<head>`:

```
<head profile="http://microformats.org/profile/hresume">
```

Because hResume uses hCard and hCalendar, be sure to include those profiles as well, separating each with a space:

```
<head profile="http://microformats.org/profile/hresume
http://microformats.org/profile/hcard http://microformats.
org/profile/hcalendar">
```

Syntax

- `hresume` is a required root property. All résumé content needs to be contained by an element assigned this `class` value. This property is used only once.

- `contact` is the other required property for hResume. It contains the person's contact information and must be marked up with hCard. And because a résumé is about a single individual, this property is used once.

- `summary` is an optional property applied to content about the person's objective, such as the job being sought and overall qualifications. You can use this property only once in a single hResume.

- The optional `skill` property is applied to content about a person's specific skills, such as XHTML and CSS. These skills can be considered tags for the résumé, so they should be links (`<a>`) assigned the rel-tag microformat.

- The optional `experience` property is applied to content about a person's previous work experience. This type of content is date-time based and, as such, can be considered an event and should be marked up with hCalendar. Additionally, `experience` content for job titles should be marked up with hCard.

- The optional `education` property contains information about a person's education. Again, such content is date-time based and should also be an hCalendar.

- The optional `affiliation` property is applied to information about organizations with which a person is affiliated, such as a professional association or group. These organizations should also be marked up with hCard.

- You should use `<cite>` to indicate any publications the person has authored. Note that this is a standard HTML element, not a property; it doesn't appear as a `class` value. Also, it is optional.

Of all of these properties (and `<cite>`), the root `hresume`, `contact`, and `summary` can be used only once. The others can be used as many times as necessary.

Practical Markup

Résumé content is, by its very nature, straightforward. In turn, the markup for résumés is (or should be) as well. You may have some headings, some lists, a few paragraphs and links—which means `<h1>`s (and/or other heading elements), `<p>`s `<a>`s, `<ul>`s maybe even `<dl>`s.

No rocket surgery or brain science here, but it's still worth taking a look at some POSH implementations of hResume.

Simple résumé

There may be instances when you have a very basic résumé, with just your contact information, objective, and skill set. Maybe it's your first résumé, so you don't have any relevant job experience. Or maybe you just want to provide the basics and have prospective employers contact you for further details. Or maybe you are lazy (I suffer from that disease myself).

```
<h1>Kaylee Frye</h1>
<h2>Mechanic</h2>
<ul>
    <li>555-123-2571</li>
    <li><a href="mailto:kaylee@shiny.com">kaylee@shiny.com
</a></li>
```

(continues on next page)

```
    <li><a href="http://shiny.com">shiny.com</a></li>
</ul>
<h2>Objective</h2>
<p>Seeking a position as a mechanic on the Firefly Transport
ship Serenity.</p>
<h2>Skills</h2>
<ul>
    <li>Firefly transports</li>
    <li>Trace compression block engines</li>
    <li>Fuel cells</li>
</ul>
```

Required root property: `hresume`

Because the root `hresume` needs to contain *all* of the résumé content,
I add a containing `<div>` with `class="hresume"` to my markup:

```
<div class="hresume">
    <h1>Kaylee Frye</h1>
    <h2>Mechanic</h2>
    <ul>
        <li>555-123-2571</li>
        <li><a href="mailto:kaylee@shiny.com">kaylee@shiny.
com</a></li>
        <li><a href="http://shiny.com">shiny.com</a></li>
    </ul>
    <h2>Objective</h2>
    <p>Seeking a position ...</p>
    <h2>Skills</h2>
    <ul>
        <li>Firefly transports</li>
        <li>Trace compression block engines</li>
        <li>Fuel cells</li>
    </ul>
</div>
```

Required property: `contact`

Because the `contact` property must contain all of the person's contact
information, I need to add another `<div>` to my markup so I can apply
that `class` value:

```
<div class="hresume">
    <div class="contact">
        <h1>Kaylee Frye</h1>
        <h2>Mechanic</h2>
        <ul>
            <li>555-123-2571</li>
            <li><a href="mailto:kaylee@shiny.com">kaylee@
shiny.com</a></li>
            <li><a href="http://shiny.com">shiny.com</a></li>
        </ul>
    </div>
    <h2>Objective</h2>
    <p>Seeking a position ...</p>
    <h2>Skills</h2>
    <ul>
        <li>Firefly transports</li>
        <li>Trace compression block engines</li>
        <li>Fuel cells</li>
    </ul>
</div>
```

Adding hCard   hResume specifies that contact also be an hCard, so
I'll add the relevant properties from hCard:

```
<div class="contact vcard">
    <h1 class="fn">Kaylee Frye</h1>
    <h2 class="title">Mechanic</h2>
    <ul>
        <li class="tel">555-123-2571</li>
        <li><a href="mailto:kaylee@shiny.com" class="email">
kaylee@shiny.com</a></li>
        <li><a href="http://shiny.com" class="url">shiny.com
</a></li>
    </ul>
</div>
```

Combining microformats: XFN   While it isn't part of the hResume
spec, the contact information provides an opportunity to combine another
microformat, XFN. If you recall, rel-me is assigned to hyperlinks that reference URLs about you, which is exactly what a website in a résumé is.

```
<li><a href="http://shiny.com" class="url" rel="me">shiny.
com</a></li>
```

Optional property: `summary`

Next I add the `summary` property to the element containing my résumé objective statement:

```
<div class="hresume">
    <div class="contact vcard">
        <h1 class="fn">Kaylee Frye</h1>
        <h2 class="title">Mechanic</h2>
        <ul>
            <li class="tel">555-123-2571</li>
            <li><a href="mailto:kaylee@shiny.com" class=
"email">kaylee@shiny.com</a></li>
            <li><a href="http://shiny.com" class="url" rel=
"me">shiny.com</a></li>
        </ul>
    </div>
    <h2>Objective</h2>
    <p class="summary">Seeking a position as a mechanic on
the Firefly Transport ship Serenity.</p>
    <h2>Skills</h2>
    <ul>
        <li>Firefly transports</li>
        <li>Trace compression block engines</li>
        <li>Fuel cells</li>
    </ul>
</div>
```

Optional property: `skill`

The `skill` property must be assigned to a link, so I have to add `<a>`s to my skill content before assigning the property:

```
<ul>
    <li><a href="/tag/firefly_transport" class="skill">
Firefly transports</a></li>
    <li><a href="/tag/trace_compression_block_engines"
class="skill">Trace compression block engines</a></li>
    <li><a href="/tag/fuel_cells" class="skill">Fuel cells
</a></li>
</ul>
```

Adding rel-tag   Note that the href values for the new links are tag spaces. That's because skill links should also be assigned rel-tag, which requires that the destination href for tag links be a tag space :

```
<ul>
    <li><a href="/tag/firefly_transport" class="skill" rel=
"tag">Firefly transports</a></li>
    <li><a href="/tag/trace_compression_block_engines"
class="skill" rel="tag">Trace compression block engines</a>
</li>
    <li><a rel="tag" href="/tag/fuel_cells"
class="skill">Fuel cells</a></li>
</ul>
```

Personally, I don't really care for this part of the hResume specification. Seems a bit link crazy. And these are links that I have a difficult time believing would be relevant to potential employers, not to mention they could take attention away from why an employer is reading my résumé.

If you feel the same way, then don't include this property. It *is* optional. But if you think skill makes sense for your résumé, now you know how to implement it (you can thank me later).

The end result

Properly marked up with hResume, our example looks like:

```
<div class="hresume">
    <div class="contact vcard">
        <h1 class="fn">Kaylee Frye</h1>
        <h2 class="title">Mechanic</h2>
        <ul>
            <li class="tel">555-123-2571</li>
            <li><a href="mailto:kaylee@shiny.com" class=
"email">kaylee@shiny.com</a></li>
            <li><a href="http://shiny.com" class="url" rel=
"me">shiny.com</a></li>
        </ul>
    </div>
    <h2>Objective</h2>
    <p class="summary">Seeking a position as a mechanic on
the Firefly Transport ship Serenity.</p>
```

(continues on next page)

```
    <h2>Skills</h2>
    <ul>
        <li><a href="/tag/firefly_transport" class="skill"
rel="tag">Firefly transports</a></li>
        <li><a href="/tag/trace_compression_block_engines"
class="skill" rel="tag">Trace compression block engines</a>
</li>
        <li><a rel="tag" href="/tag/fuel_cells"
class="skill">Fuel cells</a></li>
    </ul>
</div>
```

The logic behind the markup

Not much to explain in this example. The content dictated my markup: `<p>` for paragraph content, `<ul>` for lists, `<h1>` and `<h2>` for headings.

I could've easily used a `<dl>` for my `contact` content—with the name contained by `<dt>`—and job title, telephone, email, and website contained by `<dd>`s. This works semantically and means that I wouldn't need that non-semantic `<div>` I added. But I really want the potential SEO boost for the name and job title, so heading elements are appropriate.

Detailed résumé

For some folks, the more detailed the résumé, the better. And I would be one of those folks, so let's use an abbreviated version of my résumé:

```
<h1>Emily Paige Lewis</h1>
<img src="emilyLewis.jpg" alt="Emily Lewis" />
<p>Albuquerque, <abbr title="New Mexico">NM</abbr></p>
<ul>
    <li><a href="mailto:emily@ablognotlimited.com">emily[at]
ablognotlimited[dot]com</a></li>
    <li><a href="http://www.ablognotlimited.com">A Blog Not
Limited</a></li>
</ul>
<h2>Highlights of Qualifications</h2>
<ul>
    <li>Web designer specializing in hand-coded semantic
XHTML, cross-browser CSS, progressive enhancement
accessibility and usability</li>
```

```
    <li>Expert in the design of corporate web sites,
intranets, email campaigns and e-commerce applications</li>
</ul>
<h2>Technical Expertise</h2>
<ul>
    <li>XHTML - 10 yrs</li>
    <li>CSS - 10 yrs</li>
</ul>
<h2>Experience and Accomplishments</h2>
<h3>Web Designer</h3>
<p>Pitney Bowes Business Insight</p>
<p>December 2004 - present</p>
<ul>
    <li>Designed interfaces and developed XHTML, CSS and
graphics for main corporate site, international sites,
marketing newsletters, corporate blog, corporate intranet
and user conference site</li>
    <li>Designed interfaces and developed XHTML, CSS and
graphics for marketing email campaigns, ensuring consistent
display across popular email clients</li>
</ul>
<h2>Education</h2>
<h3>Bachelor of Arts</h3>
<p>St. Mary's College of Maryland</p>
<p>September 1992 - June 1996</p>
<h2>Affiliations</h2>
<ul>
    <li><a href="http://webuquerque.com">Webuquerque</a>
co-manager</li>
    <li><a href="http://baltimore.iabc.com/">IABC Baltimore
Chapter</a> board-member</li>
</ul>
<h2>Publications</h2>
<p><cite>Microformats Made Simple</cite>, October 2009</p>
```

Required root property: `hresume`

To assign the root hresume, I first have to add a containing <div>:

```
<div class="hresume">
    <h1>Emily Paige Lewis</h1>
```

(continues on next page)

```
    <img src="emilyLewis.jpg" alt="Emily Lewis" />
    <p>Albuquerque, <abbr title="New Mexico">NM</abbr></p>
    <ul>
        <li><a href="mailto:emily@ablognotlimited.com">
emily[at]ablognotlimited[dot]com</a></li>
        <li><a href="http://www.ablognotlimited.com">A Blog
Not Limited</a></li>
    </ul>
    <h2>Highlights of Qualifications</h2>
    <ul>
        <li>Web designer ...</li>
        <li>Expert in the design ...</li>
    </ul>
    <h2>Technical Expertise</h2>
    <ul>
        <li>XHTML — 10 yrs</li>
        <li>CSS — 10 yrs</li>
    </ul>
    <h2>Experience and Accomplishments</h2>
    <h3>Web Designer</h3>
    <p>Pitney Bowes Business Insight</p>
    <p>December 2004 - present</p>
    <ul>
        <li>Designed interfaces ...</li>
        <li>Designed interfaces ...</li>
    </ul>
    <h2>Education</h2>
    <h3>Bachelor of Arts</h3>
    <p>St. Mary's College of Maryland</p>
    <p>September 1992 - June 1996</p>
    <h2>Affiliations</h2>
    <ul>
        <li><a href="http://webuquerque.com">Webuquerque</a>
co-manager</li>
        <li><a href="http://baltimore.iabc.com/">IABC
Baltimore Chapter</a> board-member</li>
    </ul>
    <h2>Publications</h2>
    <p><cite>Microformats Made Simple</cite>, October 2009
</p>
</div>
```

Required property: `contact`

As in the first example, I need to contain all of my content with a new `<div>` assigned `class="contact"`:

```
<div class="contact">
    <h1>Emily Paige Lewis</h1>
    <img src="emilyLewis.jpg" alt="Emily Lewis" />
    <p>Albuquerque, <abbr title="New Mexico">NM</abbr></p>
    <ul>
        <li><a href="mailto:emily@ablognotlimited.com">
emily[at]ablognotlimited[dot]com</a></li>
        <li><a href="http://www.ablognotlimited.com">A Blog
Not Limited</a></li>
    </ul>
</div>
```

Adding hCard   But don't forget, it isn't just a matter of adding the contact property; you also have to add hCard:

```
<div class="contact vcard">
    <h1 class="fn n"><span class="given-name">Emily</span>
<span class="additional-name">Paige</span> <span class=
"family-name">Lewis</span></h1>
    <img src="emilyLewis.jpg" alt="Emily Lewis"
class="photo" />
    <p class="adr"><span class="locality">Albuquerque
</span>, <abbr title="New Mexico" class="region">NM</abbr>
</p>
    <ul>
        <li><a href="mailto:emily@ablognotlimited.com"
class="email">emily[at]ablognotlimited[dot]com</a></li>
        <li><a href="http://www.ablognotlimited.com" class=
"url" rel="me">A Blog Not Limited</a></li>
    </ul>
</div>
```

Note that for my n and adr subproperties, I had to add `<span>`s to contain the content. Also note that, once again, I added rel-me.

<SPAN> VS. <DIV>

Throughout all the examples in this book, there are instances where it is necessary to add nonsemantic `<span>`s and `<div>`s to contain content that needs to be assigned a property or subproperty.

Aside from any discussion about nonsemantic content (because there is no discussion, sometimes it is simply necessary), you may be wondering why I'm using a `<div>` in certain situations and a `<span>` in others.

The answer lies in the markup and content that needs to be contained.

`<div>`s can contain block-level elements, like `<h1>`, `<p>`, `<table>`, `<ul>`, and other `<div>`s. They also can contain inline elements. `<span>`s, on the other hand, can *only* contain inline elements such as `<a>` and other `<span>`s or even just plain content.

Neither `<span>` nor `<div>` have any true semantic meaning. And neither have any default browser rendering, other than `<span>`s are rendered inline and `<div>`s are rendered as blocks. So when you need to choose one over the other, ask yourself: block or inline?

Optional property: `summary`

The content in this résumé example doesn't include an objective, but it does include some highlights of qualifications, which is perfect content for the `summary` property:

```
<h2>Highlights of Qualifications</h2>
<ul class="summary">
    <li>Web designer specializing in hand-coded semantic
XHTML, cross-browser CSS, progressive enhancement
accessibility and usability</li>
    <li>Expert in the design of corporate web sites,
intranets, email campaigns and e-commerce applications</li>
</ul>
```

Optional property: `skill`

To assign the `skill` property, I once again add links to the content and assign each `rel="tag"` along with `class="skill"`:

```
<h2>Technical Expertise</h2>
<ul>
    <li><a href="/tag/xhtml" class="skill" rel="tag">XHTML
</a> - 10 yrs</li>
    <li><a href="/tag/css" class="skill" rel="tag">CSS</a>
- 10 yrs</li>
</ul>
```

Optional property: `experience`

In order to apply the `experience` property, I have to add another <div> containing all of the experience content:

```
<div class="experience">
    <h3>Web Designer</h3>
    <p>Pitney Bowes Business Insight</p>
    <p>December 2004 - present</p>
    <ul>
        <li>Designed interfaces ...</li>
        <li>Designed interfaces ...</li>
    </ul>
</div>
```

This résumé example includes only one work-experience reference (for brevity's sake—oh, and the trees), but remember that the `experience` property can be used as many times as needed

Adding hCalendar   But just adding the `experience` property isn't enough. You also need to add hCalendar because work-experience content should be considered a date-time event.

I will be the first to admit that when I learned hResume, it was this particular use of hCalendar that had me stumped. I never thought of my previous jobs as events, so it took me a while to understand hCalendar's place in hResume.

Once I did, I realized a few things:

- Job title = event name (`summary`)

- Employer = where event was held (`location`)

- Dates of employment = start and end dates (`dtstart` and `dtend`)

- Responsibilities and accomplishments = details about the event (`description`)

```
<div class="experience vevent">
    <h3 class="summary">Web Designer</h3>
    <p class="location">Pitney Bowes Business Insight</p>
    <p><span class="dtstart"><abbr class="value" title=
"2004-12-01">December 2004</abbr></span> - present</p>
    <ul class="description">
        <li>Designed interfaces ...</li>
        <li>Designed interfaces ...</li>
    </ul>
</div>
```

Note that because my experience included only date information (rather than both date and time), I'm using `<abbr>` with the value class pattern.

Adding hCard

We still aren't done with experience yet. The hResume spec requires that the job title and employer content be marked up with hCard. But wait! My content for experience doesn't include my name, which is the only required property for hCard.

What to do? Add my name to each instance of experience? Not only would that be tedious, but also I'm fairly certain that a prospective employer would see that and file my résumé under "idiot."

The solution is the include design pattern I mentioned way, way, way back in Chapter 1, which provides a means for reusing content (my name) without having to repeat it. To implement the include pattern, I first have to assign a unique id value to my name content in the contact hCard:

```
<h1 class="fn n" id="emily-hcard-name"><span class="given-
name">Emily</span> <span class="additional-name">Paige</
span> <span class="family-name">Lewis</span></h1>
```

Next, I add a link assigned `class="include"` with an `href` value equal to the `id` value for each instance of experience:

```
<div class="experience vevent">
    <a href="#emily-hcard-name" class="include">Emily
Lewis</a>
    <h3 class="summary">Web Designer</h3>
    <p class="location">Pitney Bowes Business Insight</p>
    <p><span class="dtstart"><abbr class="value" title=
"2004-12-01">December 2004</abbr></span> - present</p>
    <ul class="description">
```

```
            <li>Designed interfaces ...</li>
            <li>Designed interfaces ...</li>
        </ul>
</div>
```

And that hyperlink must contain inner text. Unfortunately, this still results in the repeated display of my name within the résumé. The solution? Hide it with a bit of CSS:

```
.include {display:none;}
```

Including a hyperlink is the preferred method for the include pattern. If, however, your publishing process or system prevents you from adding a hyperlink with inner text, you can use an alternate method with `<object>`.

For the `<object>` approach, I still have to assign an id to my name in the contact hCard:

```
<h1 class="fn n" id="emily-hcard-name"><span class="given
-name">Emily</span> <span class="additional-name">Paige
</span> <span class="family-name">Lewis</span></h1>
```

Then, instead of including a link in each instance of experience, I add an `<object>` assigned `class="include"`, which has a data value equal to the id value on my name:

```
<div class="experience vevent">
    <object data="#emily-hcard-name" class="include"></
object>
    <h3 class="summary">Web Designer</h3>
    <p class="location">Pitney Bowes Business Insight</p>
    <p><span class="dtstart"><abbr class="value" title=
"2004-12-01">December 2004</abbr></span> - present</p>
    <ul class="description">
        <li>Designed interfaces ...</li>
        <li>Designed interfaces ...</li>
    </ul>
</div>
```

This method will be understood by machines, but results in some pretty wonky browser rendering. You should resort to it only when publishing constraints keep you from using the hyperlink method.

Now let's get back to the rest of the hCard properties required for experience:

```
<div class="experience vevent vcard">
    <a href="#emily-hcard-name" class="include">Emily Lewis
</a>
    <h3 class="summary title">Web Designer</h3>
    <p class="location org">Pitney Bowes Business Insight
</p>
    <p><span class="dtstart"><abbr class="value" title=
"2004-12-01">December 2004</abbr></span> - present</p>
    <ul class="description">
        <li>Designed interfaces ...</li>
        <li>Designed interfaces ...</li>
    </ul>
</div>
```

Optional property: `education`

Because I don't have a containing element for my `education` content, I add a `<div>`:

```
<div class="education">
    <h3>Bachelor of Arts</h3>
    <p>St. Mary's College of Maryland</p>
    <p>September 1992 - June 1996</p>
</div>
```

Even though I'm showing only a single `education` instance in this example, the property can be used multiple times within an hResume .

Adding hCalendar   Like `experience`, `education` content should be considered date-time events, assuming the following:

- Type of education = event name (`summary`)

- Institution = event (`location`)

- Dates of attendance = start and end date-time (`dtstart` and `dtend`)

```
<div class="education vevent">
    <h3 class="summary">Bachelor of Arts</h3>
    <p class="location">St. Mary's College of Maryland</p>
    <p><span class="dtstart"><abbr class="value" title=
"1992-09-01">September 1992</abbr></span> - <span class=
```

```
"dtend"><abbr class="value" title="1996-06-01">June 1996
</abbr></span></p>
</div>
```

Again, I'm using `<abbr>` with the value class pattern because I'm only deal-ing with dates and I like consistency within an implementation.

Optional property: `affiliation`

My résumé example includes affiliations, so I will assign the `affiliation` property to each:

```
<ul>
    <li class="affiliation"><a href="http://webuquerque.com">
Webuquerque</a> co-manager</li>
    <li class="affiliation"><a href="http://baltimore.iabc.
com/">IABC Baltimore Chapter</a> board-member</li>
</ul>
```

Adding hCard   Per the hResume spec, the organizations referenced in each `affiliation` should be hCards:

```
<ul>
    <li class="affiliation vcard"><a href="http://
webuquerque.com" class="fn org url">Webuquerque</a>
co-manager</li>
    <li class="affiliation vcard"><a href="http://baltimore.
iabc.com/" class="fn org url">IABC Baltimore Chapter</a>
board-member</li>
</ul>
```

Optional element: `<cite>`

While hResume does not have a property to indicate publications, it does recommend the use of the `<cite>` element. Since you are reading this book and it has thus gone to print, I can add it as a publication on my résumé:

```
<p><cite>Microformats Made Simple</cite>, October 2009</p>
```

Machines will parse the content contained by `<cite>` as a publication authored by the person the résumé is about.

INSIGHT ON <CITE>

When I first familiarized myself with the hResume specification, I quickly realized that I had been using the `<cite>` element incorrectly for years. For some reason I still don't understand today, I had used <cite> for indicating quotes in my content.

Now, I'm not the smartest cookie in the jar (mmmm, cookies!), but I doubt I'm the only person who has made this particular mistake or used <cite> incorrectly. Mistakes are how I learn though, and maybe you can learn from mine.

<cite> is an inline element and should be used for references to a source; a citation if you will. It can be used in conjunction with a quote, and it can be used for a direct reference to another source:

```
<p><cite>Homer Simpson</cite> says
<q>Here's to alcohol, the cause of—and
solution to—all life's problems.</q>.</p>
```

In this example, `<cite>` contains the name of the person behind the quote (contained by the `<q>` element). I can also use `<cite>` to reference a source such as a book:

```
<p>According to my favorite resource,
<cite>The AP Stylebook</cite>,
summertime is one word.</p>
```

Now, when it comes to actual quotes, you have two choices: `<q>` for inline quotes and `<blockquote>` for large quotations that contain other block level elements. For both `<q>` and `<blockquote>`, you can also use the `cite` attribute to indicate the source (in the form of a URI) of the quotation:

```
<blockquote cite="http://en.wikiquote.
org/wiki/The_Hitchhiker%27s_Guide_to_
the_Galaxy">
    <p>The History of every major
Galactic Civilization tends to pass
through three distinct and recognizable
phases, those of Survival, Inquiry and
Sophistication, otherwise known as the
How, Why and Where phases.</p>
    <p>For instance, the first phase is
characterized by the question How can we
eat? the second by the question Why do
we eat? and the third by the question
Where shall we have lunch?</p>
</blockquote>
```

So, with that, neither your nor I have an excuse for incorrectly using the `<cite>` element. You can thank me later for this public service.

The end result

Adding all of those properties and subproperties gives us a résumé fully marked up with hResume:

```
<div class="hresume">
    <div class="contact vcard">
        <h1 class="fn n" id="emily-hcard-name"><span class=
"given-name">Emily</span> <span class="additional-name">
Paige</span> <span class="family-name">Lewis</span></h1>
        <img src="emilyLewis.jpg" alt="Emily Lewis"
class="photo" />
```

```
        <p class="adr"><span class="locality">Albuquerque
</span>, <abbr title="New Mexico" class="region">NM</abbr>
</p>
        <ul>
            <li><a href="mailto:emily@ablognotlimited.com"
class="email">emily[at]ablognotlimited[dot]com</a></li>
            <li><a href="http://www.ablognotlimited.com"
class="url" rel="me">A Blog Not Limited</a></li>
        </ul>
    </div>
    <h2>Highlights of Qualifications</h2>
    <ul class="summary">
        <li>Web designer specializing in hand-coded
semantic XHTML, cross-browser CSS, progressive enhancement
accessibility and usability</li>
        <li>Expert in the design of corporate web sites,
intranets, email campaigns and e-commerce applications</li>
    </ul>
    <h2>Technical Expertise</h2>
    <ul>
        <li><a href="/tag/xhtml" class="skill"
rel="tag">XHTML</a> - 10 yrs</li>
        <li><a href="/tag/xhtml" class="skill"
rel="tag">CSS</a> - 10 yrs</li>
    </ul>
    <h2>Experience and Accomplishments</h2>
    <div class="experience vevent">
        <a href="#emily-hcard-name" class="include">Emily
Lewis</a>
        <h3 class="summary">Web Designer</h3>
        <p class="location">Pitney Bowes Business Insight
</p>
        <p><span class="dtstart"><abbr class="value"
title="2004-12-01">December 2004</abbr></span> - present
</p>
        <ul class="description">
            <li>Designed interfaces and developed XHTML, CSS
and graphics for main corporate site, international sites,
marketing newsletters, corporate blog, corporate intranet
and user conference site</li>
```

(continues on next page)

```
            <li>Designed interfaces and developed XHTML,
CSS and graphics for marketing email campaigns, ensuring
consistent display across popular email clients</li>
        </ul>
    </div>
    <h2>Education</h2>
    <div class="education vevent">
        <h3 class="summary">Bachelor of Arts</h3>
        <p class="location">St. Mary's College of Maryland
</p>
        <p><span class="dtstart"><abbr class="value"
title="1992-09-01">September 1992</abbr></span> - <span
class="dtend"><abbr class="value" title="1996-06-01">June
1996</abbr></span></p>
    </div>
    <h2>Affiliations</h2>
<ul>
    <li class="affiliation vcard"><a href="http://
webuquerque.com" class="fn org url">Webuquerque</a>
co-manager</li>
    <li class="affiliation vcard"><a href="http://baltimore.
iabc.com/" class="fn org url">IABC Baltimore Chapter</a>
board-member</li>
</ul>
    <h2>Publications</h2>
    <p><cite>Microformats Made Simple</cite>, October 2009
</p>
</div>
```

The logic behind the markup

As in the first example, I used an <h1> for my name content in order to get a potential SEO boost. However, the use of <h2>s in this example is less for SEO and more for structure (and, admittedly, a bit of presentation). As I hope you know, heading elements help define the structure of the page in terms of sections. What I mean by this is that where I use a heading element, the content that follows is related to the heading.

Heading elements also have an added accessibility benefit. Screen-reader and keyboard-only users can use shortcuts to skip from heading to heading as they navigate.

I also like that by using heading elements for my structure and semantics, I have less CSS styling to do. The default rendering of headings in today's browsers include font sizing and weight. Of course, you can override this presentation, but I personally like my headings in bold (weight), so I don't need to specify that in my CSS.

For the remainder of the content in this example, I use list elements for `education` and `experience` content, because it makes sense to me to reference it as a list. Of course, <p>s would be perfectly acceptable and make just as much semantic sense, depending on your personal perspective.

Also, just as in the first example, I could've used a <dl> for my `contact` content, but I would've lost the SEO on my name, since a <dt> can't contain block level elements like <h1>.

Authoring Tools

Efficiency is just as important as a good résumé in today's job market and economy. And I want to help you be efficient (because I'm *that* invested in you—and I'm just cool), so check out some of these tools to make your life a bit easier when publishing hResume:

- hResume Creator: http://hresume.weblogswork.com/hresumecreator/
- Optimus Microformats Transformer (for validation): http://microformatique.com/optimus/
- CV Antix Build Your CV: http://cv.antix.co.uk/Build/
- hResume Cheatsheet: http://microformats.org/wiki/hresume-cheatsheet
- For more hResume tools, see http://microformats.org/wiki/hresume -implementations

The Journey Continues

I bet you are really feeling comfortable with microformats now. You've not only learned hResume in this chapter, you've also gotten loads of practice with rel-tag, hCard, and hCalendar.

And while we are more than halfway done with our microformats journey (at least as far as this book will take you), there is still more microformatty goodness ahead. Next up: defining syndicated content with hAtom.

Chapter 9

Defining Syndicated Content: hAtom

When I hear the word *syndication,* I immediately think of television shows—specifically *The Simpsons.* Because way back in 1994, *The Simpsons* began its syndication run, which meant I could see older episodes of my favorite show on other stations and at other times than the normally scheduled Sunday night on Fox.

That's what syndication is. With broadcast syndication, television and radio stations can purchase the rights to shows belonging to other broadcast networks. With print syndication, newspapers and magazines buy the rights to other periodicals' articles, comics, and columns.

Then there is web syndication. At its core, web syndication is similar to that for print and broadcast: web content from one site is made available to other sites and services. And there are commercial licensing models for web syndication. But beyond these core similarities, web syndication is its own unique and wonderful beast.

Most web syndication comes in the form of web feeds like RSS (Really Simple Syndication) and Atom, which users subscribe to. Content authors typically provide these feeds as a means to inform subscribers of new content, so users don't have to check the source site to see if new content is available. Instead, web feeds push new content to subscribers, who commonly access that content via a feed reader such as Google Reader, Fever, and Bloglines.

It is for this particular subscription aspect of web syndication that hAtom comes into play.

What Is hAtom?

hAtom is a draft microformat for adding structure and semantics to web content that can be syndicated. Such content includes blog posts, news articles, podcasts, and vodcasts.

Although hAtom is based on the Atom XML syndication format, it isn't a 1:1 representation of Atom. More a subset of Atom, hAtom has properties and subproperties based on Atom's corresponding elements that are most relevant to "syndicatable" web content:

- Title

- Summary

- Full content

- Author

- Published and updated dates

HTML syndication

Aside from the lovely structure and semantics (and yes, they *are* lovely), hAtom offers a powerful benefit: syndication of content directly from markup, without the need for separate RSS or Atom files.

Remember those machines? Well, some clever developers have created hAtom transformers that extract hAtom from markup and transform it into XML for an Atom or RSS feed.

- TransFormr: http://transformr.co.uk/#hatom

- hAtom-to-Atom/RSS Transcoder: http://tools.microformatic.com/help/xhtml/hatom/

- Optimus Microformats Transformer: http://microformatique.com/optimus/

Implementing these transformers is amazingly simple. With both TransFormr and hAtom-to-Atom/RSS Transcoder, you simply prepend the URL of your page containing hAtom with their transformer URL. For example, here it is for TransFormr:

```
http://transformr.co.uk/hatom/http://www.ablognotlimited.com/
```

You can then add a link to your site for users to subscribe to the feed:

```
<a href="http://transformr.co.uk/hatom/http://www.
ablognotlimited.com/" title="Subscribe to Atom feed">
Subscribe</a>
```

When a user selects this link, the transformer converts the hAtom into Atom (or RSS if you use `http://transformr.co.uk/rss2/`), and the user can then subscribe to the feed (**Figure 9.1** on the next page):

Optimus is slightly different. You reference the URL of your page containing hAtom in its query string `uri` parameter:

```
http://microformatique.com/optimus/?uri=http://www.
ablognotlimited.com
```

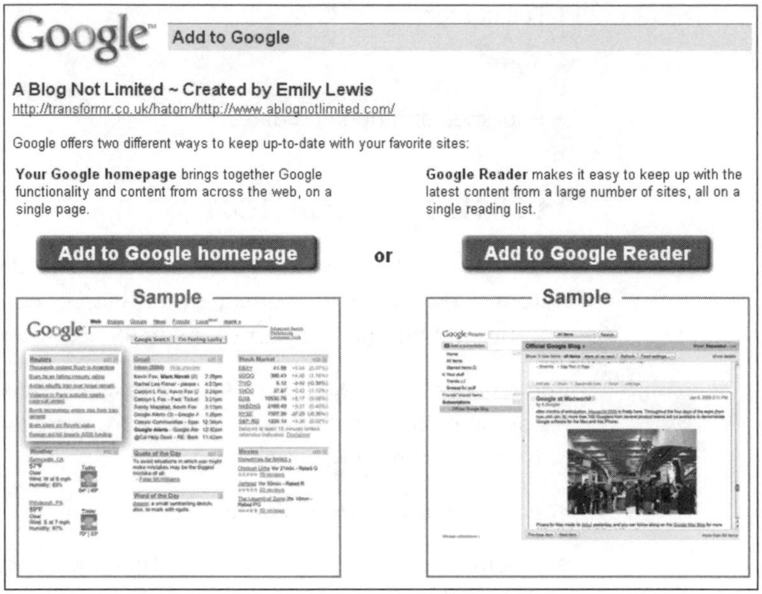

Figure 9.1
Google Reader sub-
scription prompt for
A Blog Not Limited
feed generated with
TransFormr

This will transform *all* microformats on your page into XML. To narrow the transformation to hAtom, you specify `format=rss` in the query string:

```
http://microformatique.com/optimus/?uri=http://www.
ablognotlimted.com&format=rss
```

The end result is the same as with TransFormr: if you provide this link on your site, it will generate the RSS feed that users can subscribe to.

Alternatively, you can submit your URL to Optimus, and it will transform your hAtom into an XML file you can download and work with further (**Figure 9.2**).

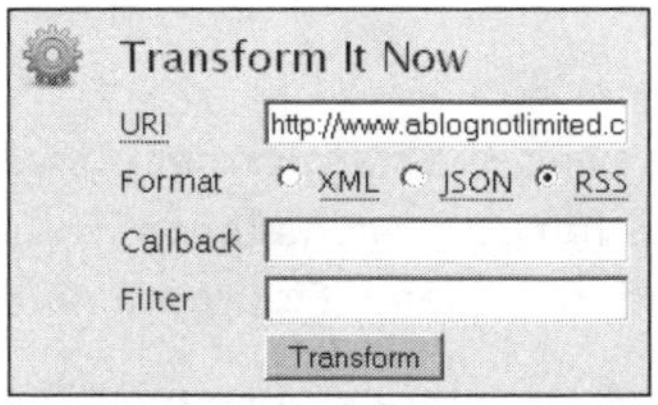

Figure 9.2
Optimus online form
to transform hAtom
content to RSS

So by using hAtom, you provide your users (the humans) the web content they want, and machines the ability to transform that content into feeds.

RSS 2.0 VS. ATOM 1.0

RSS and Atom are the two most popular feed formats used in web syndication today. They both achieve the goal of allowing your users to subscribe to your content, but they are indeed different.

RSS comes in several different versions, but the one most commonly used today is RSS 2.0. Feeds using the RSS 2.0 format have three required fields:

- Feed-level title

- Link

- Description

The description field can contain either full text or summary content; however, there is no way to indicate which is being served.

RSS 2.0 only supports plain text or escaped HTML, and doesn't offer a means to indicate which is provided. This can be a problem, as escaped HTML is just plain ugly, perhaps even confusing.

For example, the ampersand (&) will be expressed as & in the feed. So if you have a title *Fun & Games*, the RSS feed will show *Fun & Games*. There are workarounds for this, but they do require some tweaking of the RSS XML.

Additionally, RSS does not support well-formed XML, thus making it difficult (if not impossible) to reuse RSS-syndicated content.

For internationalization, RSS lets you specify the language for the feed as a whole, but not for individual entries.

Atom 1.0, by comparison, is more robust. In terms of fields, it requires both feed- and entry-level details:

- Unique identifier for both the feed and the entry

- Title for feed and entry

- Last-updated dates for feed and entry

In addition to its required fields, Atom 1.0 has optional fields to distinguish between summary content and full text. And it allows you to specify language for every element within the feed and its entries.

Finally, the other main differentiator from RSS 2.0 is that Atom 1.0 can handle a wide variety of content types, making it ideal for reusable content:

- Plain text

- Escaped HTML

- Well-formed XHTML

- Well-formed XML

- Base64-encoded binary content

- References to web content not included in the feed

I am by no means an expert in feeds (feeding my face is a different story), so I can't advise you which is better. And these are just some of the basic differences. It's up to you to do the research and decide which format is best for your purposes.

As my mother told me, I tell you: go look it up.

Not a syndication format

Although hAtom is based on Atom and it can be used to generate syndication feeds, it is *not* a syndication format. In fact, it wasn't even developed strictly for web content that can be syndicated.

As hAtom author David Janes explains:

"hAtom was never intended to be a 'syndication format,' nor [was it meant] to compete with Atom or RSS. It's simply designed to describe the micro-content on web pages, such as blog posts. We used Atom because it provides a well-defined nomenclature for describing such elements."

Although hAtom isn't a syndication format, the vocabulary used in describing hAtom content is closely tied to feeds:

• A single implementation of hAtom is referred to as a **feed.**

• The individual pieces of web content hAtom contains are referred to as **entries.**

So just because I'm referencing a feed or an entry, don't get confused. You aren't required to use HTML syndication when you publish with hAtom. It's just an added benefit.

Gaining traction

Despite its draft status and regardless of whether it is used for syndicated content or for "microcontent," hAtom has been respectably adopted:

• Google Notebook supports hAtom permalinks.

• Blogger Layouts uses hAtom by default for blogs.

• Last.fm uses hAtom for its shoutboxes.

• Internet Explorer 8's Web Slices use a combination of hAtom and the Web Slice format to define specific parts of a web page users can subscribe to.

Profile

If the idea of HTML syndication turns you on as much as it does me (and let's not forget how hawt semantics and structure are), then it is time to address the details of hAtom, starting with the profile:

```
<head profile="http://microformats.org/profile/hatom">
```

hAtom does use hCard, so you should reference the hCard profile as well:

```
<head profile=" http://microformats.org/profile/hatom
http://microformats.org/profile/hcard">
```

Syntax

Here are the properties and subproperties for hAtom:

- `hfeed`, the root property of a single feed, can contain an unlimited number of entries. It is optional and assumed (by machines) to be on the page if it isn't declared. However, if you wish to create multiple, distinct feeds on a page and, therefore, multiple `hfeed`s, you do need to include the property for each distinct feed.

- `hentry` is a required property that contains all the content for a feed entry, and it can be used as often as needed.

- `entry-title`, a required subproperty of `hentry`, specifies the title of the entry.

- `updated`, another required subproperty of `hentry`, indicates the date and time the entry was last updated.

- The required `author` subproperty contains information about the entry author and must also be marked up with hCard.

- `entry-summary` is an optional subproperty used to indicate a summary of or introduction to the entry.

- `entry-content`, also optional, is the subproperty that specifies the full content of the entry.

- `published` indicates the original publish date of the entry. It, too, is optional.

In addition to these properties, you can include a **permalink** (permanent link) to your entry content using rel-bookmark. This is particularly useful for sites that provide a summary or archive page of entries. The permalinks direct users to the main content page for each entry.

You can also specify categories for feeds and entries using rel-tag. Categories for the feed appear as rel-tag links within `hfeed` but outside `hentry`. Categories at the entry level must be contained by `hentry`.

Practical Markup

In the following POSHilicious examples, we'll take a look at hAtom in blogs and news sites. But don't take that as a restriction. hAtom is perfectly suited to any content that has, at a minimum, a title, a last-updated date, and an author (the three required properties). And it is especially ideal for content that you wish to syndicate and allow people to subscribe to.

Single blog post

Since I started this chapter mentioning *The Simpsons*, let's continue that reference with a fictional blog post from Homer:

```
<h1>The Exquisite Beauty of Duff and Donuts</h1>
<p><a href="/contributors/homer">Homer Simpson</a></p>
<p>September 28, 2009</p>
<p>Donuts are a delicious creation of bready, sweet
goodness. Duff beer is a delicious creation of hops and
yeast. Together they make the perfect meal.</p>
<p>And you have so many options. Try Duff with that powdered
concoction calling your name. Or with the cruller that will
melt in your mouth. Forget the coffee, dip your donuts in
Duff and see how that gets your day started.</p>
<p>Can't write. Eating. Drinking.</p>
<ul>
    <li><a href="/tags/food">food</a></li>
    <li><a href="/tags/beer">beer</a></li>
    <li><a href="/tags/donuts">donuts</a></li>
    <li><a href="/tags/Duff">Duff</a></li>
</ul>
```

Optional root property: `hfeed`

For this example, there is only one feed (which happens to contain one entry), so I don't need to include the root `hfeed` property because it is assumed to be on the page.

Required property: `hentry`

I do, however, need to contain my entry content with `hentry`, which means I also need to add a containing `<div>`:

```
<div class="hentry">
    <h1>The Exquisite Beauty of Duff and Donuts</h1>
    <p><a href="/contributors/homer">Homer Simpson</a></p>
    <p>September 28, 2009</p>
    <p>Donuts are a delicious creation ...</p>
```

```
    <p>And you have so many options. ...</p>
    <p>Can't write. Eating. Drinking.</p>
    <ul>
        <li><a href="/tags/food">food</a></li>
        <li><a href="/tags/beer">beer</a></li>
        <li><a href="/tags/donuts">donuts</a></li>
        <li><a href="/tags/Duff">Duff</a></li>
    </ul>
</div>
```

Required property: `entry-title`

Next, I designate the title of my entry with `entry-title`:

```
<h1 class="entry-title">The Exquisite Beauty of Duff and
Donuts</h1>
```

Required property: `author` with hCard

Not only do I need to add the `author` property to the element containing Homer's name, I also need to mark up his information with hCard:

```
<p class="author vcard"><a href="/contributors/homer"
class="fn url">Homer Simpson</a></p>
```

Required property: `updated`

Then I indicate the last-updated date with the required `updated` property. I also need to add the ISO 8601 machine data for date-time information using the value class pattern:

```
<p class="updated"><span class="value-title" title="2009-09-
28T13:00:00"> </span>September 28, 2009</p>
```

Since the machine ISO 8601 information is both date and time, I'm using the empty `<span>` method for the value-title subset of the value class pattern. This avoids the non-human-friendly browser tooltips and screen-reader expansion.

Optional property: `published`

For some content, particularly blog posts, there isn't really a last-updated date. Most typically, the date that is included within an entry is the publish date.

And hAtom gives you an option for such cases: where there isn't an `updated` date specified, machines use the `published` value. For these cases, you can just add the `published` property (again, making sure to supply the ISO 8601 date-time information):

```
<p class="published"><span class="value-title" title="2009-
09-28T13:00:00"> </span>September 28, 2009</p>
```

So while `updated` is required, it sorta isn't if you include `published`. However, I've noticed some inconsistencies in how machines deal with this caveat, so I personally recommend you include both properties but apply them to a single date-time value:

```
<p class="updated published"><span class="value-title"
title="2009-09-28T13:00:00"> </span>September 28, 2009</p>
```

Optional property: `entry-content`

Next, I want to indicate the full content of my post by containing it with the `entry-content` property. Because the content in this example is a series of `<p>`s, I add a `<div>` to contain them all:

```
<div class="entry-content">
    <p>Donuts are a delicious creation of bready, sweet
goodness. Duff beer is a delicious creation of hops and
yeast. Together they make the perfect meal.</p>
    <p>And you have so many options. Try Duff with that
powdered concoction calling your name. Or with the cruller
that will melt in your mouth. Forget the coffee, dip your
donuts in Duff and see how that gets your day started.</p>
    <p>Can't write. Eating. Drinking.</p>
</div>
```

Optional property: `entry-summary`

Bloggers often present their feed-entry content as a summary or an introduction. Users can then click through to the website to read the full content. This is where `entry-summary` is useful, and I apply it to the first paragraph of `entry-content`:

```
<p class="entry-summary">Donuts are a delicious creation of
bready, sweet goodness. Duff beer is a delicious creation of
hops and yeast. Together they make the perfect meal.</p>
```

Optional permalink

In addition to providing summary content for a feed, `entry-summary` is useful for archive or summary pages. I do this on my own blog by listing three posts on the home page, each with just the summary content and a link to the full post.

However, in such situations, you should provide a permalink within your `hentry` to that full post. As such, I need to add a link with an `href` referencing the permanent URL.

```
<h1 class="entry-title"><a href="http://thesimpsonsblog.com/
posts/exquisite-beauty-duff-donuts">The Exquisite Beauty of
Duff and Donuts</a></h1>
```

And then I add rel-bookmark to that link:

```
<h1 class="entry-title"><a href="http://thesimpsonsblog.
com/posts/exquisite-beauty-duff-donuts" rel="bookmark">The
Exquisite Beauty of Duff and Donuts</a></h1>
```

Optional categories

Lastly, my post includes a list of tags that describe the content. hAtom considers these categories and recommends they be marked up as links using rel-tag:

```
<ul>
    <li><a href="/tags/food" rel="tag">food</a></li>
    <li><a href="/tags/beer" rel="tag">beer</a></li>
    <li><a href="/tags/donuts" rel="tag">donuts</a></li>
    <li><a href="/tags/Duff" rel="tag">Duff</a></li>
</ul>
```

And because these are nested within `hentry`, they are categories for the individual entry, not the feed. If I wanted to specify categories to the feed as a whole, I would nest them within the `hfeed` root property but outside of `hentry`.

The end result

```
<div class="hentry">
    <h1 class="entry-title"><a href="http://thesimpsonsblog.
com/posts/exquisite-beauty-duff-donuts" rel="bookmark">The
Exquisite Beauty of Duff and Donuts</a></h1>
```

(continues on next page)

```
    <p class="author vcard"><a href="/contributors/homer"
class="fn url">Homer Simpson</a></p>
    <p class="updated published"><span class="value-title"
title="2009-09-28T13:00:00"> </span>September 28, 2009</p>
    <div class="entry-content">
        <p class="entry-summary">Donuts are a delicious
creation of bready, sweet goodness. Duff beer is a delicious
creation of hops and yeast. Together they make the perfect
meal.</p>
        <p>And you have so many options. Try Duff with that
powdered concoction calling your name. Or with the cruller
that will melt in your mouth. Forget the coffee, dip your
donuts in Duff and see how that gets your day started.</p>
        <p>Can't write. Eating. Drinking.</p>
    </div>
    <ul>
        <li><a href="/tags/food" rel="tag">food</a></li>
        <li><a href="/tags/beer" rel="tag">beer</a></li>
        <li><a href="/tags/donuts" rel="tag">donuts</a></li>
        <li><a href="/tags/Duff" rel="tag">Duff</a></li>
    </ul>
</div>
```

The logic behind the markup

OK, now let's take a look at the markup. I chose `<h1>` for my title to give me that potential SEO boost. And I added the permalink to the title: For me, that makes the most semantic sense. But a permalink could be applied to date-time content, as well and if I'd taken that approach, it wouldn't have required the addition of a `<span>` to indicate date-time with the value class pattern:

```
<p class="updated published"><a class="value-title" title=
"2009-09-28T13:00:00" href="http://thesimpsonsblog.com/
posts/exquisite-beauty-duff-donuts" rel="bookmark">September
28, 2009</a></p>
```

Note that I apply the `value-title` property for the value class pattern to my `<a>`, rather than the `<span>`. Of course, this does result in a relatively non-human-friendly browser tooltip. But that's why there are so many value class pattern options. Pick the one best suited to your audience and content.

For the rest of the entry, I use `<p>`s because that's what the content is. If my example had also included list content, then I would've used the appropriate list element(s) as well. If it had included images, then `<img />` elements would be included. And so on, and so on.

Finally, for the categories (tags), they just make sense to me as list items, rather than a bunch of separate <p>s or even comma-delimited text contained by a <p> (though that would work just fine).

WEB SLICES WITH INTERNET EXPLORER 8

I don't really hate Internet Explorer. I have a very "special" relationship with IE 6: it borks on good, valid CSS, and I beat it into submission while bitching and moaning about how horrible it is.

But IE has come a long way since IE 6 (hear that, folks: time to upgrade!), and IE 8 is the closest Microsoft has come to supporting web standards. Even better, IE 8 supports hAtom with its Web Slices feature.

Web Slices are a way for content authors to indicate different parts (slices) of their web pages that are available for subscription. Users of IE 8 can then subscribe and be notified within the browser when updates to that content are available.

And because Web Slices leverage hAtom (along with the Web Slices format), you only need to add a single class value and unique identifier to your hAtom content:

- `hslice` defines the Web Slice content and can be applied as another `class` value to the same element `hentry` is applied to.

- Each element assigned `class="hslice"` must also be assigned a unique `id`.

Applied to my blog post example, it looks like this:

```
<div class="hentry hslice" id="slice1">
```

Web Slices then use the rest of the hAtom properties to define the title and content of the slice. And that's it. Except to give a nod to Microsoft for embracing existing standards rather than creating a new, proprietary technology.

News-article archive using <ol>

Now let's turn to news content. But this time, rather than focusing on a single news article (which would be marked up identically to a single blog post), we're going to look at an example featuring several articles (entries).

```
<h1>Good News Archive</h1>
<ol>
    <li>
        <h2><a href="http://goodnews.com/archive/daily-
affirmations-help-slacker">Daily Affirmations Help Slacker
Reach Full Potential</a></h2>
        <p>June 15, 2009</p>
```

(continues on next page)

```
    <p><a href="http://doggoneitpeoplelikeme.com">Stuart
Smalley</a></p>
    <p>Joe Schmoe spent his whole life as a couch
potato. Boob tube, video games and naps occupied his entire
life. Until Joe began daily affirmations. Six months later,
he is now the lead mayoral candidate of his town.</p>
  </li>
  <li>
    <h2><a href="http://goodnews.com/archive/cat-
rescues-mouse">Cat Rescues Mouse</a></h2>
    <p>June 14, 2009</p>
    <p><a href="http://practicalcats.com">Bustopher
Jones</a></p>
    <p>Jerry, the beloved pet mouse of Mr. and Mrs.
Smith, was trapped in a sewer drain for 55 hours. Fire and
Rescue were unable to retrieve Jerry despite their best
efforts. Fortunately, the Smith's cat, Tom, came to the
rescue and retrieved Jerry. Once arch enemies, the two are
now best friends.</p>
  </li>
  <li>
    <h2><a href="http://goodnews.com/archive/chocolate
-helps-weight-loss">Chocolate Helps Weight Loss</a></h2>
    <p>June 13, 2009</p>
    <p><a href="http://allchocolateallthetime.
com">Milton Hersey</a></p>
    <p>New research has surfaced indicating that
chocolate can help you lose weight. But it isn't eating
chocolate that has this effect. Instead, bathing in
chocolate has helped study particpants lose an average of
50 pounds.</p>
  </li>
</ol>
```

Optional root property: `hfeed`

Once again, we are dealing with a single feed, so you can omit the root property `hfeed`. But if you feel the need to add it, you would apply it to the parent element containing all of the individual entries (`<ol>`):

```
<ol class="hfeed">
```

Required property: `hentry`

We do, however, need to assign the `hentry` property to the containing element (`<li>`) for each entry's content:

```
<ol class="hfeed">
    <li class="hentry">
        <h2><a href="http://goodnews.com/archive/daily
-affirmations-help-slacker">Daily Affirmations Help Slacker
...</a></h2>
        <p>June 15, 2009</p>
        <p><a href="http://doggoneitpeoplelikeme.com">Stuart
Smalley</a></p>
        <p>Joe Schmoe spent ...</p>
    </li>
    <li class="hentry">
        <h2><a href="http://goodnews.com/archive/cat-rescues
-mouse">Cat Rescues Mouse</a></h2>
        <p>June 14, 2009</p>
        <p><a href="http://practicalcats.com">Bustopher
Jones</a></p>
        <p>Jerry, the beloved pet ...</p>
    </li>
    <li class="hentry">
        <h2><a href="http://goodnews.com/archive/chocolate
-helps-weight-loss">Chocolate Helps Weight Loss</a></h2>
        <p>June 13, 2009</p>
        <p><a href="http://allchocolateallthetime.com">
Milton Hersey</a></p>
        <p>New research has surfaced ...</p>
    </li>
</ol>
```

Required property: `entry-title`

The title content for each entry needs the `entry-title` property:

```
<li class="hentry">
    <h2 class="entry-title"><a href="http://goodnews.com/
archive/daily-affirmations-help-slacker">Daily Affirmations
Help Slacker ...</a></h2>
    <p>June 15, 2009</p>
```

(continues on next page)

```
    <p><a href="http://doggoneitpeoplelikeme.com">Stuart
Smalley</a></p>
    <p>Joe Schmoe spent ...</p>
</li>
```

Required property: `author` with hCards

Next, I assign `author` to the author content and add hCard:

```
<li class="hentry">
    <h2 class="entry-title"><a href="http://goodnews.com/
archive/daily-affirmations-help-slacker">Daily Affirmations
Help Slacker ...</a></h2>
    <p>June 15, 2009</p>
    <p class="author vcard"><a href="http://doggoneitpeople
likeme.com" class="fn url">Stuart Smalley</a></p>
    <p>Joe Schmoe spent ...</p>
</li>
```

Required property: `updated`

For the date information, I apply the `updated` property and add the ISO 8601 machine data:

```
<li class="hentry">
    <h2 class="entry-title"><a href="http://goodnews.com/
archive/daily-affirmations-help-slacker">Daily Affirmations
Help Slacker ...</a></h2>
    <p class="updated"><abbr class="value" title="2009-06-15">
June 15, 2009</abbr></p>
    <p class="author vcard"><a href="http://doggoneitpeople
likeme.com" class="fn url">Stuart Smalley</a></p>
    <p>Joe Schmoe spent ...</p>
</li>
```

Again, because I'm dealing with just a date (no time), I can use `<abbr>` with the value class pattern.

Optional property: `published`

In this example, as with the blog post, let's assume the publish date and last-updated date are the same. So we also add the `published` property to the date-time content:

```
<li class="hentry">
    <h2 class="entry-title"><a href="http://goodnews.com/
archive/daily-affirmations-help-slacker">Daily Affirmations
```

```
Help Slacker ...</a></h2>
    <p class="updated published"><abbr class="value"
title="2009-06-15">June 15, 2009</abbr></p>
    <p class="author vcard"><a href="http://doggoneitpeople
likeme.com" class="fn url">Stuart Smalley</a></p>
    <p>Joe Schmoe spent ...</p>
</li>
```

Optional property: `entry-summary`

The content in this example is a new archive; I'm only listing summary content for each entry. As such, I apply the `entry-summary` property:

```
<li class="hentry">
    <h2 class="entry-title"><a href="http://goodnews.com/
archive/daily-affirmations-help-slacker">Daily Affirmations
Help Slacker ...</a></h2>
    <p class="updated published"><abbr class="value"
title="2009-06-15">June 15, 2009</abbr></p>
    <p class="author vcard"><a href="http://doggoneitpeople
likeme.com" class="fn url">Stuart Smalley</a></p>
    <p class="entry-summary">Joe Schmoe spent his whole life
as a couch potato. Boob tube, video games and naps occupied his
entire life. Until Joe began daily affirmations. Six months
later, he is now the lead mayoral candidate of his town.</p>
</li>
```

Optional permalink

My content already includes links to the entries' permalinks, so I go ahead and add rel-bookmark:

```
<li class="hentry">
    <h2 class="entry-title"><a href="http://goodnews.
com/archive/daily-affirmations-help-slacker"
rel="bookmark">Daily Affirmations Help Slacker Reach Full
Potential</a></h2>
    <p class="updated published"><abbr class="value"
title="2009-06-15">June 15, 2009</abbr></p>
    <p class="author vcard"><a href="http://doggoneitpeople
likeme.com" class="fn url">Stuart Smalley</a></p>
```

(continues on next page)

```
        <p class="entry-summary">Joe Schmoe spent ...</p>
    </li>
```

The end result

Let's take a look at the whole thing:

```
<h1>Good News Archive</h1>
<ol class="hfeed">
    <li class="hentry">
        <h2 class="entry-title"><a href="http://goodnews.com/
archive/daily-affirmations-help-slacker" rel="bookmark">
Daily Affirmations Help Slacker Reach Full Potential</a></h2>
        <p class="updated published"><abbr class="value"
title="2009-06-15">June 15, 2009</abbr></p>
        <p class="author vcard"><a href="http://doggoneit
peoplelikeme.com" class="fn url">Stuart Smalley</a></p>
        <p class="entry-summary">Joe Schmoe spent his
whole life as a couch potato. Boob tube, video games and
naps occupied his entire life. Until Joe began daily
affirmations. Six months later, he is now the lead mayoral
candidate of his town.</p>
    </li>
    <li class="hentry">
        <h2 class="entry-title"><a href="http://goodnews.com/
archive/cat-rescues-mouse" rel="bookmark">Cat Rescues
Mouse</a></h2>
        <p class="updated published"><abbr class="value"
title="2009-06-14">June 14, 2009</abbr></p>
        <p class="author vcard"><a href="http://
practicalcats.com" class="fn url">Bustopher Jones</a></p>
        <p class="entry-summary">Jerry, the beloved pet
mouse of Mr. and Mrs. Smith, was trapped in a sewer drain
for 55 hours. Fire and Rescue were unable to retrieve Jerry
despite their best efforts. Fortunately, the Smith's cat,
Tom, came to the rescue and retrieved Jerry. Once arch
enemies, the two are now best friends.</p>
    </li>
    <li class="hentry">
        <h2 class="entry-title"><a href="http://goodnews.com/
archive/chocolate-helps-weight-loss" rel="bookmark">
Chocolate Helps Weight Loss</a></h2>
```

```
    <p class="updated published"><abbr class="value"
title="2009-06-13">June 13, 2009</abbr></p>
        <p class="author vcard"><a href="http://allchocolate
allthetime.com" class="fn url">Milton Hersey</a></p>
        <p class="entry-summary">New research has surfaced
indicating that chocolate can help you lose weight. But
it isn't eating chocolate that has this effect. Instead,
bathing in chocolate has helped study particpants lose an
average of 50 pounds.</p>
    </li>
</ol>
```

The logic behind the markup

I chose an ordered list as my containing element because, at least in this example, the entries are listed according to date. Thus, the sequential nature of <ol> is appropriate. If, however, the entries weren't listed in any particular order, then <ul> would've been my element of choice.

And I could've dropped the list container entirely, and just marked up each entry with a containing <div>:

```
<div class="hentry">
    <h2 class="entry-title"><a href="http://goodnews.com/
archive/chocolate-helps-weight-loss" rel="bookmark">
Chocolate Helps Weight Loss</a></h2>
    <p class="updated published"><abbr class="value"
title="2009-06-13">June 13, 2009</abbr></p>
    <p class="author vcard"><a href="http://allchocolate
allthetime.com" class="fn url">Milton Hersey</a></p>
    <p class="entry-summary">New research has surfaced ...
</p>
</div>
```

Another option could be a definition list, with each entry contained by a <dl>:

```
<dl class="hentry">
    <dt class="entry-title"><a href="http://goodnews.com/
archive/chocolate-helps-weight-loss" rel="bookmark">
Chocolate Helps Weight Loss</a></dt>
    <dd class="updated published"><abbr class="value"
title="2009-06-13">June 13, 2009</abbr></dd>
```

(continues on next page)

```
    <dd class="author vcard"><a href="http://allchocolate
allthetime.com" class="fn url">Milton Hersey</a></dd>
    <dd class="entry-summary">New research has surfaced
...</dd>
</dl>
```

Note that the entry title is contained by the <dt>, while the other content elements of the entry are contained by <dd>s.

The only drawback of this approach is that I lose the potential SEO of the <h2> on the title in my original example.

Authoring Tools

As much as I am a fan of hand-coding (don't ask me why, I'm just uptight that way), I'm sad to report there isn't a whole hell of a lot available to make your life easier when authoring hAtom. Fortunately, hAtom is uncomplicated, so adding it to your markup by hand shouldn't elicit suicidal thoughts. Still, you can check out these tools:

- hAtom Cheatsheet: http://microformats.org/wiki/hatom-cheatsheet

- Sandbox Theme for WordPress: http://www.plaintxt.org/themes/sandbox/

- hAtom WordPress (for those who use WordPress but don't want to use Sandbox): http://fberriman.com/2006/08/07/implementing-hatom-the-entries-code/

- Optimus Microformats Transformer (for validation): http://microformatique.com/optimus/

- For more hAtom tools, see http://microformats.org/wiki/hatom-implementations

Up and hAtom

Now you know how to publish with hAtom, so get to it! Got a blog? A news site? Trying your hand at podcasting? Then drop in hAtom and experiment. I'm making this a requirement for the Microformats Are Way F'n Cool Club t-shirts.

Next, we'll take a look at hReview, which is the microformat for reviews of products, services, places, . . . anything.

Defining Reviews: hReview

Everyone has an opinion about something. And what better medium to share those opinions than the Internet? Of course, there's an abundance of opinions on the web that I, personally, wish I never had the "pleasure" of reading or hearing. But there are always those opinions that can be valuable: reviews of products, services, places—anything, really.

How many times have you considered purchasing a book and turned to Amazon's reviews to help you make your decision? Or what about booking a trip to a far-off destination? Even deciding whether to see a particular band?

Other people's opinions, at times, can sway you one way or another. And it is for this type of content that hReview is intended.

What Is hReview?

hReview is a draft microformat for adding semantics to web reviews of just about anything. Got a blog post where you talk about how much you love the latest Harry Potter? Mark it up with hReview. A news article where you review the latest software offering from Microsoft? Turn it into an hReview. Does your corporate website include customer reviews of your products? hReview can help you do more with that content.

Unlike some of the microformats we've covered—like hCard, hCalendar, and hAtom—that are based on a representation of another existing technology, hReview was developed according to the review content most commonly found on the web today, including the following:

- Name of the item being reviewed

- Name of the person authoring the review

- Date of the review

- Summary and full description for the review

- Rating of the item being reviewed

Distributed reviews

One of the intended benefits of hReview is to provide an open standard for the distribution of reviews. There are already popular sites—Amazon, Best Buy, Rotten Tomatoes, to name a few—that offer review content for a wide variety of products and services. These reviews are relatively easy to find, as those sites provide a central location for their own review content.

But what about reviews that exist on personal blogs, corporate sites, or even in forum comments? These reviews may be more difficult to find, because they may exist independent of a "review system." hReview provides a mechanism for that review content to be more easily shared, aggregated, and distributed.

To date, there is just a handful of tools and applications (machines!) that offer this service. But because hReview provides the necessary foundation for those applications to be developed, I believe there will be many more in the future. What would such applications look like?

Let's consider small-scale first: a corporate site that promotes products and services and allows customers to write reviews about those products and services. These reviews may be found in different sections of the website. But a developer could create an application that indexes all of the hReviews on the site and provides results in a single area, without having to replicate the review content. Users could access reviews from a single area, rather than having to navigate from product to product or service to service.

On a larger scale, such as a search engine, reviews marked up with hReview across the entirety of the web could be indexed, providing users with reviews from a broad range of sources, not just the product or service owner. This would give users more information to help them make better-informed decisions.

Google gets in the game

Speaking of hReview aggregation on a large scale, Google's Rich Snippets indexes hReview-microformatted content to provide summary information (snippets) in its search results. So content marked up with hReview will display in Google's search results with a snippet that provides summary detail of the review, including the rating (**Figure 10.1**).

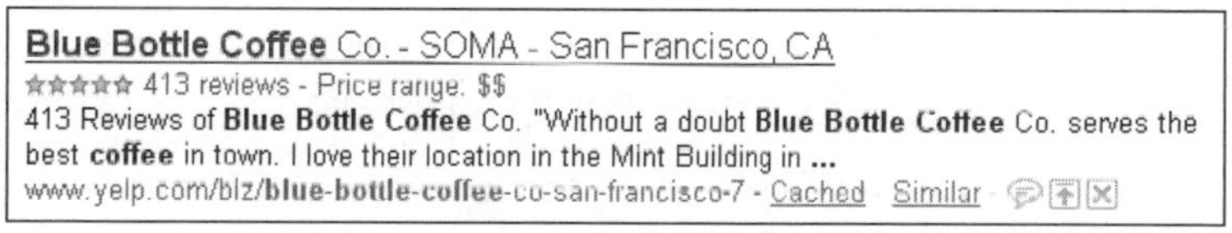

Figure 10.1
Google's Rich Snippets displays ratings and summary details of web reviews marked up with hReview.

Blue Bottle Coffee Co. - SOMA - San Francisco, CA
☆☆☆☆☆ 413 reviews - Price range: $$
413 Reviews of **Blue Bottle Coffee** Co. "Without a doubt **Blue Bottle Coffee** Co. serves the best **coffee** in town. I love their location in the Mint Building in ...
www.yelp.com/biz/**blue-bottle-coffee**-co-san-francisco-7 - Cached   Similar

You may have noticed that I wrote "*will* display." That's because, as of this writing, Google is still rolling out this feature. Not all users see Rich Snippets yet. However, as with hCard, which is also used in Rich Snippets, Google's move to begin consuming microformats and using them to display results signals a strong support for structured data like microformats.

And for content authors using hReview, having support from one of the major players in search means that their content will be exposed to search users in a more meaningful fashion. This can lead to more click-throughs, which could lead to greater profit.

Before Google

Long before Google began embracing hReview, there were many other companies that recognized its value. From a publishing perspective, there are thousands (if not more) sites that mark up their reviews with hReview, including these:

- Yahoo! Local publishes user feedback and ratings of places in its search results with hReview.

- Yahoo! Tech adds hReview to all the reviews of its more than 300,000 technology products.

- Cork'd, the wine community site, publishes reviews with hReview.

- Is It Any Good uses hReview for all product reviews.

- MicroRevie.ws takes reviews from Twitter updates, marks them up with hReview, and provides an aggregated display.

And there are many, many more, from personal blogs to magazine and news sites. Although hReview is a draft, many people recognize its value and are implementing it today.

There are also tools that consume microformats:

- LouderVoice aggregates hReviews from blogs and publishes them in hReview.

- Scrugy, the wine information search engine, aggregates and parses hReviews from wine-related sites and blogs.

- Yahoo! SearchMonkey uses hReview to make its Gallery search results more contextually relevant to its users.

- Yelp, in response to Google's Rich Snippets, now publishes its reviews with hReview.

- The Tails Export add-on for Mozilla Firefox identifies hReview on web pages, and gives users a quick view of the rating and an export feature of the hReview markup (**Figure 10.2**).

Figure 10.2
The Tails Export 0.3.5 add-on for Mozilla Firefox identifies hReview on pages, such as wine reviews on Cork'd.

Profile

Now that you know hReview's benefits, I'm sure you are itching to be in the same company as some of these great sites that support it. It's time to learn how to publish hReview, starting with the profile in your document `<head>`:

```
<head profile="http://microformats.org/profile/hreview">
```

hReview can include hCard and hCalendar, as well as rel-license. So if you also use these microformats, be sure to include their profiles too.

Syntax

You've got the profile; next let's go over the properties and subproperties of hReview:

- `hreview` is the required root property for hReview. It must be assigned to the element containing all of the review content.

- `item` is the required property assigned to the content about whatever is being reviewed. It has three subproperties:
  - `fn` is required and indicates the name of the item being reviewed.
  - `url` is an optional subproperty and is applied to the URL of the item being reviewed.
  - `photo` is the last subproperty of `item` and is optionally applied to an `<img />` element that references a photo or image of the item.

- `version`, an optional property for hReview, indicates the version of the hReview specification that is being used. For the examples in this chapter, we are referencing version 0.3.

- `summary` is the optional property assigned to the content that summarizes the review, most commonly the review title.

- `type` is the optional property that indicates the type of item being reviewed—a `product`, `event`, `business`, `person`, `place`, `website`, or URL.

- `reviewer` is the optional property assigned to the content about the person who wrote the review. This should also be an hCard.

- `dtreviewed` is the optional property that indicates, in ISO 8601 format, the date of the review.

- `rating` is the optional property assigned to the rating of the item being reviewed. This can be a value on an integer scale, where 1.0 is the lowest value and 5.0 is the highest, with ranges on the decimal point such as 2.5. Alternatively, you can use a scale with the `rating` subproperties of `best` and `worst`.

- `description` is the optional property that indicates the full text of the review.

- If a review includes keywords or phrases, you can optionally mark those up with rel-tag.

- If the review is licensed, you can optionally assign rel-license to that content.

Along with these properties and subproperties, you also have the option to indicate the permalink of the review. As you may recall from Chapter 9, the permalink is the permanent URL for the review.

If you choose to specify a permalink, you must assign `rel` values of `bookmark` and `self` to the `<a>`.

Reviews of people and events

As you've seen many times in the previous chapters, you can (and should) combine microformats. It is just another way to further structure your content and add semantic value.

And hReview requires that you include hCard when marking up review content about people, places, and organizations. When dealing with content about events, hReview requires that you also include hCalendar. In these situations, both hCard and hCalendar are applied to the element that is assigned `class="item"`.

If the review is about a person, place, or business, then the element assigned `class="item"` should also be assigned the hCard root property `vcard` along with any relevant subproperties. In these cases, the `fn` subproperty of `item` is also treated as the `fn` property of hCard.

For reviews about events, the element assigned `class="item"` should be assigned the hCalendar `vevent` property, as well as the relevant subproperties.

Practical Markup

Now let's put all of these hReview properties and subproperties to work in some POSH examples.

Book review

I'm a book lover. Have been since I could read. And one of my favorite books of all time is Douglas Adams' *Hitchhiker's Guide to the Galaxy*. So, let's pretend that I actually found the time to post a (very short) review on my blog:

```
<h1><a href="/articles/Review-Hitchhikers">Review of
<cite>Hitchhiker's Guide to the Galaxy</cite></a></h1>
<p>March 11, 2009</p>
<p>Rated 5 stars by <a href="http://ablognotlimited.
com/">Emily Lewis</a></p>
<p>Do you love science fiction and Monty Pythonesque
irreverence? Then Douglas Adams' <cite>Hitchhiker's Guide to
the Galaxy</cite> is the book for you.</p>
```

Required root property: `hreview`

In order to assign the root `hreview`, first I add a `<div>` to contain all of the review content:

```
<div class="hreview">
    <h1><a href="http://ablognotlimited.com/articles/Review
-Hitchhikers">Review of <cite>Hitchhiker's Guide to the
Galaxy</cite></a></h1>
    <p>March 11, 2009</p>
    <p>Rated 5 stars by <a href="http://ablognotlimited.
com/">Emily Lewis</a></p>
    <p>Do you love ...</p>
</div>
```

Required property: `item`

The only other required property is `item`, which you add to the element containing information about the item being reviewed. In this example, you add it to the `<h1>` since it contains the book name:

```
<h1 class="item"><a href="http://ablognotlimited.com/
articles/Review-Hitchhikers">Review of <cite>Hitchhiker's
Guide to the Galaxy</cite></a></h1>
```

Required subproperty: `fn`

Although `item` has three subproperties, only one, `fn`, is required. It indicates the name of the item being reviewed. Remember, subproperty values must be contained by the parent property, so I add `fn` to the `<cite>` element contained by the `<h1>`:

```
<h1 class="item"><a href="http://ablognotlimited.com/
articles/Review-Hitchhikers">Review of <cite class="fn">
Hitchhiker's Guide to the Galaxy</cite></a></h1>
```

Optional property: `summary`

The `summary` property should be assigned to a brief synopsis of the review, which is commonly the title of the review. The title in this example is contained by the `<h1>`, so I add `summary` alongside `item`:

```
<h1 class="item summary"><a href="http://ablognotlimited.
com/articles/Review-Hitchhikers">Review of <cite class="fn">
Hitchhiker's Guide to the Galaxy</cite></a></h1>
```

Optional property: `type`

This review is for a book, so of the seven legal values for `type`, `product` is the most appropriate. I don't have the actual word *product* in my review, but I do reference that it is a *book*.

So I indicate the `type` value using the value class pattern. In this example, I have to add a few `<span>`s to contain the word *book* and indicate the machine data (`product`):

```
<p>Do you love science fiction and Monty Pythonesque
irreverence? Then Douglas Adams' <cite>Hitchhiker's Guide to
```

the Galaxy</cite> is the <span class="type"><span class=
"value-title" title="product">book</span></span> for you.</p>

Note that the value class pattern allows me to retain the original content
for my human users, but indicate the correct `product` value in the `title`
attribute of the inner `<span>`.

And, of course, you could use the empty `<span>` method for the value-title
subset of the value class pattern if you are concerned about tooltip display.

Optional property: `reviewer` with hCard

To specify the name of the person who wrote the review, I need to assign
the `reviewer` property to that content. But if you recall, the `reviewer`
also needs to be an hCard. As such, I cannot assign `reviewer` to the `<a>`
because the root `vcard` cannot be combined with any of its properties
like `fn` and `url`, which would naturally be assigned to the `<a>`. So I add
a `<span>`:

```
<p>Rated 5 stars by <span class="reviewer vcard">
<a href="http://ablognotlimited.com/">Emily Lewis</a>
</span></p>
```

Then I add the required `fn` property for `vcard` and the optional `url` property to the `<a>`.

```
<p>Rated 5 stars by <span class="reviewer vcard">
<a href="http://ablognotlimited.com/" class="fn url">
Emily Lewis</a></span></p>
```

Adding rel-me While it isn't a requirement for hReview or hCard, I
can also add `rel="me"` to the `<a>`, since in this example I am the reviewer,
and the link is to my blog, and presumably posted on my site:

```
<p>Rated 5 stars by <span class="reviewer vcard">
<a href="http://ablognotlimited.com/" class="fn url"
rel="me">Emily Lewis</a></span></p>
```

Again, this is not necessary, but I encourage you to look for these little
opportunities to combine microformats even when the specification
doesn't require it. The more semantic and structured, the better, as far as
I'm concerned. And if you want to be in the club and get your T-shirt, you
should feel the same way.

Optional property: `dtreviewed`

For the date of the review, I add the `dtreviewed` property and indicate the ISO 8601 date information via the value class pattern, using the empty `<span>` method of the value-title subset:

```
<p class="dtreviewed"><span class="value-title" title="2009-
03-11"> </span>March 11, 2009</p>
```

Optional property: `rating`

Of course, I give my favorite book five stars. And then I add the `rating` property to that content, after first adding a `<span>` to contain the actual value:

```
<p>Rated <span class="rating">5</span> stars by <span class=
"reviewer vcard"><a href="http://ablognotlimited.com/">Emily
Lewis</a></span></p>
```

If I didn't want to use the default 1.0–5.0 rating scale, I could indicate a different scale using the `best` or `worst` subproperties of `rating`:

```
<p>Rated <span class="rating"><span class="value">20</span>
stars out of <span class="best">20</span></span> by <span
class="reviewer vcard"><a href="http://ablognotlimited.
com/">Emily Lewis</a></span></p>
```

Note that for this alternate scale, the rating value is contained by `<span class="value">`, and the best possible value is contained by `<span class="best">`, both of which are contained by a parent `<span class="rating">`.

Optional property: `description`

For the full text of this review, I assign the `description` property:

```
<p class="description">Do you love science fiction and
Monty Pythonesque irreverence? Then Douglas Adams' <cite>
Hitchhiker's Guide to the Galaxy</cite> is the <span class=
"type"><span class="value-title" title="product">book
</span></span> for you.</p>
```

Optional rel-tag

As it happens, the description content of my example review includes a few key phrases that would make ideal tags. But, as you may recall, in order to implement rel-tag, those tags must be contained by links with destination hrefs that are tagspaces. So let's first add those links:

```
<p class="description">Do you love <a href="/tag/science
-fiction/">science fiction</a> and Monty Pythonesque
irreverence? Then <a href="/tag/Douglas-Adams/">Douglas
Adam</a>s' <cite>Hitchhiker's Guide to the Galaxy</
cite> is the <span class="type"><span class="value-title"
title="product">book</span></span> for you.</p>
```

Then assign each rel-tag:

```
<p class="description">Do you love <a href="/tag/science
-fiction/" rel="tag">science fiction</a> and Monty
Pythonesque irreverence? Then <a href="/tag/Douglas-Adams/"
rel="tag">Douglas Adam</a>s' <cite>Hitchhiker's Guide to the
Galaxy</cite> is the <span class="type"><span class="value
-title" title="product">book</span></span> for you.</p>
```

Optional permalink

This example also includes a permanent link to this review, so I indicate that by assigning the necessary rel values (bookmark and self) to the permalink <a>:

```
<h1 class="item"><a href=" http://ablognotlimited.com/
articles/Review-Hitchhikers" rel="bookmark self">Review of
<cite class="fn">Hitchhiker's Guide to the Galaxy</cite>
</a></h1>
```

The end result

And now we have a complete hReview:

```
<div class="hreview">
    <h1 class="item"><a href="http://ablognotlimited.com/
articles/Review-Hitchhikers" rel="bookmark self">Review of
<cite class="fn">Hitchhiker's Guide to the Galaxy</cite>
</a></h1>
```

(continues on next page)

```
    <p class="dtreviewed"><span class="value-title"
title="2009-03-11"> </span>March 11, 2009</p>
<p>Rated <span class="rating">5</span> stars by <span
class="reviewer vcard"><a href="http://ablognotlimited.com/"
class="fn url">Emily Lewis</a></span></p>
    <p class="description">Do you love <a href="/tag/
science-fiction/" rel="tag">science fiction</a> and Monty
Pythonesque irreverence? Then <a href="/tag/Douglas-Adams/"
rel="tag">Douglas Adam</a>s' <cite>Hitchhiker's Guide to the
Galaxy</cite> is the <span class="type"><span class="value-
title" title="product">book</span></span> for you.</p>
</div>
```

The logic behind the markup

The markup in this example is pretty straightforward. As in many of the examples in this book, I use the `<h1>` on content for which I'd like to get a bit of SEO, which is also semantically appropriate for the title.

I did add the nonsemantic `<div>` as a parent element for the root `hreview`. Since this example is just a single review, that makes the most semantic sense to me. However, if I were listing several reviews on a page, I could easily use a list element, with each review contained by an `<li class="hreview">`.

For the actual review content, my example is but one `<p>`. If I had multiple paragraphs, then I would've needed to add a containing `<div>` in order to assign the `description` property.

However, I've seen some people use a containing `<blockquote>` element because, from their semantic perspective, the review is what a person is saying and it can contain other block-level elements. Personally, I don't agree with this, but that doesn't mean it isn't correct. Semantics can and often do have nuance based upon the content author's perspective.

The only other element that may be worth explaining is `<cite>`. You will notice that I contain each reference to the book name in `<cite>` elements. This is because (as I mentioned in Chapter 8) `<cite>` indicates the source being cited.

Combining hReview and hAtom

Because the *Hitchhiker's* book review example is one that appears as a blog post, it makes sense to also apply hAtom to encourage syndication of this review. So let's add all of the relevant hAtom properties you learned about in the last chapter:

```
<div class="hreview hentry">
    <h1 class="item entry-title"><a href="http://ablognot
limited.com/articles/Review-Hitchhikers" rel="bookmark
self">Review of <cite class="fn">Hitchhiker's Guide to the
Galaxy</cite></a></h1>
    <p class="dtreviewed updated published"><span class=
"value-title" title="2009-03-11"> </span>March 11, 2009</p>
<p>Rated <span class="rating">5</span> stars by <span class=
"reviewer vcard author"><a href="http://ablognotlimited.
com/" class="fn url">Emily Lewis</a></span></p>
    <p class="description entry-content">Do you love <a
href="/tag/science-fiction/" rel="tag">science fiction
</a> and Monty Pythonesque irreverence? Then <a href=
"/tag/Douglas-Adams/" rel="tag">Douglas Adam</a>s' <cite>
Hitchhiker's Guide to the Galaxy</cite> is the <span class=
"type"><span class="value-title" title="product">book
</span></span> for you.</p>
</div>
```

Authoring Tools

There are a few tools available to help you publish your content with hReview if you aren't into the hand-coding thing:

- hReview Creator: http://microformats.org/code/hreview/creator

- G-Tools helps you create reviews of Amazon products and includes an option to publish with hReview: http://goodpic.com/mt/aws/index_us.html

- hReview Dynamic Template helps you author hReview in Windows Live Writer: http://tech.niques.info/projects/wlw-template-hreview/

- If you use WordPress, these two plug-ins can help you publish your review in hReview: http://www.aes.id.au/?page_id=28 and http://sungnyemun.org/wordpress/?p=22

- For more hReview tools, see http://microformats.org/wiki/hreview-implementations

Let Your Voice Be Heard

Now that you know how to implement hReview (and I'm sure you are going to start publishing right away), your reviews have the potential to reach a wide audience. Your reviews can become key resources to help other people make decisions about what books to read, what restaurants to frequent, what bands aren't worth the money to see, and much more. Everyone benefits.

And this brings us to the end of the chapters in which we focus on one microformat at a time. In the next chapter, I'll brief you on four relatively new draft microformats.

Chapter 11

Speed Round

Over the past nine chapters, I've detailed the ins and outs of 16 micro-formats, giving you the fundamentals, as well as exploring various POSH implementations.

You're welcome.

It is now time to put that fundamental knowledge to the test. In this chapter, I'm going to cover the last four draft microformats: hAudio, hRecipe, hProduct, and hMedia. But unlike in previous chapters, I'm just going to give you the basics for each.

Why? Well, for one reason, these four drafts are newer than the other draft microformats we've discussed. Their specifications are far less stable, with a fair amount of experimental properties and subproperties (meaning they may change or be removed entirely). As such, there is just less to cover.

Another reason is that I'd like you to consider this speed round as an opportunity to learn the basics of a microformat, and then see where you can take it on your own.

Without further ado, let's get started!

hAudio: Defining Audio Recordings

hAudio is a draft microformat that adds metadata (semantics FTW!) to audio recordings. The added semantic context hAudio provides is intended to encourage sharing, distribution, syndication, and aggregation of audio content on the web.

As a music lover (*addict* is more accurate), I initially think of audio record-ings as music. But hAudio isn't just for music. It is for any and all audio on the web, including the following:

- Speeches
- Audio books
- Podcasts
- Sound effects

Profile

As with all the microformats, I recommend you add the profile to your document `<head>`:

```
<head profile="http://microformats.org/profile/haudio">
```

And if you are using hAudio with other microformats in your document, just include the profiles for those microformats along with that for hAudio, making sure to separate each with a single space.

Syntax

Now let's take a look at the properties and subproperties for hAudio:

- `haudio`, the required root property of hAudio, must be assigned to the element that contains all of the content about the audio recording.

- To define the name or title of the audio recording, you can use either the `fn` (for a single recording) or the `album` (for a collection of recordings) property. Your hAudio implementation must have at least one of these values and can have both, if contextually relevant.

- The optional `item` property indicates a part of the main hAudio, such as a track or song of an album or a section of a podcast. In a way, it is a more discrete hAudio element contained by the parent hAudio. However, you do not need to specify the root `haudio` element for items. You can, though, indicate the name/title of the `item` using an `fn` subproperty. And `item` can be used multiple times within the root `haudio`.

- `position` is an optional subproperty of `item` that indicates the position of an `item` in a list, such as a track number for an album, a position in a playlist, or a chapter of a podcast. There can be only one `position` per `item`, and the inner content of an element assigned `position` must be a number or sequential identifier.

- The optional `contributor` property indicates any person involved in the creation of the audio recording, such as artist, producer, or composer. You can use `contributor` as many times as your content dictates. The specification also recommends (but doesn't require) that you mark up instances of `contributor` with hCard.

- The optional `published` property specifies the published date of the recording, such as the day a speech was given or the day an album went on sale. While not required, the date information should also include the ISO 8601 machine data, so you would use the value class pattern for this property.

- The `category` property is used to indicate keywords that describe the genre or style of the audio recording. These keywords can also be considered tags, so you can also apply rel-tag. `category` can be used as many times as needed.

- You apply the optional `sample` property to an `<a>` element with an `href` destination that is the URI for an excerpt of the recording. You use the rel design pattern for this property, applying `rel="sample"` to the `<a>` element. hAudio can have multiple instances of `sample`.

- You can use the optional `enclosure` property to indicate the URI for the full recording, again with the rel design pattern where the `<a>` is assigned `rel="enclosure"`. You can have multiple instances of enclosure per hAudio.

- The optional `payment` property indicates a URI where the recording may be purchased. Once again, you use the rel design pattern, assigning `rel="payment"` to the `<a>` element. You can use `payment` multiple times within hAudio.

- If you have one or more images associated with your audio recording—album cover, photo of a speaker, picture from a concert—you can use the optional `photo` property assigned to the `<img />` elements.

- You use the optional `duration` property to specify the length of the audio recording. This property has three optional subproperties to indicate hours (`h`), minutes (`min`), and seconds (`s`). If you don't care to use these subproperties, you can specify the duration information with ISO 8601 data in the value class pattern.

- The optional `price` property specifies the currency amount to purchase the audio recording. You can use `price` multiple times within hAudio, and it can include the optional subproperties `currency` (assigned to the currency symbol with an ISO 4217 `title` value, such as USD) and `amount` (assigned to a numerical value of the amount of currency).

- You assign the optional `description` property to content that provides a description of the hAudio content, such as a description of a sound effect or the meaning of a song. You can use `description` multiple times within an hAudio and, in such cases, machines concatenate all instances into a single `description`.

Practical markup

To say that I liked Def Leppard while growing up would be an understatement. I was obsessed. I burned out my record player (yes, I'm that old) on all of their albums, in particular *Pyromania*. So, let's use that as an example for our hAudio markup, which includes the required root `haudio` property and the required `album` property:

```
<div class="haudio">
    <h1 class="album">Pyromania</h1>
    <img src="/images/Pyromania.jpg" alt="Pyromania cover
art" class="photo" />
    <dl>
        <dt>Def Leppard</dt>
            <dd class="contributor">Joe Elliot, vocals</dd>
            <dd class="contributor">Steve Clark, guitar</dd>
            <dd class="contributor">Phil Collen, guitar</dd>
            <dd class="contributor">Rick Savage, bass</dd>
            <dd class="contributor">Rick Allen, drums</dd>
    </dl>
    <dl>
        <dt>Release date:</dt>
            <dd class="published"><span class="value-title"
title="1983-01-20"> </span>January 20, 1983</dd>
        <dt>Genre(s):</dt>
            <dd><a href="/tags/pop-metal" class="category"
rel="tag">Pop metal</a>, <a href="/tags/hard-rock"
class="category" rel="tag">hard rock</a>, <a href="/tags/
rock" class="category" rel="tag">rock</a></dd>
        <dt>Length:</dt>
            <dd class="duration"><span class="value-title"
title="PT44M57S"> </span>44 minutes, 57 seconds</dd>
        <dt>Price:</dt>
            <dd class="price"><abbr class="currency"
title="USD">$</abbr><span class="amount">15.00</span></dd>
        <dt>Available for purchase:</dt>
            <dd><a href="http://www.amazon.com/Pyromania
-Def-Leppard/dp/B000001F2V" class="payment">Amazon</a></dd>
    </dl>
    <p class="description">Pyromania is the third album from
Def Leppard, released in 1983. Heavily produced by <span
class="contributor">Robert John "Mutt" Lange</span>, the album
sold more than 10 million copies in the United States.</p>
    <h2>Tracks</h2>
    <ol>
        <li class="item"><a href="/samples/RockRock.mp3"
class="fn" rel="sample">Rock! Rock! (Till You Drop)</a></li>
        <li class="item"><a href="/samples/Photograph.mp3"
class="fn" rel="sample">Photograph</a></li>
```

(continues on next page)

```
        <li class="item"><a href="/samples/Stagefright.mp3"
class="fn" rel="sample">Stagefright</a></li>
        <li class="item"><a href="/samples/TooLate.mp3"
class="fn" rel="sample">Too Late for Love</a></li>
        <li class="item"><a href="/samples/DieHard.mp3"
class="fn" rel="sample">Die Hard The Hunter</a></li>
        <li class="item"><a href="/samples/Foolin.mp3"
class="fn" rel="sample">Foolin'</a></li>
        <li class="item"><a href="/samples/RockAges.mp3"
class="fn" rel="sample">Rock of Ages</a></li>
        <li class="item"><a href="/samples/UnderFire.mp3"
class="fn" rel="sample">Comin' Under Fire</a></li>
        <li class="item"><a href="/samples/Action.mp3"
class="fn" rel="sample">Action! Not Words</a></li>
        <li class="item"><a href="/samples/BillyGun.mp3"
class="fn" rel="sample">Billy's Got a Gun</a></li>
    </ol>
</div>
```

The rest of the properties and subproperties I used in this example are optional. But the content is there, so why not add the extra semantic goodness. Think of it as frosting for your content cake. Cake is so much better with frosting, no?

Adding hCard

As I mentioned for the `contributor` property, the hAudio specification recommends that it also be an hCard, so let's do that for my favorite member of Def Leppard (I wonder if he ever got my fan club letter …):

```
<dd class="contributor vcard"><a href="http://defleppard.
com/band/joe.asp" class="fn url" rel="crush">Joe Elliot</a>,
<span class="role">vocals</span></dd>
```

Note that I added XFN to this example with the `rel` attribute (and the `crush` value) because XFN is appropriate for this person's hCard `url`. And because a 12-year-old girl's rock-star crush never truly dies.

Combining microformats

With the addition of hCard and XFN above, you can see that hAudio demonstrates one of my favorite things about microformats: they can be used together. But beyond hCard, think about some other opportunities for combining hAudio with other microformats.

For my *Pyromania* example, I could easily include a review of the album (five stars, of course). That makes it a great candidate for adding hReview. If you were using hAudio to mark up a podcast, what about using hAtom too? What if your content is a schedule of events, each of which has an associated audio recording of a speech? You could embed hAudio within hCalendar.

Just remember that whenever you are publishing a microformat, pay close attention to your content to see if there are other microformats you could include. You want your content to be rich and powerful, don't you?

hRecipe: Defining Food and Beverage Recipes

I love food. Cooking it, eating it, experimenting with it. Same with drinks, especially those of the "happy hour" persuasion. And I love sharing my recipes.

The web is full of folks like me. Folks who publish their favorite recipes on their blogs. Entire sites devoted to food and beverage recipes. It is for these folks or more specifically, their content—that hRecipe was developed.

hRecipe is a draft microformat for adding semantic richness to food and beverage recipe web content, which, in turn, helps make that content more distributable.

Profile

As of this writing, there isn't yet a profile URI for hRecipe. However, you can find the XMDP profile on the Microformats Wiki: http://microformats. org/wiki/hrecipe. Be sure to reference the specification when you are publishing hRecipe.

Syntax

The properties and subproperties of hRecipe were developed based on content most commonly found in recipes:

- The root `hrecipe` property is required and must be assigned to the element that contains all of the recipe content.

- The required `fn` property is assigned to content that is the name or short description of the recipe.

- You use the required `ingredient` property to specify the ingredients in a recipe. You can use `ingredient` as many times as necessary within an hRecipe, but there must be at least one. The `ingredient` property also has two optional subproperties: `value`, to indicate the amount of an ingredient, and `type`, to indicate the unit of measurement for the value.

- `yield` is an optional property that specifies the quantity of a recipe, such as *serves four people* or *makes ten cupcakes*.

- The optional `instructions` property is assigned to the actual instructions or method for making the recipe.

- The optional `duration` property specifies—via the value class pattern—how much time it takes to prepare the recipe.

- If you have a photo for the recipe, such as a picture of the final preparation, you can optionally assign the `photo` property to the `<img />` element. hRecipe can include as many instances of `photo` as your content dictates.

- The optional `summary` property can be applied to a short introduction or statement about the recipe.

- Use the optional `author` property if the recipe has an author. The hRecipe specification recommends that you mark up `author` with hCard. You may use `author` as many times as necessary for your hRecipe.

- The optional `published` property indicates when the recipe was published and should include the ISO 8601 machine date-time information via the value class pattern.

- You can use the optional `nutrition` property for nutritional information about the recipe (such as calories, fat content, and so on). You can use this property multiple times within hRecipe. It also has two subproperties: `value`, for the amount of a given nutrition item, and `type`, for the nutrition unit of measurement.

- If the recipe contains keywords or phrases, you have the option of turning those into links (`<a>`) assigned rel-tag. Remember, links that are "tags" must have an `href` value that is a tag space.

Practical markup

Thanks to my mother and paternal grandmother—both of whom cooked amazing food and spent hours teaching me their recipes—I'm a pretty decent cook. Lately I've been experimenting with game hens, and I finally got the recipe perfected. Lucky you, I'm sharing it with you in the name of microformats:

This hRecipe markup is styled with CSS in Chapter 12 (page 284).

```
<div class="hrecipe">
    <h1 class="fn">Roasted Rock Cornish Game Hens</h1>
    <img src="/images/gamehens.jpg" alt="Roasted cornish
game hens" class="photo" />
    <p class="summary">A simple recipe for creating savory
game hens with crispy skins and tender, juicy meat.</p>
    <ul>
        <li class="duration"><span class="value-title"
title="PT90M"> </span>90 minutes</li>
        <li class="yield">2-4 servings</li>
        <li class="author">Created by Emily Lewis</li>
        <li class="published"><span class="value-title"
title="2009-05-25"> </span>May 25, 2009</li>
    </ul>
    <h2>Ingredients</h2>
    <ul>
        <li class="ingredient"><span class="value">1</span>
<span class="type">tablespoon</span> poultry seasoning</li>
        <li class="ingredient"><span class="value">1</span>
<span class="type">teaspoon</span> garlic powder</li>
        <li class="ingredient"><span class="value">1</span>
<span class="type">tablespoon</span> sea salt</li>
        <li class="ingredient"><span class="value">1</span>
<span class="type">teaspoon</span> fresh ground pepper</li>
        <li class="ingredient"><span class="value">1/2</
span> <span class="type">teaspoon</span> paprika</li>
        <li class="ingredient"><span class="value">1</span>
clove garlic, finely chopped</li>
        <li class="ingredient">Fresh thyme</li>
        <li class="ingredient">Fresh rosemary</li>
        <li class="ingredient"><span class="value">1</span>
small Vidalia onion, quartered</li>
        <li class="ingredient">Olive oil</li>
```

(continues on next page)

```
        <li class="ingredient"><span class="value">2</span>
cornish game hens</li>
    </ul>
    <h2>Instructions</h2>
    <ol class="instructions">
        <li>Rinse <a href="/tags/game-hens" rel="tag">game
hens</a> and dry thoroughly.</li>
        <li>Mix all dry ingredients together to create the
seasoning rub.</li>
        <li>Rub cavity of hen with chopped garlic. Then
season the cavity with the rub. Add a small sprig of
rosemary and two sprigs of thyme to the cavity. Then stuff
each cavity with 1/2 of the Vidalia onion (break apart the
pieces).</li>
        <li>Lightly coat the outside of the hen with olive
oil and season with the rub.</li>
        <li>Place hens breast side up on a roasting pan.</li>
        <li>Heat oven to 450 degrees and cook the hens at
this high temperature for 18 to 20 minutes to crisp the skin
and seal in juices.</li>
        <li>Drop the heat down to 375 degrees (do not open
the oven) and cook for an additional 40 minutes.</li>
        <li>Check the hens at 40 minutes to see if juices
run clear and inner temp is 165 degrees. If not, baste the
hens with any drippings and cook for an additional 5 to 8
minutes.</li>
        <li>Once the hens are done (inner temp of 165
degrees, though I check based on whether the juices are
clear), let them set/rest for 10 minutes.</li>
    </ol>
</div>
```

Combining microformats

Since the specification recommends that `author` also be marked up with hCard, let's add it:

```
<li class="author vcard">Created by <a href="http://
ablognotlimited.com" class="fn url">Emily Lewis</a></li>
```

What other microformats could come into play with hRecipe? What about hReview? Yep, that would work.

hProduct: Defining Consumer Products

One of the biggest parts of today's web is its consumer marketplace. Selling, buying, trading. All online. It can be difficult to sort through it all, especially when you are looking for a particular product and want to compare information from different sites.

hProduct was developed to help address this challenge—to add semantics to consumer product information, making it easier to share, distribute, and aggregate that information.

Profile

Like hRecipe, there isn't yet a profile URI for hProduct. The XMDP profile, however, can be found on the Microformats Wiki: http://microformats.org/wiki/hproduct. Please be sure to reference the online specification before publishing hProduct.

Syntax

hProduct properties and subproperties were developed based on common information among today's consumer products, while still allowing for a wide variety of product-specific details:

* All of your product content must be contained by an element assigned the required root hproduct property.

* For the product name, use the required fn property once.

* The optional brand property indicates the brand of the product. In some cases, this may be the manufacturer and would also be marked up with hCard.

* To specify the product category (such as *car* or *T-shirt*), use the optional category property, which you can use multiple times within hProduct. You can also turn category content into tags by creating links for each and assigning rel="tag" to the <a>s.

* The optional price property specifies how much it costs to purchase the product. The inner content of the element assigned class="price" can appear in currency format.

- Use the optional `description` property for the content that describes the product.

- You can assign the optional `photo` property to any images or links to images within your product content. You can use `photo` as many times as needed.

- The optional `url` property is assigned to a link that directs to a web page containing further product details.

- You can use the optional `review` property if your content includes a review of the product. The hProduct specification also recommends that `review` be marked up with hReview.

- You can use the optional `listing` property if your content also includes listing details for the product (such as those for listing services like Craigslist and eBay). The specification recommends that `listing` be marked up with hListing (http://microformats.org/wiki/hlisting). However, hListing hasn't made it beyond the proposal stage yet, so I would recommend implementing it with some caution.

- The optional `identifier` property is assigned to unique, identifying information about the product. You can have multiple instances of `identifier` within hProduct. `identifier` also has two subproperties: `type` and `value`. `type` indicates the specific identifier, such as *model*, *MPN*, *UPC*, *ISBN*, *ISSN*, *EAN*, *JAN*, *VIN*, *SKU*, and *sn*. And yep, those examples are valid types. The second subproperty, `value`, is the corresponding value of the `type`—for example, the numbers that make up a car's Vehicle Identification Number (VIN).

Practical markup

Since I just mentioned a car in the last section, why don't we use a car for our hProduct example? And let's get all Earth-friendly with it:

```
<div class="hproduct">
    <h1 class="fn">Prius</h1>
    <img src="/images/Prius.jpg" alt="Toyota Prius"
class="photo" />
    <p class="description">Mid-size, electric <a href="/
tags/hybrid-car" class="category" rel="tag">hybrid car
</a> from <a href="http://toyota.com" class="brand">Toyota
</a> starting at <span class="price">$22,000</span>. For
```

```
more information, visit the <a href="http://www.toyota.com/
prius-hybrid/" class="url">Prius site</a>.</p>
</div>
```

Combining microformats

Let's go ahead and add hCard to our brand content (as the specification recommends), since the brand in this example is a manufacturer:

```
<p class="description">Mid-size, electric <a href="/tags/
hybrid-car" class="category" rel="tag">hybrid car</a>
from <span class="brand vcard"><a href="http://toyota.
com" class="org fn url">Toyota</a></span> starting at
<span class="price">$22,000</span>. For more information,
visit the <a href="http://www.toyota.com/prius-hybrid/"
class="url">Prius site</a>.</p>
```

Other than hCard, what other microformats would work here?

If you have a retail site and you publish your product information with hProduct, what additional value could you add to encourage sales? Do you have product reviews? Then add hReview to your hProduct.

Do you have "deals of the day?" Maybe hCalendar would be appropriate.

Are you listing your product for sale or trade on a listing site like Craigslist? You could experiment with adding the proposed (not yet at draft stage) hListing to your hProduct.

As long as you focus on your content and what you want it to do, figuring out the appropriate microformats is easy.

hMedia: Defining Media Files

Throughout this book, we've focused on content—most often from the high-level perspective of a large block of content. From a narrower perspective, content is made up of individual bits of content: the text, images, audio, and video

hMedia was developed to add semantic richness to those individual bits of content that are media files—the images, audio, and video.

Profile

Once again, there's no profile URI for hMedia, but the XMDP profile can be found at http://microformats.org/wiki/hmedia. And once again, be sure to reference the online specification before publishing hMedia.

Syntax

The properties for hMedia are intentionally simple and minimal (as are all microformats) in order to provide a means to describe the information common to a range of media files:

• The root `hmedia` property is required and must contain all of the content about the media file.

• The required `fn` property can be used once within hMedia and indicates the name of the media file.

• Use the optional `contributor` property to specify any people or organizations that contributed to the creation of the media file. And, while it isn't required, you should mark up any instances of contributor with hCard, as well.

• You can apply the optional `photo` property to any images about or related to your media file.

• If the media content is an embedded file (such as a video or movie), you assign the optional `player` property to the element (often `<object>`) that references the embedded file. You can use `player` only once within hMedia.

• If the media content is a link to a downloadable file, use the optional `enclosure` property by assigning `rel="enclosure"` to the `<a>`. Additionally, the `<a>` should have a specified `type` value, such as `type="image/png"`.

Practical markup

For Webuquerque, the community group I co-manage, we record our presentations and post the videos to my blog. A video is exactly what hMedia is meant for, so let's use one of our videos for this example (and yes, a bit of blatant promotion):

```
<div class="hmedia">
    <h1 class="fn">The Battle of Development Frameworks &
Libraries</h1>
    <p><span class="contributor">Webuquerque</span>'s
August event, presented by <span class="contributor">Mark
Casias</span>, was a review of tools for creating killer web
applications.</p>
    <p>The video is <a href="http://www.viddler.com/
explore/webuquerque/videos/9/" rel="enclosure" type="video/
mp4">available on Viddler</a>:</p>
    <object classid="clsid:D27CDB6E-AE6D-11cf-
96B8-444553540000" id="viddler_7ff41f95" width="437"
height="370" class="player">
        <param name="movie" value="http://www.viddler.com/
player/7ff41f95/" />
        <param name="allowScriptAccess" value="always" />
        <param name="allowFullScreen" value="true" />
    </object>
</div>
```

Combining microformats

The hMedia spec recommends marking up instances of contributor with
hCard, so let's be good microformat monkeys and do it:

```
<p><span class="contributor vcard"><a href="http://
webuquerque.com" class="fn org url">Webuquerque</a></span>'s
August event, presented by <span class="contributor vcard">
<a href="http://www.markiesinter.net/" class="fn url">Mark
Casias</a></span>, was a review of tools for creating killer
web applications.</p>
```

What other microformats could you include? Using hMedia for a podcast or
vodcast? Then use hAtom too. Want to give the thumbs down for a video?
Add hReview. Is an image associated with an event? Don't forget hCalendar.

What about hAudio?

By this point, you may be wondering why audio files are included in
hMedia, since we already have hAudio. The distinction is that hMedia
provides a simple and minimal description of the audio file itself, while

hAudio allows for more detail about the audio recording, including price, description, and summary.

But why not use the two together? In fact, like many microformats, they share property and subproperty names, so it is only a matter of adding a few others. Let's see that in action with one of the songs from my hAudio example:

```
<li class="item hmedia"><a href="/samples/RockRock.mp3"
class="fn" rel="sample enclosure" type="audio/mpeg">Rock!
Rock! (Till You Drop)</a></li>
```

hMedia tools

Media on the web is hawt, and tools are already available that help process and beautifully present hMedia on your pages:

- Oomph's plug-in for Internet Explorer supports browsing hMedia audio, video, and photos. Oomph also offers a jQuery extension that any web author can include on their web pages to provide a nice user interface for their hMedia (http://microformats.org/wiki/oomph).

- The Transformr web-service (http://transformr.co.uk) extracts hMedia and hAtom to produce MediaRSS.

- For more hMedia tools, see http://microformats.org/wiki/hmedia -implementations

Finish Line

Whew! You made it to the end of the speed round. I knew you would.

You've also made it to the end of our journey into the beauty that is micro-formats. You've learned about the benefits, the details of each specification, and various implementations for publishing.

But lest you be too disappointed, you are not at the end of your journey with this book. In the next chapter, I'll be talking about CSS and showing you that microformats do not restrict your ability to style your content any way you can imagine.

Chapter 12

Because Looks Matter

If you've been in the web industry for even just a few days, I'm sure you've heard the mantra "content is king." Whether you agree with it or not, it would be impossible to have any sort of website without content.

And content is what we've focused on in this book:

- How to identify content that is well suited for microformats

- How to structure content with POSH

- How to enrich your content by publishing microformats

But content alone just isn't enough, especially with today's web filled with tons of competing information. Content should—or, I hazard to say, *must*—look good. I mean, even kings have fancy clothes, right?

This is where CSS comes into play. If you are following today's web standards (if not, then shame on you), you are using CSS to control the look of your website. And microformats do not restrict your ability to use CSS. In fact, the sets of `class` values from microformats provide nice, semantic styling hooks you can use instead of or in addition to custom `classes`.

The process of styling microformatted content is the same as that of styling non-microformatted content. If you have the CSS ability, you can style microformats any way you can imagine. I'll prove it to you.

My friend Jason Nakai worked up a few designs for some of the microformat examples in this book. I've translated each into CSS, using the markup from the examples so you can see the wide range of presentation options you have and, hopefully, imagine a few more for your own content.

Now, I won't be going into detail about the CSS. I'll just be showing you the style rules and end results. Remember, this book is about microformats, not CSS.

Styling Links

Some of the easiest microformats to style are those used to define links, primarily because links are so simple. A link is just some text, and most CSS for links focuses on color, decoration such as underlines, and font weight.

A trend I've seen for some links, though, includes little icons preceding certain links to give users more context about those links. Our link-based microformats are perfect cases to apply this little design element.

XFN

As you may remember, XFN is really just one or more specific `rel` values assigned to links, indicating a social relationship with the people behind those links. If you'd like to make your XFN links stand out from your other links, you can use CSS attribute selectors to present an icon before these links.

Lucky you (and me, since I suck at pixel work), Wolfgang Bartelme created a few sets of microformats icons you can use for just such a purpose: http://bartelme.at/journal/archive/microformats_icons.

I'm going to use one of his XFN icons to style an example from Chapter 4 (pages 67–68) for a link to a `friend` (remember that value?).

The CSS

The CSS is extremely simple. I add a few declarations to make the link text itself look nice. Then, using attribute selectors, which I can use to target links with specific `rel` values, I indicate the icon should appear before the link text:

It is worth mentioning that CSS attribute selectors are supported only by modern standards-compliant browsers; that would not be Microsoft Internet Explorer 6. And while it is more standards-compliant, IE 7 doesn't support the CSS :before generated content selector.

```
a {
    color: #3773ca;
    font: 110% Verdana, Arial, Helvetica, sans-serif;
    text-decoration: none;
    }
a[rel~="friend"]:before {
    content: url(images/xfn-friend.png);
    padding-right:5px;
    }
```

The end result

And with that little bit of CSS, any links that have a `rel` value of `friend` will appear as such (**Figure 12.1**).

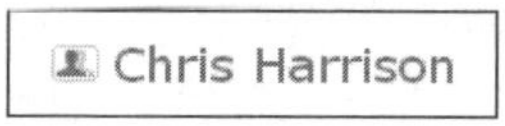
Chris Harrison

Figure 12.1
Browser rendering of styled XFN `friend` link

VoteLinks

We can take this approach and apply it to any links with specific attribute values, including VoteLinks, which uses the `rev` attribute. Wolfgang Bartleme's microformats icon collection includes a set for VoteLinks (which are adorable), but you can use anything you like. For this example from Chapter 3 (page 55), we'll use the one Jason made for us.

The CSS

Once again, CSS attribute selectors come to the rescue:

```
a {
    color: #000;
    font: 110% Arial, Helvetica, sans-serif bold;
    text-decoration: none;
    }
a[rev~="vote-against"]:before {
    content: url(images/vote-against.png);
    padding-right: 5px;
    }
```

The end result

So, without having to add any `classes` to my link, I get this cute little icon (**Figure 2.2**) before any links assigned `rev="vote-against"`:

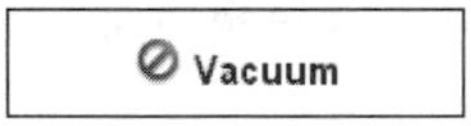

Figure 12.2
Browser rendering of styled VoteLinks `vote-against` link

⊘ Vacuum

Styling hCard

It isn't really common practice to style contact information as a business card on a website, but that doesn't mean you can't do it. So let's! We're going to use the hCard for the Badass Tattoo Company from Chapter 6 (pages 131–140).

The CSS

Here are the styles I chose to use:

```css
.vcard {
    background: #000;
    color: #fff;
    font: bold 80% Arial, Helvetica, sans-serif;
    height: 351px;
    padding: 15px;
    position: relative;
    width: 170px;
    }
.vcard a, .vcard a:link, .vcard a:visited {
    color: #fff;
    text-decoration: none;
    }
.vcard a:hover, .vcard a:focus, .vcard a:active {
    text-decoration: underline;
    }
.vcard ul {
    list-style-type: none;
    margin: 0;
    }
.vcard abbr {
    border: 0;
    }
.logo {
    position: absolute;
    top: 55px;
    left: 25px;
    z-index: 0;
    }
.adr .label, .tel:last-child, .tel .type {
    display: none;
    }
.fn {
    background: url(images/business-card-name.png)
no-repeat;
```

The last-child *pseudo-class isn't recognized by IE 6, 7, or 8.*

(continues on next page)

```
        display: block;
        height: 103px;
        left: 20px;
        position: absolute;
        text-indent: -5000px;
        top: 20px;
        width: 156px;
        z-index: 2;
        }
.adr.geo {
        bottom: 20px;
        left: -55px;
        position: absolute;
        text-align: center;
        }
.tel, .email {
        bottom:80px;
        font-size:90%;
        font-weight:normal;
        left:-65px;
        position:absolute;
        -moz-transform: rotate(-90deg);
        -webkit-transform: rotate(-90deg);
        }
.email {
        bottom:105px;
        left:120px;
        -moz-transform: rotate(90deg);
        -webkit-transform: rotate(90deg);
        }
```

Right now, the transform property is only recognized by Mozilla Firefox 3.5 and later, Google Chrome, and Apple Safari—and only when you use their prefixes, -moz-transform and -webkit-transform.

The end result

I hope you noticed that the CSS for this example only uses the elements of my markup and the classes from hCard as the selectors. I didn't have to add any additional markup, classes, or ids.

Figure 12.3
Browser rendering of
styled hCard

I will mention, though, that the CSS for this business card design (**Figure 12.3**) really only renders as intended in Safari, Chrome, and Firefox due to the rotated text. So, this may not be an ideal implementation. Nonetheless, I'm digging the text rotation.

And, of course, IE 6 and 7 have some issues with positioning on top of not supporting the text rotation. But that's what conditional comments are for, right? And there are some filters you can use to get IE to cooperate with the text rotation.

Styling hCalendar

Calendars, just like any content, can come in a wide variety of presentational flavors. For the `<table>`-based calendar from Chapter 7 (pages 181–192), we are going to create a clean and simple grid appearance.

The CSS

Here are the styles I chose to use:

```
table {
    background: #9ed0e8 url(images/calendar-background.png)
repeat-x;
    border: 1px solid #9ed0e8;
```

(continues on next page)

Currently, no browsers support the CSS3 `border-radius` property. However, Firefox and the WebKit-based browsers (Chrome, Flock, and Safari) will render rounded corners using their prefixes, `-moz-border-radius` and `-webkit-border-radius`, respectively. All other browsers will ignore these rules and render square corners.

Only Safari, Chrome, and Opera render the `text-shadow` property. All other browsers will render the plain text.

```
    -moz-border-radius: 8px;
    -webkit-border-radius: 8px;
    color: #fff;
    margin: 10px auto;
    padding-top: 55px;
    position: relative;
    width: 1120px;
    }
caption {
    background: #fff;
    border:1 px solid #bfe0f0;
    -moz-border-radius: 8px;
    -webkit-border-radius: 8px;
    color: #4ba2e5;
    font: bold 200% Georgia, "Times New Roman", Times,
serif;
    padding: 10px;
    position: absolute;
    text-shadow: #666 2px 2px 2px;
    top: 25px;
    }
td, th {
    border: 1px solid #fff;
    -moz-border-radius: 8px;
    -webkit-border-radius: 8px;
    color: #4ba2e5;
    font: bold 120% Georgia, "Times New Roman", Times,
serif;
    padding: 10px;
    width: 130px;
    }
th {
    background: #fff;
    }

td {
    background: #fff url(images/calendar-cell-background.
png) repeat-x 0 100%;
    height: 130px;
    vertical-align: top;
    }
```

```css
.today {
    background-image: url(images/calendar-today-background.
png);
    }
.otherMonth {
    background: none;
    border: 0;
    }
.vevent {
    color: #000;
    font: 60% Arial, Helvetica, sans-serif;
    }
.vevent h3 {
    font-weight: normal;
    float: right;
    margin: 12px 0 10px;
    width: 95px;
    }
.vevent a, .vevent a:link, .vevent a:visited {
    color: #000;
    text-decoration: none;
    }
.vevent a:hover, .vevent a:focus, .event a:active{
    text-decoration: underline;
    }
.vevent dl {
    float: left;
    width: 25px;
    }
.vevent dt, .vevent dd {
    display: none;
    }
.vevent .dtstart {
    display: inline;
    font-weight: bold;
    margin: 0;
    }
```

Both IE 6 and IE 7 bork just a bit on this CSS. And interestingly (or not if you've been dealing with IE for a while), the problems are the same:

- Neither display the `<caption>` element positioned absolutely inside the `<table>`. Instead, the `<caption>` appears immediately before the `<table>`.

- Both render the `<h3>` content in a larger font size than is declared, apparently ignoring the cascade and the font size applied to the containing `<div>`.

For me, these issues aren't deal breakers. However, especially if you work for an organization that requires IE 6 to look as close to the other browsers as possible, these issues should be resolved—to an extent.

Personally, I'd leave the `<caption>` display as is. The content renders just fine, and that is what is truly most important. As for the font size, I would use conditional comments to create IE-specific CSS.

The end result

For this look, I only had to add a couple of additional `class`es to certain `<table>` cells. For the `<td>` that would contain the current day's information, I added `class="today"`. And for the last few `<td>`s that aren't part of the displayed month, I added `class="otherMonth"`. I also added the `cellpadding` attribute to the `<table>`.

But nothing additional was needed for the hCalendar data itself. I just use the `vevent` property as my styling hook for that information. And voilà (**Figure 12.4**):

Figure 12.4
Browser rendering of styled hCalendar

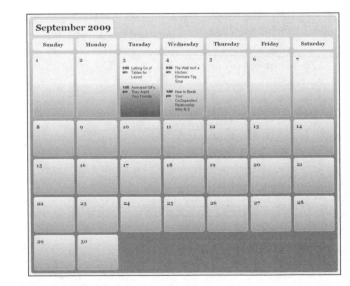

Styling hAtom

Now let's style an hAtom example, using the fictional Homer Simpson blog post from Chapter 9 (page 228–232).

The CSS

Here are the styles I chose to use:

```
.hentry {
    background: #f90 url(images/blog-post-background.png)
no-repeat 0 100%;
    border: 2px solid #399;
    -moz-border-radius: 11px;
    -webkit-border-radius: 11px;
    color: #23383e;
    font: bold 95% Verdana, Arial, Helvetica, sans-serif;
    margin: 50px auto;
    padding: 30px;
    position: relative;
    width: 190px;
    }
a, a:link, a:visited {
    color: #23383e;
    text-decoration: none;
    }
a:hover, a:focus, a:active {
    text-decoration: underline;
    }
ul {
    background: url(images/blog-post-tags-background.png)
no-repeat;
    bottom: -30px;
    height: 93px;
    list-style-type: none;
    padding:0;
    position: absolute;
    margin: 0;
    right: -30px;
    width: 374px;
    }
```

(continues on next page)

IE 6 and 7 do not support the inline-block value.

```css
ul li {
    display: inline-block;
    padding: 45px 10px 0;
    }
.entry-title {
    background: url(images/blog-post-title.png) no-repeat;
    height: 78px;
    left: -62px;
    position: absolute;
    text-indent: -5000px;
    top: -50px;
    width: 550px;
    }
.author {
    background: url(images/blog-post-author-background.png)
no-repeat;
    font-style:italic;
    height:48px;
    left:0;
    padding: 17px 0 0 110px;
    position:absolute;
    top:33px;
    width:472px;
    }
.updated {
    background: url(images/blog-post-date-background.png)
no-repeat;
    color: #fff;
    font-size: 85%;
    height: 55px;
    left: -132px;
    padding: 7px 0 0 25px;
    position: absolute;
    top: 104px;
    width: 177px;
    -moz-transform: rotate(90deg);
    -webkit-transform: rotate(90deg);
    }
.entry-content {
    font-weight:normal;
    margin-top: 70px;
```

IE 6 also doesn't support pseudo-element selectors like :first-letter.

```
    }
.entry-summary:first-letter {
    font-size: 170%;
    font-weight: bold;
    }
a[rel~="tag"] {
    color: #fff;
    font-size: 85%;
    font-style: italic;
    }
a[rel~="tag"]:before {
    content: "*";
    }
```

The end result

I didn't have to add a single class, id, or additional markup element for this presentation (**Figure 12.5**):

Figure 12.5
Browser rendering of styled hAtom

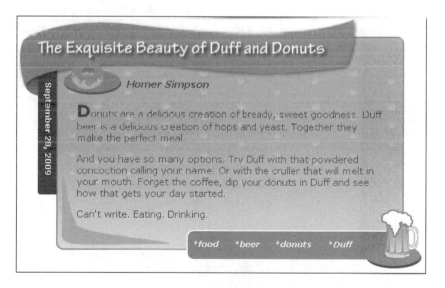

However, as in the hCard example, I'm using text rotation, which renders only in Safari and Firefox. So again, as in the hCard example, this particular CSS might not be ideal for you folks seeking cross-browser consistency. The rounded corners, though, nicely degrade to square corners for browsers that don't support border-radius.

With the expected exceptions of IE 6 and IE 7 (both of which choke a bit on the positioning), the rest of the design translates identically across browsers.

Styling hRecipe

Last, but certainly not least, we're going to style the hRecipe example from Chapter 11 (page 263).

The CSS

Here are the styles I chose to use:

```
.hrecipe {
    background: #243b42;
    border: 1px solid #243b42;
    -moz-border-radius: 15px;
    -webkit-border-radius: 15px;
    color: #243b42;
    font: 80% Arial, Helvetica, sans-serif;
    margin: 30px auto;
    padding: 15px;
    position: relative;
    width: 594px;
    }
.hrecipe div {
    background: #e3d6af;
    border: 2px solid #e58a00;
    -moz-border-radius: 15px;
    -webkit-border-radius: 15px;
    padding: 15px;
    }
h1, h2 {
    background: url(images/recipe-headings.png) no-repeat 0 0;
    height: 35px;
    margin: 0;
    text-indent: -5000px;
    width: 365px;
    }
h2 {
    background-position: 0 -120px;
```

```css
    clear: left;
    padding-top: 5px;
    width: 122px;
    }
.instructHead {
    background-position: 0 -240px;
    }
a, a:link, a:visited {
    color: #243b42;
    }
a:hover, a:focus, a:active {
    color: #96320e;
}
ul, ol {
    list-style-type: none;
    margin: 0;
    padding: 0;
    }
li {
    padding-bottom: 7px;
    }
ol li {
    padding-bottom: 10px;
    }
h2 + ul, .instructions {
    background: #fff;
    border: 2px solid #e58a00;
    -moz-border-radius: 10px;
    -webkit-border-radius: 10px;
    margin-top: -4px;
    padding: 15px;
    }
h2 + ul {
    float: left;
    }
h2 + ul li {
    float: left;
    margin-right: 15px;
    width: 245px;
    }
```

IE 6 does not support the adjacent sibling selector.

(continues on next page)

```
.photo {
    position: absolute;
    right: 15px;
    top: 15px;
    }
.summary {
    font-style: italic;
    font-weight: bold;
    width: 365px;
    }
.duration, .yield, .author, .published {
    color: #96320e;
    font-size: 90%;
    float: left;
    margin-left: 15px;
    width: 200px;
    }
.author, .published {
    clear: left;
    color: #243b42;
    }
.published {
    clear: none;
    }
```

The end result

To achieve this look, I did have to add a nonsemantic `<div>` inside my `<div class="hrecipe">`, containing all the other content. I also added a `class` to one of the `<h2>`s (`instructHead`), so I could target it for the image replacement.

Other than that, I relied entirely on the elements from the original markup example and the `classes` from the hRecipe example.

This particular look renders identically across standards-compliant browsers with the exception of the rounded corners, which display only in Firefox and WebKit browsers.

Figure 12.6
Browser rendering of
styled hRecipe

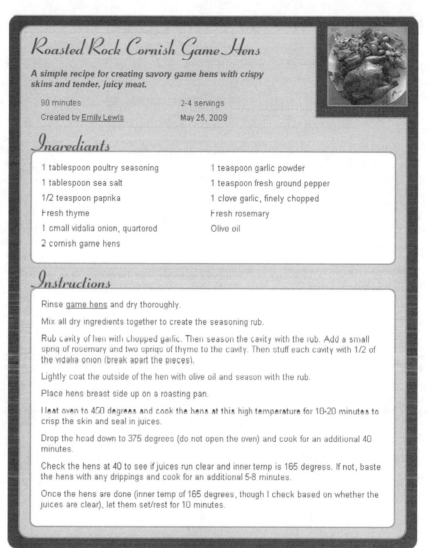

IE 6, as one would expect, doesn't recognize the advanced selectors and, as I'm sure you are aware, doesn't support alpha transparency in the PNG used for headings.

But the content still renders beautifully; users can get the information they need. If IE 6 needs to look closer to how the other browsers render the presentation, turn to conditional comments.

Limited Only to Your CSS Skills

These are but a few examples of different looks for microformatted content. And while you may prefer a different approach to your CSS to achieve these looks, the point is *anything you can do with CSS can be applied to microformatted content*.

You are limited only by your imagination and your CSS skills.

That's All Folks!

We are now at the end of the journey. At the part where, in a movie, the voice-over kicks in, recapping the events and foretelling adventures to come. But in reality your microformats journey isn't over. It is just beginning.

You now know everything you need to enrich your content with microformats:

- The global benefits of semantics and structured data, like SEO and extensible publishing
- The specific benefits of each microformat, from search to improved user experiences with downloadable business cards and calendars
- Each and every property and subproperty for 20 microformats, drafts and all
- Practical POSH examples you can apply to your own content or just use for inspiration
- Authoring tools for different microformats to make your life easier and spare your fingers any extra work at the keyboard

I also hope you've recognized the beauty of microformats, their simplicity, and their power.

Half the Battle

You have the knowledge—now what do you do with it?

First and foremost, take a look at your content and identify where microformats make sense. And then publish those microformats.

Also focus on your markup; come up with your own POSHy examples. Don't muddy your microformats with crap markup. Semantic metadata and semantic markup make an excellent couple.

You can also get involved with and help the microformats initiative:

- Talk about microformats. Advocate them. Evangelize them. Pick an action verb about communication and do that with microformats.
- Pick something from the Microformats Wiki to-do list (http://microformats.org/wiki/to-do) and do it.
- Get into the "machines" business and develop a tool for microformats.

- Subscribe to and participate in the microformats mailing lists (http://microformats.org/wiki/mail).

If you are nodding your head, palms sweaty with the anticipation of putting all you've learned to work, eager to see what you can do and how you can contribute, then I have but one thing left to say to you:

Welcome to the Microformats Are Way F'n Cool Club!

Index